HAND
FO
CARE
ASSISTANTS

A practical guide to working
with older people

**Edited by Lynne Phair
and Sue Benson**

HPL

PRC LIBRARY

00056252

This sixth edition printed in 2003

First published in 1989 by
Hawker Publications Ltd
Culvert House
Culvert Road
London SW11 5DH

Reprinted 1990 (twice), 1991
2nd Edition 1992, 3rd Edition 1993
4th Edition 1995, 5th edition 2000

British Library Cataloguing in Publication Data
*A catalogue record for this book is available
from the British Library*

ISBN 1 874790 69 8
(ISBN 1 874790 50 7 Fifth Edition)

Designed by
Andrew Chapman

Printed and bound in Great Britain by
Premier Press, Southend-on-Sea

Acknowledgements
*The chapters of this book are based on the units of the AgeCare Award Core Skills
©AgeCare, Royal Surgical Aid Society 2003
The case scenarios 'Who should decide?', 'Reassuring a worried resident' and 'Finding sensitive
solutions' are taken from the AgeCare Award workbooks, © AgeCare – The Royal Surgical Aid Society
Workbooks compiled by Lynne Phair and Anne McKenzie (2002).
Parts of the section on Managing aggression (pp35-36), and all practical procedures and good
practice guidance (in shaded boxes) on Personal hygiene and grooming in Chapt er 9 are taken from
AgeCare's policies on these topics (2002).*

Other titles in this series:
The Care Assistant's Guide to Working With People with Dementia
Fourth Edition 2002. ISBN 1 874790 37 X
The Handbook for Community Care Assistants and Support Workers
1994. ISBN 1 874790 18 3
A Practical Guide to Working with People With Learning Disabilities
Second Edition 1994. ISBN 1 874790 12 4
The Handbook for Hospital Care Assistants and Support Workers
1993. ISBN 1 874790 10 8

Contents

Contributors

Sue Benson BA (Hons), SRN has a background in nursing. For several years she has edited books, educational projects and journals, including the *Journal of Dementia Care*, for Hawker Publications.

Wendy Goodman BSc (Hons) Nursing, SRN, DN Cert, DPNS, ENB 7300, 978, A57 is Senior Practitioner – District Nursing at Eastbourne Downs Primary Care Trust, involved with the professional development and supervision of community nursing staff, which includes supporting nursing auxiliaries through NVQ programmes. She has a specialist interest in the nursing management of older people, particularly within the residential care home setting and with continence problems.

Jane Hall MSc, GradDipPhys, MCSP works as a physiotherapist for AgeCare homes. She has worked as a physiotherapist with older people for many years both in the UK and Australia. As part of her MSc in Gerontology she completed a dissertation exploring the links between dementia and exercise.

Hazel Heath MSc Advanced Clinical Practice (Older People), BA (Hons 1st Class) Nursing Older People, DipNursing(London), FETC, CertEd, ITEC, RGN, RCNT, RNT is an independent nurse consultant and editor of *Nursing Older People*. Following many years of national level work in a range of roles, she is currently completing doctoral research on work with older people in care homes.

Katrina Levett is Training Coordinator and health and safety representative at High Broom Residential Home, AgeCare. She holds the NEBOSH certificate and diploma (part 1) in health and safety; and an Advanced Certificate in Health and Safety and Group Training Certificate from CIEH.

Buz Loveday Dip Couns runs Dementia Training and Consultancy Services, devising and delivering training in a wide variety of care settings. She is co-author (with Tom Kitwood) of *Improving Dementia Care – A Resource for Training and Professional Development*.

Professor **Brendan MCormack** D Phil (Oxon) BSc (Hons) PGCEA RNT RMN RGN is Director of Research, Practice Development and Clinical Education in the Royal Hospitals, Belfast and manages these activities across all specialties, while maintaining his specialist practice focus on gerontological nursing. He leads a number of practice development and research projects in Ireland and the UK that utilise action learning and action research. In addition he is the leader of the School of Nursing's 'Working with Older People' Recognised Research Group, coordinating research and development activity in this area.

Clare Morris is a speech and language therapist and personal construct psychotherapist, specialising in therapeutic work with people with dementia, both individually and groupwork. Since 1997 she has been working for The National Prion Clinic at St. Mary's Hospital in London, supporting families affected by all forms of CJD. She also provides a counselling service to younger people with dementia and their families who attend the Specialist Cognitive Disorders Clinic at the National

Hospital for Neurology and Neurosurgery, and is involved in education, training and supervision.

Adrian Muir is Lead Internal Verification Co-ordinator at the AgeCare Assessment Centre. His role involves visiting and supporting external organisations, ensuring the standard and quality within them for the AgeCare Award. He also coordinates the training of all assessors. He holds NVQ Levels 2 & 3 in Care, NVQ level 3 in Management, D32/D33 Assessor and D34 Internal Verifier.

Tracy Packer is Nurse Consultant for Dementia Care at North Bristol NHS Trust, and Visiting Research Fellow at the University of the West of England. She is currently involved in working with acute sector staff to develop skills and confidence in their care of people with dementia and their relatives.

Lynne Phair MA BSc(Hons) Nursing RMN RGN DPNS Advanced Cert in Health & Safety, D32/33 D34 is Project Director AgeCare Awards project, working for AgeCare (The Royal Surgical Aid Society) London. This project is an exciting innovative approach to BTEC and NVQ in care specialising in training to care for older people. Lynne has always worked with older people, in the NHS Mental Health Services for older people and Voluntary Sector.

Phil Russell MA MSc BA RNT RN has a nursing background and has developed special expertise in bereavement counselling. He is a Senior Lecturer at the University of Portsmouth.

Ruth Sander MSc BA RN PGCE D32/33 has a nursing background. She is Senior Lecturer in Care of Older People at the University of Portsmouth and has a special interest in care homes.

Jane Slack MSc Health Studies, Diploma in Health and Social Welfare, RGN is Nurse Consultant – Care of the Older Person, United Bristol Healthcare Trust.

Foreword

Mike Nolan
Professor of Gerontological Nursing
University of Sheffield

It is a great privilege to have been asked to write the foreword to the sixth edition of this important book. Why do I think this book is so important? Well, there are several reasons.

Firstly, supporting older people and their families is one of the most challenging, but also one of the most exciting and rewarding areas in which to work. Secondly, those who work in care homes have the opportunity to make a very real difference to the quality of life of some of the frailest and most vulnerable members of society.

Thirdly, care assistants provide the vast majority of 'hands-on care' – and research has shown that what you do and how you do it is probably one of the most important factors influencing the quality of care provided. Make no mistake: your contribution to care is essential. Care assistants therefore need a very special book. A book like this one.

Although the aim is to provide a practical guide, practice must be based on sound principles. Probably the most important principle of all is captured in the title *Handbook for care assistants – A practical guide to working with older people*. 'Working with' suggests a partnership between equals. It recognises that even though a person may be old and frail, they still have a great deal to offer. The contents of this book reflect this belief, quite rightly starting with the need to value older people and adopt a person-centred approach before considering more practical issues.

Of course, partnerships are not just about your relationships with residents, as the family also has a key role to play. Together you can combine your expertise and knowledge to provide genuinely person-centred care.

So go on, don't just read this book but absorb its key messages, apply them in your daily work, and see what a difference you make.

Introduction

To the sixth edition

Lynne Phair & Sue Benson

Caring for older people should be one of the most rewarding occupations a person can ever have the opportunity to do. However no one can just 'do' caring; everyone needs to be given the chance to learn how to care and why care should be delivered in a certain way. We also need to understand why we feel the way we do, so that we can understand how that affects our views and feelings towards older people.

This book has been written in a way that we hope will address all of these points. We want care staff in all care environments to look beyond the practical tasks they have to complete, and be able to understand why you do things in a particular way, and more importantly why you should challenge outdated and sometimes unacceptable ways of working.

Everything you do when working with older people should show that you have considered them first, that they are at the centre of your thoughts and actions, that your work is person-centred.

Each chapter has been carefully written to give you all the underpinning knowledge you need for the Induction and Foundation standards and NVQ level 2 in care, in respect of older people. Practical tips for good practice are also included, but every chapter will, we hope, make you reflect and think about your own values, beliefs and attitudes towards older people.

The book has been planned specifically to cover the number of units required for your NVQ, and the reference guide on page 180 will guide you to the underpinning knowledge for other NVQ units.

We are grateful to AgeCare (Royal Surgical Aid Society) for permission to use case scenarios from the AgeCare Awards workbooks (in chapters 1 and 2), and sections of good practice guidance from AgeCare policies (in chapters 3 and 9).

The book also offers cross referencing to the other two important government documents currently in use in the care of older people: *The Essence of Care* and *The National Service Framework for Older People.*

Care assistants play a key role in providing high quality care for older people in all care settings. We hope this book will provide a resource which will enable each individual to fulfill their potential at work and in their future career.

MICHAEL CORP/AGECARE

CHAPTER 1

Valuing older people

Lynne Phair

- *Stereotyping: what it is and why you should avoid it*
- *The rights of every citizen* • *Relatives and consent*
- *Data protection and you*
- *Rights and responsibilities of care staff*

To be able to work with older people, we must first think about our own attitudes – in particular whether we value them as full and equal members of society. We need to understand our own feelings about older people if we are to be true and sincere when offering them care and support.

Perceptions of old age change as we grow up. To a child, someone who is 40 or 50 may seem very old indeed. Our understanding of old age is also affected by our background. The culture in which we live, the images the television and media give to us and our own experiences all shape our views.

Stereotyping

Stereotyping is the name given to the thoughts you may have which group people together or which help to form your view or opinion of a group of people. These views and opinions may have arisen from stories, impressions or misunderstandings, or from your own experience. You may decide, for example, that a person has certain abilities or disabilities or level of intelligence if they are from another country or a different ethnic group, have a different skin colour or a physical disability.

It is impossible to avoid hearing and sometimes being influenced by stereotypical views. Maturity and wisdom are achieved when we begin to understand why we hold such beliefs and seek to change them.

The media

Many views and opinions of others are formed from the different types of media we are exposed to. The organisations delivering the information can place a slant on the television or newspaper article by leaving out some pieces of information or only giving us one opinion. For example, it is not uncommon for television programmes to focus on the negative aspects of old age, and to give an impression this is the norm.

Advertising companies do not often use older people to advertise products unless they are targeted at that generation. This means the image of an older person driving the latest sports car or buying a highly technical computer is not one the public sees. So the media reinforces the negative images of older age even though, in May 2000, the charity Age Concern found four million people over 50 owned a computer and each spent an average of nine hours a week using it.

Diversity and culture

Everyone is different and everyone knows that! Yet we often forget this fact when we are working with people or caring for someone who is from a different culture. The United Kingdom is a country made up of a diverse population. In 2000, there were 10.7 million people over 60 years of age. And seven per cent of the UK population of people over 65 was from an ethnic minority. Of those 15 per cent were Black-Caribbean, 10 per cent Indian, nine per cent Chinese and seven per cent Pakistani people.

The UK population will continue to become more cosmopolitan, so it is important to ensure older people from every culture can receive care and support in a way that is appropriate to them.

Everyone has a cultural background; it is not just linked to ethnicity. It is important to recognise the cultural diversity which is present because of the location, or area where people live. Each region of the UK has some unique cultural ways, such as local foods or festivals. In other areas, the type of work, for example mining or farming, or the lack of it, as in inner city estates, may have affected and developed the culture. This means culture is something everyone has, or is affected by, but which we may not always be aware of because we live within it.

First impressions

When an advertising company designs a poster it only adds as much information as can be absorbed in about 15 seconds, because this is how long we take to form a first impression.

Such an impression is made by your brain collecting information very quickly from what you see, hear, smell, feel or

The powerful effects of stereotyping

Your beliefs can affect your attitudes and actions more than you realise. If, for example, you believe that all older people are incontinent, you will design or adapt the environment to manage incontinence – plastic chair covers, vinyl flooring, overuse of incontinence aids. If however you accept and understand that in fact 85 per cent of older people are not incontinent, your attitude and approach to care and the care environment will be very different.

taste and using information stored from previous experiences or previous impressions and our own cultural background.

In these ways, stereotypical views and the influence of the media affect the first impression someone has of an older person. If we are aware of the effect these influences can have and understand our own views and feelings and beliefs about older people, we can work towards ensuring that our understanding is positive and is not influenced by incorrect information.

Legal rights of older people

In the UK, you can consent to heterosexual relationships at the age of 16, learn to drive at 17 and vote at 18. Every citizen has legal and civil rights. Children are protected by the Children's Act, so they too have legal rights. It is a common misconception that older people – particularly those who live in a care environment – do not have the same rights as anybody else. They *do* have exactly the same rights, so it is important to understand what those rights are.

The Human Rights Act

The Human Rights Act 1998 gives every citizen the same human rights. These affect every aspect of our lives as the Act applies to any service which is supplied. For example, any service supplied by the Government, NHS or Social Services. The main ones are:

- the right to life
- prohibition of slavery and forced labour
- right to liberty and security
- right to a fair trial
- right to respect for privacy and family life
- freedom of thought, conscience and religion
- right to free elections
- right to marry
- abolition of the death penalty
- right to education
- prohibition of discrimination.

Discrimination

Discrimination is the term used to describe when a person is denied something because of their race, gender, sexuality or disability. The Human Rights Act makes it unlawful for a person to discriminate against another.

A number of other laws help protect people against discrimination:

- The Equal Pay Act 1970
- The Sex Discrimination Act 1975
- The Race Relations Act 1976
- The Disability Discrimination Act 1995.

All are designed to protect people from decisions being taken against them simply because of who they are. They attempt to help ensure everyone is accepted as an equal.

The right to vote

Everyone has the right to vote in local and national elections. It is important that a person living in a care home is given the opportunity to exercise that right. Councils and the Government offer postal votes in advance of election days, which makes this easier. However, some people may wish to visit the polling station, and this should be organised for them.

Consent

Consent is the legal term used to describe a person's right to decide whether they wish to do something.

It is a very important issue. Older people should have the right to make decisions for themselves about the life they lead. They should be supported in their wish to make decisions themselves if they are able to. Their right to give consent is not affected by physical frailty. However, asking a question in a certain way can force a person to give their consent, and a lack of options may make someone feel they do not have a choice.

Competence and capacity

Competence and capacity are the legal terms used to describe a person who has the ability to decide whether or not they wish to do something. If a person is unable to make decisions because they are mentally unable, 'their competence and capacity is affected'.

The ability to make decisions may vary depending on the situation, the type of decision and how the person is asked to be involved in that decision. Only a doctor can decide that a person is not able to make legal decisions. But all older people should be encouraged to make decisions for themselves if they are able to.

Involvement of relatives in the issues of consent

It is not only staff who have to accept and understand that consent is important and that people, even those living in a care environment, must be able to exercise their rights of individual decision-making. Some relatives find it very hard to understand that, although frail physically, a person may be mentally able to decide what is to happen to them. Relatives also need to understand that older people should be encouraged and supported to make decisions for as long as they are able to.

A situation may arise where perhaps a relative is trying to help the resident but their opinion is rather misguided, as in the example *Who should decide?* in the box opposite.

In this example, the correct answer is that the doctor should talk to Miss Black and judge how important the operation is to her in respect of pain, discomfort and immobility. The doctor should then discuss the situation with the niece, but then make the decision. Relatives do not have the right to decide, although their concerns and consideration should be fully considered when making medical and caring decisions about the older person. It is important that relatives or friends who are important to the older person are fully involved in decisions about care. However, it must be established whether or not that resident wants that particular relative/friend to be involved.

Enduring power of attorney

The example also introduces the concept of Enduring Power of Attorney. This document gives the relative, or another named individual, the right to manage the person's financial and business affairs. It has to be signed and agreed while the resident is still mentally able to make that decision and only comes into power when the person loses the ability to manage their own financial affairs. Currently the enduring power of attorney does not cover a person's care, although UK law is about to change and

in Scotland new laws are being implemented to offer care decision powers to others. It is important that medical staff consider the balanced needs of everybody, but in the end decisions made about care and treatment have to be done in what is believed to be the best interests of the resident.

Care directives – living wills

It is now common for people to write a living will to decide in advance what treatment they wish to have if they become seriously ill, in case they are unable to state their views at the time. Living wills do not have a legal status in the UK; however, they are often closely considered when treatment or care is being planned.

Confidentiality and the Data Protection Act 1998

Confidentiality is the term used to describe the need to 'keep a confidence' – to keep information about others secure and not discuss information received inappropriately. However, it is important to understand that confidentiality will be applied at different levels in different situations. For staff working in the care home environment the need for confidentiality is paramount. However, that confidentiality is between you and the resident and you and the organisation or your senior staff. Thus, if a resident informs you of something you do have a duty to pass that information on to the relevant person; you should not keep it to yourself. This is because you are working for the organisation. You do not have the levels of knowledge, expertise and responsibility required to decide what if any action should be taken on information given to you in confidence by a resident.

Confidentiality is protected under the Data Protection Act 1998. This came into the UK to comply with European legislation for the protection and use of personal information. It is very important that you understand the Act and how it applies to your workplace. There should be a policy describing the procedures of how data will be protected.

The Data Protection Act applies to:

1. computer-held records
2. records kept in manual files
3. all records that relate to a person which can be identifiable. This person is called a 'data subject'.

Information covered by the Data Protection Act includes identifying details such as, name, address, postcode, telephone number, age, sex, date of birth. It is information that can be used to identify a living individual. It can be from any type of media: manual or computer records, video or CCTV footage or x-rays.

A data subject is an individual who is the subject of personal information. In a care environment this is anyone who gives data to the care environment including employees, residents, clients, even volunteers. All these people have

Who should decide?

Miss Black is a retired teacher aged 74 who has dementia. She is unable to remember much detail, but is able to say what she wants on a day to day basis. She has a niece who is her enduring power of attorney. Miss Black needs a hip replacement. The doctors says she is fit enough medically and that she is in a lot of pain when walking. The niece, however, says no. She believes there is no point as a new hip will not help her aunt's memory and that she is better off sitting still. Who has the right to consent? Does the medical team have a right to overpower the aunt? Who should they listen to?

rights to be protected.

You need to ensure the data is secured properly:

• Close doors and windows at nights and weekends so that people cannot access computer records or manual records.
• Keep information secure; lock it in a drawer when it is not in use.
• Take care when discussing information or disclosing it to others. Ask yourself, is it appropriate for this person to have that information?
• Make sure lockable cabinets have keys and are locked.
• Don't write down passwords or access codes if you have access to computer records
• Make sure information is transported securely, for example when carrying resident records to a hospital.
• Ensure records are always in a closed envelope when being transported so that they cannot fall out accidentally and be read by others.

Access to records

Individuals have rights of access to information held about them, whether it is on computer, in manual files or on video. All residents and employees should be informed about what information is held. It must be adequate, relevant and not excessive for the purpose for which it has been collected. It is also important that information is accurate, kept up to date and not held for longer than is necessary. The Data Protection Act is simple and sensible. It is about storing information correctly, not gathering information that is not really required and not telling people anything they do not have the right to know. The Act also covers destroying information correctly by shredding or parcelling it up so that people who do not have the right to access it, cannot read it.

SUE BENSON/AGECARE

We need to understand our own feelings about older people if we are to be true and sincere in offering care and support.

Personal accountability

The term personal accountability refers to your responsibilities as an adult to ensure the action you take is correct and lawful. Although when you work in a care environment, others more senior will have responsibility and accountability, you have personal accountability for your own actions. Thus, if you carry out an action that is incorrect or unlawful and you knowingly do this, you are responsible and accountable. So, for example, if you are asked to undertake work you don't have training for, or you do not feel is part of your role, it is important for you to say so to the person asking you to do the task. If you do something that you know you are not trained to do, you are accountable for your actions.

Record keeping

It is a legal requirement that records are kept of all care and support given to a person in a care setting. Whether you have responsibility to make those records will vary depending on the care environment you work in. However, it is important that they are kept legibly and accurately, and that if there is an incident, you make a record at the time. All residents will also have an assessment from which a written care plan is drawn up. This care plan must be regularly referred to and regularly updated. It is important that you understand and become familiar with the way the care plan system works in your care environment. Every aspect of care should be written down so everyone understands what the resident requires. It is also very important that the resident is involved in the process of planning their own care.

There are many other documents that need to be written up, because the care home is required to keep these records. These include bath and fridge temperatures, and the storage and monitoring of

drugs and medicines. When making records it is important that you:
- use a black pen
- write clearly
- do not use white opaque correction fluid to cover up mistakes
- add accurate and correct information to care notes
- sign each record you make
- ensure each is dated and timed
- always inform the person in charge that you have made an entry.

If it is not your responsibility to write in the care notes, ensure you inform the person in charge of any changes, observations or significant pieces of information, however small or trivial they might appear. The senior staff are trained to identify how information slots together to form important knowledge about the person's care needs.

The Mental Health Act 1983

This Act of Parliament is designed to protect people with a severe mental illness and the public.

Most people with mental health problems are able to understand the need for care and treatment. However sometimes people become so ill they are not able to understand that they need care and treatment. If the psychiatrist believes someone is a danger to themself or others, they may be detained under the Mental Health Act to be assessed and possibly treated.

People detained under this Act can appeal against their detention to the Mental Health Tribunal. This panel assesses the situation and decides whether the person is well enough to be released. It needs to ensure:
- the person who has been mentally ill is not discriminated against or "labelled" because they have had a mental illness, and
- that the public is protected.

The Care Standards Act 2000

All residents of a care home are now protected under the Care Standards Act. This sets the minimum standards which are designed to determine whether a care home meets the needs and secure the welfare and social involvement of the people who live there. The standards are used by the National Care Standards Commission to measure the quality of life and care being delivered in a care home environment.

The standards are grouped under key topics, which were chosen by groups of older people when the government consulted them. The topics are:
- choice of home
- health and personal care
- daily life and social activities
- complaints and protection
- environment
- staffing
- management and administration.

NHS and Community Care Act 1990

This Act gives older and disabled people rights about the services they are entitled to from the NHS and social services. All older people are entitled to be assessed to see what services they need to help them live. However their ability to receive the services will depend on the local arrangements and rules about who can receive them. It may also depend on how much money the person has in savings.

Every social services department produces a community care plan which details what services a person may be able to receive. However, community services are expensive and sometimes the budgets available do not match the needs in the area, in which case the rules change so the services can target those who are most needy.

Carers (Recognition and Services) Act 1995

This Act is concerned with carers who provide or intend to provide a substantial amount of care on a regular basis. The term carer refers to a family member or friend who is not paid to give that care.

Under this Act, a carer is entitled to an assessment by social services when they carry out an assessment of the person being cared for. The results of the carer's assessment should be taken into account when social services are making decisions about the services to be provided to the user.

However, the carer has to ask for this assessment and the social services department cannot be forced to give services to the carer to meet their needs. The Act only means that social services have to bear the needs of the carer in mind.

Chapter 1 - Valuing older people: rights and responsibilities

ESSENCE OF CARE								
Record Keeping Factors								
1	2	3	4	5	6	7		
Privacy & dignity Factors:								
1	2	3	4	5	6	7		

NMS								
14.5	37.1	37.2	37.3	17.1	17.2	17.3		

NSF								
1.2	1.7	1.12	1.17	1.19	1.20			
2.1	2.2	2.8	2.13	2.14	2.15	2.16	2.17	2.18	2.18
2.24	2.27	2.28	2.29	2.31	2.34			

TOPSS						
Induction						
3.3.1	3.1.2	3.2.1				
2.1.1	2.2.1	2.3.1	2.3.2			
1.1.1	1.1.2	1.2.1	1.2.2	1.4.1	1.4.2	
Foundation						
5.1 all	5.2 all					
2.5.3						
1.1.1	1.1.1	1.2.1	1.3.1	1.4.1	1.4.2	

NVQ 2 CARE
Element O1.1
All range All performance Criteria
Element O1.2
All range All performance criteria
Element O1.3
All range All performance Criteria   All knowledge and understanding

Compiled by Adrian Muir

CHAPTER 2
Person-centred care
Lynne Phair

*• The philosophy of person-centred care • The 'new culture of care'
in practice • Your approach really matters • Challenging routines and rituals
• Sensitive solutions to meet individual needs*

Many homes and care environments have mission statements. A mission statement is a specific philosophy of care by which the home and all its staff work. A philosophy of care should be a way of life, influencing the way you conduct yourself and relate to other people, especially the residents you work with.

Person-centred care is an approach and philosophy which was developed to support people with dementia. Its basic principle is that the person with dementia should be respected as a human being who happens to have a special need, and that care staff should be aware that the way they talk and behave will have a positive or negative effect on that person. This means recognising that the actions, words and approaches of a member of care staff will have an effect on the person's well-being (happiness) or ill-being (unhappiness) and can cause damage and distress.

We can all be affected by the words and actions of others. If someone is particularly nasty or unkind to us, we can bounce back and ignore them. Or we can talk to a friend about it and put the situation into context, which makes us feel better. People with dementia do not necessarily have this ability. They may not be able to understand why someone has spoken or acted towards them in a certain way. If this happens, especially if it happens over and over again, damage is done and continues to erode the person's belief in themself.

The principle of person-centred care can be applied to any care environment because every older person, whether they have dementia or not, needs to know that he or she is valued as an individual.

Traditional care

Tom Kitwood* described the way staff in care environments have traditionally seen themselves as a group of people who were able, competent, kind and knew what was best for older people. They felt they had skills to 'manage' people's illnesses and 'challenging' behaviour – and therefore they should decide how best a

*Tom Kitwood was head of Bradford Dementia Group and Professor of Dementia Studies at Bradford University until his sudden death in 1998. His clear and persuasive writing, both academic and for practitioners, gave a vital boost to the development and growth of a person-centred approach to dementia care. Useful publications include: *Person-Centred Care*. Ed. Sue Benson, Introduction and concept, Tom Kitwood. Hawker Publications, London. *The New Culture of Dementia Care*. Ed. Tom Kitwood and Sue Benson, Hawker Publications, London. Information (including other publications) from Bradford Dementia Group - see p175.

person should be cared for. In short, staff believed that any difficulties the person had were different from the difficulties staff had, that staff were in control and always knew what was best.

The new culture of care

Tom Kitwood also described an improved care environment, which he called 'The new culture of care'. It marks an important change of attitude, to the belief that older people have the ability and the right to say how their care should be given, even – especially – those who have difficulty communicating their feelings and preferences. It acknowledges that we all have strengths and weaknesses, and supports working together using the skills we have to help people in the best way possible. The new philosophy advises that staff should not assume they are more able than or superior to the resident, simply because they can go home at night.

Tom Kitwood has identified five statements which, if accepted, show that we do value someone as an individual:

1. We respect each person as an individual and understand that we are all very different.
2. We recognise that everyone makes a contribution to society in some way.
3. We acknowledge that everyone has needs which we should try and meet.
4. We understand that we should value someone and respect him or her simply for being the person they are, and not make judgements about the person we think they should be.
5. We agree that everyone has rights, in society, in law, and as a human being.

If we all hold these values and work with them, we can start to work and live the principles of person-centred care when caring for older people.

Practical examples of person-centred care in everyday life

Tom Kitwood identified positive actions which can demonstrate that care staff understand and are living the philosophy of person-centred care. Respect for the person should be the cornerstone of the life of a care home. No matter how well furnished the home, or however clean and well fed the resident, if attention is not paid to the emotional well-being of that individual, he or she is not being valued as a whole person.

There are six principles staff can learn to work to:

1. Holding
This means both physical and psychological holding: supporting a resident with a hug, holding their hand, or giving emotional support by showing you understand their feelings.

2. Validation
This is acknowledging the person's experience and emotion. It is real to them and it should not be denied. Denying their experience denies their feelings.

MICHAEL CORP/AGECARE

The cornerstone of care is the emotional and physical well-being of each individual.

3. Facilitation

This means enabling a person to do what they can do for themselves. Staff should not just do something because it is easier or quicker for them to do so than for the resident to do it.

4. Celebration

This means care staff and an older person should enjoy life together, working in partnership and as equals.

5. Timulation

This word was invented by Tom Kitwood. It describes how the senses can be stimulated which then gives pleasure, through seeing, smelling or hearing.

6. Relaxation

The atmosphere of a care home should be calm for both staff and residents.

The philosophy of person-centred care also identifies the negative aspects of attitude and behaviour, which can damage an older person's feeling of well-being or self worth.

Tom Kitwood identified 17 components of what he called *malignant social psychology*. Each can occur in degrees from mild through to severe. The damage could be instant or it may build up slowly but, as with any human being, it will affect their self-esteem, confidence and, eventually, their belief in themself.

The philosophy of person-centred care identifies these 17 components:

Treachery: being dishonest or deceiving residents to obtain compliance.

Disempowerment: doing something for a person who is quite capable of doing it for themself.

Infantilisation: implying that the person has the mentality of a child by speaking in a condescending manner.

Condemnation: blaming the resident or accusing him or her of something.

Intimidation: using mild threats, which is an abuse of power even if only in a small way.

Objectification: This means talking about residents or dealing with them as if they are an object.

Stigmatisation: suggesting the older person is different, that there is something wrong with them.

Outpacing: giving information too quickly and not bearing in mind the needs and abilities of the person to whom you are speaking.

Invalidation: ignoring the feelings of the person.

Banishment: removing the person, either physically or psychologically, from the area they are in.

Ignoring: talking about the person in their presence, as if they were not there.

Imposition: forcing the person to do something.

Withholding: refusing to respond when a person asks for help.

Accusation: blaming the person for failures that arise due to their lack of ability.

Disruption: disturbing a person suddenly and without respect.

Mockery: making fun of a person's unusual behaviour.

Disparagement: telling a person they are failing.

Not all of Kitwood's philosophy can be proved, but it is accepted that these negative elements of communication or interaction damage self-esteem, no matter how well or ill the person who is subjected to them.

It is also important to understand that this philosophy of care is about a way of living. It is about a way of approaching our own life and our attitude towards older people. We have all accidentally said or done something that has hurt someone's feelings. Taking a person-centred approach means we recognise this, and try to make amends and improve our actions.

Reassuring a worried resident

Mrs Andrews is physically independent but she becomes anxious and worried if she cannot meet the routines of the home. She has been invited to a garden fête but will not be back until 7pm. Mrs Andrews becomes anxious she will miss her supper and that doing so would be inconvenient for the staff. A person-centred approach means reassuring Mrs Andrews that she could have her supper at any time: that it could be reheated, if appropriate and safe to do so, or that a cold supper could be arranged. This shows you are validating her feelings, treating her as an individual and looking at ways by which she can be helped.

Using person-centred care

It is important to start actively living person-centred care. You can do this just by sitting in the lounge of the care environment and watching life from the residents' point of view for a while. You will see whether residents are being cared for as people, or as residents who have something wrong with them. In the traditional style of care, it is not unknown for staff and nurses to call people 'the Parkinson's disease' or 'the person with the stroke'. Person-centred care means thinking of them as, for example, 'Bert, a retired motor mechanic who happens to have dementia'.

Watching how staff and relatives interact with residents, and how the residents interact with each other, can help to build up the skills of person-centred care. Sitting in the lounge for an hour watching the life in a care home may show some very positive aspects. You may see a hug from a care assistant to a resident or a compliment on their choice of clothes; a member of staff chatting with a resident; or a conversation between two residents resulting in them sharing a biscuit. However, you might also see residents calling for assistance and being ignored; being moved with a hoist without being told why, or asking for a cup of tea and being told it's not possible because it's not time.

Once you have begun to get a flavour of life in the care home lounge, you can begin to help other staff to examine their practices and attitudes towards the residents.

The first and most important principle to establish among all staff is to understand and believe that staff and residents are equals and that any negative language or actions should be stopped. Once this belief system is established, then the care can develop into the philosophy of person-centred care.

In your everyday practice you can judge whether person-centred care is working in your care environment by observing and perhaps counting how many times you see examples of well-being or ill-being. You may see this kind of observation being done in a formal evaluation of care using Dementia Care Mapping (Bradford Dementia Group).

Signs of well-being in a resident include: people appearing happy; humour – from staff, residents and relatives; residents being encouraged to be helpful and to work as part of the care home life; shows of affection, both physical touching and emotional bonding; initiating of social contact; people behaving in a relaxed way as if they are at home in the care environment.

Indications of ill-being include: anxiety; expressions of worry and concern from residents; fear; tentativeness; unhappiness in a person's eyes; boredom; sitting staring into space; or suffering physical discomfort or pain that is not being attended to.

Sometimes a person may suffer ill-being because there is no one to communicate with and nothing to engage with. It is important to remember that different activities call for different levels of ability. This means that someone who is physically unable to participate in an activity, may still be able to get involved by watching, talking, listening and engaging with staff and other residents.

Person-centred care in your own approach to work

Try to use the philosophy of person-centred care throughout your professional life and to work from this approach. Remember the six principles and that you, your attitude and your approach to residents, make a difference.

You do not always have to refer to a senior member of staff. See the boxes on this and the previous page: – *Reassuring a worried resident*, and *Finding sensitive solutions*.

Routines and rituals

Person-centred care should also be part of the philosophy of how a home is organised. The routines and rituals of a care home can automatically make staff approach people in a certain way or encourage fixed ideas and ritualistic behaviour. For example, homes may have a list that states which day a person can have a bath which may be just once a week. Perhaps all the chairs are plastic – as it is assumed that older people are incontinent. The time for serving an early morning cup of tea may be fixed; residents may not be allowed in a pantry kitchen which was actually designed for their use, because it is quicker for staff to make the tea and it is assumed that older people could burn themselves.

Using the principles of person-centred care encourages looking at practices in the care home and deciding whether a routine and ritual is required because there is evidence to support the need for it, or if it is a system that has been set up purely to suit the organisation.

These are difficult things to address, but it is important for ritualistic practice to be eliminated if a care home environment is to make real progress towards person-centred care.

Involving residents in decision-making

There are many examples of residents being involved in decision-making processes. This is an extension of the philosophy of person-centred care. For example, it is now quite usual for residents to be involved in decisions about their choice of clothes (the National Minimum Standards says every resident should wear their own). However, in

Finding sensitive solutions

Mr Thomas is a dignified man who used to be a lawyer. He has had a stroke and cannot use his right hand. He also cannot speak very well. Mr Thomas wants to feed himself but tips the food down his shirt. His wife comes in and tells him he looks a mess. In a person-centred approach you can delicately suggest to his wife it is important Mr Thomas continues to feed himself if this is what he wants to do. You can ask Mr Thomas how he would like to be protected, whether with a napkin, an apron or cloth or paper towels. You can suggest he could use other eating utensils and demonstrate this equipment to him. The most important thing is that Mr Thomas should not be reminded he is failing, instead he should be supported in finding alternative ways of managing his life.

some care home environments, they are not involved in the choice of life in the care home in many other ways.

If an organisation is to develop its care home environment and the carers are to develop their own approach to person-centred care, it is important that every aspect of decision-making is looked at to ensure residents are involved as far as possible.

Examples of good practice include involving residents in:
• menu planning, every two weeks and with the chef
• discussing what type of social activities the staff can organise, and perhaps in helping with the organisation
• deciding the new decoration schemes

for their own room or for an area of the home
• interviewing potential staff. Residents would have to be taught equal opportunities policies and the legal requirements of interviewing, and understand them. But mentally able residents can make a constructive contribution to this aspect of the home life.

For managers and owners of care environments, person-centred care is underpinned with good recruitment procedures, attitude-focused induction programmes, philosophy-focused training and education, good staff communication, good staff support, and regular reviews of how the philosophy of the home is being lived.

Chapter 2 - Valuing older people: putting a philosophy into practice

ESSENCE OF CARE

Privacy & Dignity Factors

1	2	3	4	5	6	7

NMS

3.3	2.2	4.1	4.2	4.3	4.4	7.6

NSF

2.1	2.2	2.3	2.4	2.5	2.6	2.7	2.8	2.9
2.10	2.11	2.13	2.14	2.16	2.17	2.18	2.19	
2.20	2.21	2.24	2.29					
2.30	2.34	2.39						
2.40	2.43	2.44	2.47	2.48				
2.51								

TOPSS

Induction

1.1.1	1.1.2	1.2.1	1.2.2	1.4.1	1.4.2
2.3.1	2.3.2				
3.1.1	3.1.2	3.2.1			

Foundation

1.1.1	1.1.2	1.2.1	1.3.1	1.4.1	1.4.2		
4.1.1	4.3.1	4.3.1					
5.1.1	5.1.2	5.1.3	5.1.4	5.2.1	5.2.2	5.2.3	5.2.4

NVQ 2 CARE

Element O1.1
All Range met   All performance criteria met
Element O1.2
All Range met   All performance criteria met
Element O1.3
All Range met   All performance criteria met   All Knowledge requirements met   *Compiled by Adrian Muir*

CHAPTER 3

Communication

Lynne Phair and Clare Morris

Language and cultural differences • Levels and types of communication – use of eyes, gestures, appearance, touch, personal space, the environment, verbal and non-verbal communication • Skilled questioning • Active listening and observation • Making sense of the world • Security, choice and control • Hallucinations and delusions • Positive skills in response to aggression

We have all been communicating all day every day since birth in many different ways, and have become very skilled already. Arguably it is impossible *not* to communicate. We send out messages all the time – sometimes we intend to and at other times we give away small clues about the way we are feeling whether we want to or not. Communication is so much more than what we say to each other. Relationships of all kinds are central to being human and getting our communication right or wrong is something that will arouse strong feelings, whether this is in our private lives or at work.

Largely we feel good when people listen to us, try to understand, respond to what we want, and agree with us. We are likely to be unnerved when people ignore us, seem bored or distracted, point out our shortcomings, or dismiss what we are trying to say. It is true that our perception of these situations may not be what the other person intends, but we react according to our own understanding of the situation. For example, not noticing someone or being preoccupied with something else could be experienced by the other person as being ignored.

Language changes

Language has changed over the centuries. The words used by Shakespeare or Chaucer, for example, are not easily understood by today's young people. Language has changed even over one or two generations. What one generation might describe as 'wicked' or 'cool' (words which have very different meanings for older people) another generation might well have called 'spiffing'.

Language has to change to keep pace with changes in our daily lives. We now have stereos and CDs for example, not record players or wirelesses. It is important to ensure that you understand the words and language used by the person you are caring for (perhaps by discussion with the resident, or with older relatives or members of staff).

Cultural differences

Different cultures communicate in different ways. The French are famous for kissing each other on the cheek; in Russia it is more than acceptable for men to kiss each other, whereas in the UK it is uncommon and often frowned upon for men to kiss each other in public. Japanese people greet each other with a deep, respectful bow; Thai and

Indian people use a 'hands together in prayer' gesture.

An awareness of differences in the way people from other cultures communicate will help you become more person-centred in communicating with and helping individuals.

Ways of communicating

Communication is often thought of as being the language we speak; however, we communicate in a variety of different ways. We communicate through speech, type of language, tone of the voice, the volume of the voice, the way we move, our hand gestures, our eye movements, the space between people, how we hold things, and other methods of communication which have developed through the culture in which we live.

Messages are sent and received all the time between two people who are communicating. These messages are both verbal and non-verbal. A message is sent with an intention – something the person sending it wishes to communicate. However, other 'messages' sent at the same time – for example from tone of voice, body language and posture – may complicate the communication, or even change its whole meaning. So it is important to be aware that a person may well not receive exactly the same information from a message that the sender believes he or she sent.

Levels of communication

Communication occurs at different levels. *Intra*personal communication is how you communicate with yourself – the way you think, the way you move, how you give yourself information. *Inter*personal communication is how you communicate with one or two other people, how messages are sent and received by you to them and from them to you. Public communication is how you communicate with a wider audience, how you perform, how you communicate at work, how you communicate with people with whom you do not have a close relationship or a one-to-one opportunity. At work that might be communicating in the dining room or lounge, or in the staff meeting.

Verbal communication

Verbal communication includes the words that are used, the tone of voice and the volume at which the statement is given. For example, if a person wants to show that they understand and appreciate another person's predicament, they may answer quietly, fairly slowly and in a warm tone of voice. However, if the person is disapproving or unsympathetic, exactly the same words could be used but they could be said sharply, loudly and/or quickly. The same words would be used but the message delivered would be completely different.

Shouted communication can be especially hard for any of us to interpret. A person may shout because they are angry; on the other hand they may be shouting because they are themselves hard of hearing or believe their listener to be, because they need to communicate over a long distance, or because their voice has a naturally loud volume.

Non-verbal communication

Non-verbal communication means all communication other than speech and language. It includes what you do while you are talking – where you put your hands, what you do with your head, how you sit or stand, for example. Whether you are nervous, feel intimidated or are confident can all be expressed through non-verbal communication and through body signals.

It is important to have some awareness of what you are communicating to oth-

Making sense of the world as 'personal scientists'

A simple framework for understanding the way people go about the task of living may be helpful in developing a person-centred approach to your work. This framework can also provide a way of checking and reflecting on what we are doing. Person-centred care is often not straightforward, and there will always be those residents we find easier to work with than others.

The task of all living things is to make sense of the world and events around them in order to be able to predict what will happen next in the huge range of situations that we face. We could liken this to the process of science. As a 'personal scientist' we have a theory of events, which we test out from minute to minute with our behaviour. The outcome of our behaviour (the experiment to test out our theory of the world) either confirms our theory or proves it wrong. If our theory is confirmed, we are *validated*; if it is proved wrong we are *invalidated*.

Validation of our way of seeing things feels good and encourages us to continue 'experimenting' along similar lines. For example, when we care for an elderly person and they respond well to us, we are validated, and may well come to know that resident better than some others and spend that little bit longer with them. The resident will feel validated too, because you have approached them as a fellow human being, not just a body to be washed, fed, etc.

When we get it wrong, such as when we approach an elderly person with physical affection and this is rebuffed, we may feel hurt, defensive or even cross. There are four main reactions people may have to this *invalidation*:

• We can treat the rebuff as an exception (the resident got out of bed the wrong side) and be affectionate again the next time.

• We may redefine our theory of the way this person likes to be approached and next time greet the person more formally (changing our theory and starting again).

• We could decide that this particular resident doesn't like us, and decide to keep out of their way, encouraging another carer to look after them (avoiding putting our theory to the test, withdrawing).

• In some cases we may deny any responsibility for our approach and label the resident as aggressive (refusing to change our theory, becoming defensive and blaming other people/things).

In the first and second scenarios we may well make the resident feel validated – and valued – so long as we are attempting to stand in their shoes and adjusting our behaviour to take into account how the resident might be making sense of the situation. In the other cases, we may need to reflect on the circumstances and all the possible reasons for them by discussion it with our co-workers. In this way it is possible to develop a team approach to situations we find difficult, and in this way bring about greater validation for both resident and carer. If you as the carer feel validated, you will have a great deal more satisfaction in the important work you do.

Time and time again it is evident that it is not so much 'getting it right' that is important in a care-giving relationship, as the attempt to 'stand in the other person's shoes'. By reflecting on your communication with residents and trying out different ways of approaching your work, you are making the attempt to stand in their shoes and this in itself is a respectful stance that is validating for residents.

Security, choice, control

It is frightening to find yourself unsteady on your feet, 'suddenly' living among strangers in The Home which you have always dreaded. Maybe it is the first time you have had to share your living space with anyone new for a long time. Being in pain and being aware of getting closer to death are likewise issues that shake very important ways of seeing ourselves. We cannot change these 'facts'; however, we can adjust our communication in order to help the person deal with them.

Being unable to choose for yourself what you do and when is deeply disturbing. Seemingly insignificant issues like which chair you sit in, choosing an item of clothing, whether you want sugar in your tea today, can take on huge importance in helping the person feel more secure because they are having some control, some effect on events around them. It helps if we can create as many choices as possible, however small, to help increase that sense of having some choice and control over events, and thereby feeling more like a 'person'.

For example, you may notice that a new resident is particularly agitated, is asking if the bus is coming to take her home as 'the peas are on the stove'. You know she has no choice about going home and that the bus isn't coming to pick her up. Perhaps the woman has an inkling too, and is very frightened of that. It is likely to help to say gently she will be staying here tonight, that everything at home is taken care of so she doesn't need to worry, and to ask what you can do to make her feel better. Perhaps to watch TV or sit down and tell you about her family? To have some kind of choice is better than no choice at all, and the process of making the choice can really bring about a sense of control.

ers in this way – it may be far from the message you think you are sending. For example, some say that having your hands in your pockets means you are withholding information or keeping a secret. However, you may simply have cold hands, or be getting some change from your pocket. Scratching your nose while talking or listening has been interpreted by psychologists as meaning the person is lying or covering up their emotions – but you may just have an itchy nose!

Folding your arms or sitting with legs crossed during conversation can give the impression that you are feeling very defensive or actually threatened by the communication. These positions are seen as indicating uncertainty and lack of confidence – though they may arise from habit or nervousness.

Other very common gestures used in our culture are rubbing hands together to indicate anticipation, clapping to show approval, thumbs down to show disapproval, shrugging shoulders to show lack of interest, pretending to shoot ourselves when we realise we have made an error. We wave hands to say goodbye and we rub our tummies when we are hungry. These are very conscious body language gestures.

Use of eyes

Eyes communicate a lot of messages to other people. Sometimes this is deliberate and sometimes subconscious. The eye gaze plays an important part in any conversation. Looking at another or looking away, looking down, avoiding eye contact – all give messages to the person we are communicating with. If a person avoids eye contact while talking to you, it may mean that they feel uncomfortable or that they feel guilty. Some people may look down while talking about embarrassing, difficult or shameful activities. However, in some cultures it is rude to look directly at another person.

When people are thinking about things, often their eyes will move up to the top of their head, as if looking into their brains to find the answers. And the eyes tell us whether someone is smiling. Some people smile genuinely and the whole of their face lights up. But if someone is trying to force a smile, their eyes will not move so easily. The length of the gaze when having a conversation can also indicate how interested the person is or how bored they are with the topic.

Gestures

People often move their hands when they are talking – sometimes this can reveal emotions, or modify the meaning of what is being said. Some gestures have direct meanings as described earlier, other gestures arise from habit and yet others are unconscious. Gestures may be used as sign language, understood by members of a certain groups or different cultures.

Gestures may be used to control a group. Some gestures, such as salutes, denote a power structure. Gestures are very heavily affected by the culture of the person using them; a gesture in one culture may indicate approval but the same hand movement in another could be insulting.

Many hand-to-face gestures are largely unconscious. A person may put their hand over their mouth when they do not really want to be saying something, when they feel embarrassed about what they are saying, when they are trying to hide something or when they are trying to conceal a yawn, perhaps because they are bored.

However, some of these movements may purely and simply be nerves. So it is important to think of all of these types of communication in the context of what is being said, what is being seen and what is being done.

Appearance

People communicate a great deal through the way they appear to others in their style of dress, the way their hair is done, the jewellery they wear, whether they have positive or negative odour. For example, uniforms worn by care staff can communicate a number of messages. Some people believe that uniforms are important in care homes as they inform residents who the care staff are, and some residents like to see people in uniform because it gives them a sense of safety – they know who to go to for help. Some staff do not feel they can do their job properly unless they are wearing their uniform – it reminds them of the professional manner in which they should behave at work. Others argue that a uniform reinforces the power care staff undoubtedly have over residents, and creates an 'us and them' barrier.

Other professions have uniforms: a judge will wear his wig and gown, many police wear uniforms, as do other service professionals. This tells us all immediately who they are and what job they do.

Touch

In the UK, touch is less a part of how we communicate than in many other countries. Touch is very common among children and as an expression of affection in relationships. But touch as a general method of communication is often felt to have some intimate overtones. Some research has shown that as people get older and move into care environments, the only type of touch they receive is when physical care is being given. Touch is important to all of us. It can be a way of demonstrating that we understand what the person is saying, that we want to understand how they are feeling; it gives warmth and shows that we care. However, touch could also indicate that a person wants to take advantage of

Are you paying attention?

In order to hear and understand, we first need to attend to what is said. How often have you been aware of someone talking to you but have been distracted by something else? If you are in pain, or have any changes in thinking, memory, perception or language you will be very preoccupied in dealing with them. So it is important always to make sure you have the resident's attention before you speak or perform any care tasks.

Also, we tend to take for granted that we can do a lot of things at the same time – can chat away while we walk or cook, for example, because much of what we do is 'automatic'. For someone with memory, language or perceptual difficulties this ability to do two things at once can become impossible.

Somebody who has difficulty with language and walking will tend to stop and talk, or walk and be silent. Someone who has difficulty with visual perception and language will be concentrating so hard on making sense of what they see that they won't be able to attend to what you are saying. In a similar way, giving long instructions to someone with memory and language problems puts a greater load on processing, making understanding much less likely.

another, or to become intimate – so touch could carry a negative message or be misunderstood, especially by someone from a different culture.

Handshakes communicate messages. A strong, firm handshake can inspire confidence. However, a very powerful handshake where the fingers are squeezed can actually intimidate. On the other hand a 'dead fish' handshake, in which the person does not hold the hand properly, can communicate a lack of confidence and a lack of security.

Personal space

Animals in the wild and domestic cats are well known for marking their territories. Humans also have a way of marking out their space. Think about sitting on a train: people alone always try to find a seat away from others, to have as much space as possible around them, often putting their bag beside them to make it more difficult for someone else to sit down.

Some authors describe this as a 'portable air bubble' that a person creates around them. The size of the bubble depends on the density of the population in the space in which they grew up, in relation to the space in which they are now.

It is helpful to think of personal space as a number of different zones around our body into which we are comfortable for people to enter, depending on the circumstances (see diagram, right).

In western cultures these are:
• The intimate zone, between 15 and 45 centimetres (six to 18 inches), which is normally entered by people who are close friends or relatives, people who are making sexual advances, or an intruder. People often feel uncomfortable when packed into a train or tube if people are standing very close to them. If someone enters your intimate zone, for example on a social occasion, you may well move backwards away from them.
• The personal zone, between one and two metres (three to six feet), in which people who are friends stand for social functions, parties and friendly gatherings.
• The social zone – between one and a half and three metres (four to twelve feet) is where we stand with strangers or people who have come to the house, perhaps the plumber or carpenter, or people we have never met before.
• The public zone – around three metres (12 feet) – is used when addressing a large group of people.

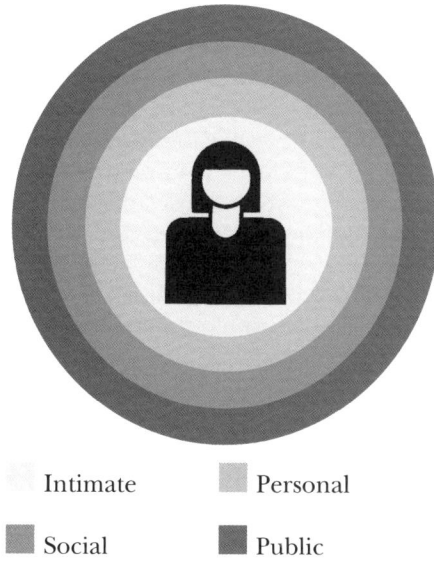

Intimate   Personal

Social   Public

So when you are caring for somebody, you will be entering their intimate zone to offer personal care. It is important to communicate positively and sensitively about what you are intending to do and why you are intending to do it. Even people who seem unaware of what is happening to them will still intuitively understand that they are receiving someone into their intimate zone.

The environment

The environment itself sends powerful messages. The way a care home is decorated, whether it smells, whether it is warm, whether there is appropriate music playing, whether there are photographs around, whether there is a smell of cooking, whether it a positive smell or a negative smell – all communicate vital information, not only to the residents and staff but to people who are visiting.

Communication through the arts

Communicating with residents in other ways could include music and drama, hand massage, arts and crafts, flower

Hallucinations, delusions

Hallucinations are images seen or heard by a person without any obvious reason. These experiences are often generated purely within the brain. A delusion is a belief the person has which is untrue but which to them is very real, and cannot be altered by persuasion. Sometimes people can become deluded due to an understandable reaction to the sense they make of events, given their life history, their disabilities, and events around them. What is important is that these experiences are real to the person having them, and that they can be very frightening.

Vera was convinced that a fellow resident was raping her, and that last night she had to 'box him off'. She could identify the perpetrator of the 'crime' without fail. This belief became more and more fixed and the nursing staff's assurance that it had not taken place did not help. When asked whether she had been very frightened, she confirmed that she was and talked at length about 'what happened'. Then she heaved a sigh of relief and whispered, 'You know I can't really be sure it actually happened.'

This elderly woman had extensive visual difficulties and a traumatic history of rape and torture at Auschwitz. The man in question was very confused, regularly taking all his clothes off and wandering in and out of the ladies' rooms. It is not difficult to see how her 'delusion' developed, and what helped was not to deny her experience with reassurance but to focus on her feelings about the situation.

Being 'reassured' that something did not really happen can be unhelpful, as this brings with it the suggestion that you 'are not in your right mind' or going mad. Most people will react defensively in this situation.

arranging, the use of photographs or objects from the past. These are all ways of communicating with people, and for people to communicate with others, if the normal avenues of communication are more difficult for them.

Communication techniques
Questions

It is important that the person who wants to send a message or communicate with another person is able to listen and understand the information or the response given in reply. To obtain a useful answer you need to ask the right sort of question:

• An **open question** is one which starts with one of the following words: what, why, when, how, where or who. This kind of question encourages the person to give more information in their answer.

• A **closed question** is one which only invites a 'yes' or 'no' response.

For example, 'What would you like for lunch today, Mr Brown?' invites Mr Brown to choose what he wants from a wide range of options – this is an open question. However, if the carer says 'Do you want steak and kidney pie?' the answer has to be yes or no. This is a closed question and also a 'leading' one because no other choices are offered. If a simple yes or no answer is required – 'Do you need the toilet, Mr Brown?' – that may be the best way to ask.

Active listening skills

Active listening means showing you are alert and interested in that individual, listening and trying to understand what is being said to you. This means you need to think about the way you are sitting, the way you look at the person, and the way you show you agree or disagree with what they say. Looking at the person, nodding and saying 'hmm' or 'yes' will all communicate that you are actively listening to what they have to say. It is also good to sit next to the person, facing them with your body turned towards them. If your legs are crossed, they should be crossed towards the person. You should lean forward slightly with your hands resting on your lap rather than having them folded in front of you.

When the person has finished speaking it may be helpful to summarise what you think they said, so that they can tell whether you have understood what they were talking about or their point of view. Try to use their own words whenever possible when you do this.

For older people who have communication difficulties, it may be helpful also to place a hand on their arm, so that you can communicate through touch that you understand how they are feeling. You may sometimes need to develop skill in picking out a person's words and linking them together. It can be an even more skilled process to understand what a person with dementia is trying to communicate. Unhurried active listening, giving the person plenty of time to respond, is very important.

Listening and observing

In order to understand something of the unique way a person is making sense of things around them, we need to listen carefully, sometimes trying to 'read between the lines' particularly when (for reasons of disability) people cannot express themselves in the normal or expected way. What is the general feeling behind what is said? What does the person *do*? When do they *not* do those things? Many clues will be non-verbal and we may understand as much from observing how residents behave in different situations as we do by listening to what is actually said.

One word of caution: be careful to

Checklist of strategies for effective communication

- Ensure adequate lighting
- Approach the person within their field of vision and let them know you are there
- Make sure you have eye contact or the person's attention before you speak
- Position yourself with the light on your face
- Reduce background noise
- Be careful not to raise your voice, but speak clearly
- Supply information in case the person is unsure who you are, eg 'Hello, it's Clare from... it is time for...'
- Give instructions in small chunks
- If you need to say something again, instead of simply repeating what you said try saying it in a different way. Try cueing the person into the topic or general theme of what you want to convey. The more information you give, the more help in boosting understanding you will achieve
- Make use of non verbal cues. Show the person what you mean
- If the person loses the thread of their conversation, try saying back what you have understood so far
- One-to-one conversation is easier than trying to follow conversations in a group. In a group setting, people who have difficulty with communication will benefit from having the main points of the conversation conveyed to them, and being invited to contribute. For example 'Did you hear that, Margaret? George thinks... Would you agree with that?'
- Allow time to respond to any request or question
- Provide alternatives if the person is struggling to find a word, rather than speaking for them
- Think about different ways in which to get your message across
- Focus on the 'message' rather than the accuracy of what is said
- Be aware that the person may say 'yes' and shake their head meaning 'no'. Gestures are often more reliable than what is said
- Ask the person how you can help if they are struggling, rather than making assumptions and doing it for them
- Gather information about when a difficult behaviour is happening and when it is not happening, and generate a theory about the circumstances in which it makes sense
- Acknowledge and respond to the feelings behind what is said
- Be aware of the role of touch and non-verbal communication
- Distraction – suggesting another activity such as a walk or a cup of tea – can *sometimes* be useful
- Reminiscence – most people enjoy trips down 'memory lane' – people who have memory problems may find this the most comfortable way to make conversation
- Beware the temptation of going along with something said that is obviously wrong, but avoid correcting the person unless they invite you to do so
- Listen for clues and try to find out more about how events might look to the resident concerned
- Use language that is appropriate for the person.

avoid the temptation to stand watching the residents. One gentleman described nurses and care assistants on a hospital ward for older people with mental health problems as 'prison officers'. You could see his point: the nurses stop him leaving, sometimes even lock the door, and stand at the side of the room watching every move he makes! Except of course when 'the others' come and then they sit in that little room with the window. Then it is really quite easy to leave...

If we start with the assumption that all behaviour makes sense in the light of how that person sees the situation, we can use our imagination and our knowledge of the possible disabilities that can arise to develop a 'theory', and then test it out.

Special difficulties

Chapter 6 describes how the process of normal ageing affects communication. Having a stroke, Parkinson's disease or dementia (see chapter 7) or physical disability will all affect a person's ability to communicate through both speech and body language. For example, if they are unable to dress themself, do their own hair or make-up, their appearance could be affected. They may be unable to ensure that their face, hands and clothes are clean after eating or drinking. All these things affect the message that the person would prefer to communicate to others.

Stroke, dementia, and other neurological diseases can also cause *dysarthria*. The muscles of speech can be affected in the same way as muscles in the rest of the body. This causes 'slurring' of speech, and may be due to a number of different problems arising from damage to different parts of the brain.

Use and care of a hearing aid

If a person has a hearing aid it is important to ensure that they wear it. A record should be made in the care plan of which

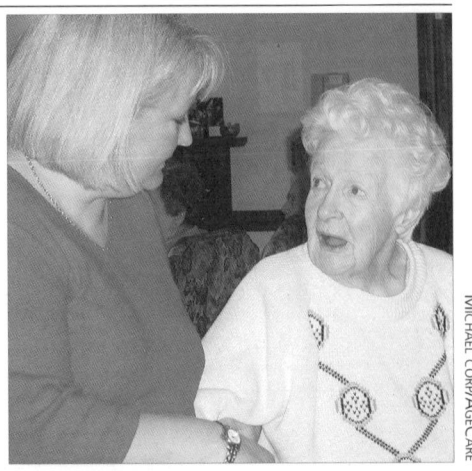

MICHAEL CORR/AGECARE

We need to listen carefully, and sometimes read 'between the lines' when people are talking.

ear the aid is worn in, and when the battery should be checked and changed.

There are many varieties of hearing aid, using different methods of transmission. It is important to obtain a copy of the maintenance instructions from the manufacturer, in order to care for the aid correctly.

Batteries may need replacing, or the ear piece may need cleaning to remove excess wax. A high pitched whistle is a sign of feedback, showing that the aid is not properly fitted. It may just require repositioning – but if this does not solve the problem the local hospital audiology department should be contacted. A hearing aid that is ill-fitting or not working is worse than useless and should not be worn.

Spectacles and contact lenses

For people who wear glasses, being without them is a very frightening and disturbing experience. It is very important therefore to ensure that the person always has their glasses with them. People should also be offered an opportunity to have their vision checked by an optician every two years.

Damaged, scratched or lost glasses can profoundly affect a person's ability to communicate effectively, so glasses should always be treated with great care – kept in a case when not in use, and never placed lens down.

Glasses should be cleaned with warm water and a little liquid soap if they are smeared with grease.

Older people may also use contact lenses. These are thin transparent oval disks which a person usually puts in themselves. However, a care assistant may need to assist a person in removing them. This is done by putting the head forward and pushing the corners of he eye gently together. The contact lens will then pop out. When not in the eye, lenses should always be kept in a special solution to prevent them drying out (unless they are disposable).

Dentures

Many older people wear dentures. Are they being worn? Do they fit? Are they comfortable? Teeth play an important role in speaking clearly.

So when thinking about communication it is important to know about all its different aspects, and to consider how age or a person's illness or disability will affect them. The next step is to find out from them how you can help them communicate in a way that suits them, and makes them feel valued.

Writing and the telephone

Written communication may be used in a care home to inform older people about something, and is used daily by staff to communicate with each other. There are clear rules about communicating in writing and how it should be done. Every resident should have a care plan and an assessment. Staff should write down observations and record the

Communicating with people with dementia

When working with people with dementia, staff need to use the same positive communication skills that have been described in order to communicate effectively with all older people.

However, time and patience are even more important, and the care assistant must be very sensitive to the person's difficulties. Dementia may have affected their ability to understand the spoken word, non-verbal communication and information from the environment alike. You will need to observe and think about how your communication is being received, and adjust what you say and how you say it according to the person's abilities.

The list of good practice points in the panel on page 31 can help identify which communication skills may be needed when communicating with a person with dementia.

All of these good practice points apply to people who have all types of dementia. Using the senses of touch, taste and smell may also help to communicate if a person has lost their ability to use words. However, the key point to remember is that it is the staff's challenge to discover the best way of communicating with someone who has difficulties: successful communication is *your* responsibility.

information in the care plan or evaluation sheet, so that:

- there is a record that something happened
- the information can be passed on to other people coming on duty
- if any questions are ever asked about the care that has been delivered, there is a record of what has happened.

Records should always be written in a

manner that is respectful and factual.

Written communication can also send messages that are not intended. For example, writing in a red pen is often seen as being angry or aggressive. Writing in block capitals is also interpreted as being aggressive.

Whenever a letter is being written, whether it is to the employer, to a relative or about another business matter, it should always be written clearly and as neatly as possible on plain paper, usually with a black or blue pen.

Black pen should always be used in a care home environment to ensure that any notes can be photocopied clearly.

Using the phone

When answering the telephone, first impressions can influence how the person phoning feels you are caring for their relative or friend. Good communication skills on the telephone should always include the following good practice points:

- when answering always give the name of the phone and your own name, and say good morning, good afternoon or good evening
- find the person most appropriate to deal with a telephone call
- do not give out information about residents unless you have been authorised to do so.

Always ensure that a written message is taken and left in the appropriate place. Remember that when communicating by telephone you rely on the words you use and the tone and volume of your voice to get your message across – the visual and spatial aspects of communications are lost. It is important to be aware that the meaning of a message can be changed because some of the methods of communication cannot be used.

Email

Email has become a very popular method of communicating, particularly between staff and departments in a large care organisation. It is a very quick and easy way to communicate, especially if factual information is being given. Sometimes, however, this speedy communication can seem abrupt or even insulting to the person receiving it – so it is important to read over and think about how you would feel receiving the message, before you send it.

Storage and confidentiality

If information is going to be used to enable good communication and benefit the resident, it must be stored correctly. The correct method of storage will depend on the type of information and whether it is on paper or a computer.

Any information about residents should be stored in their file or care plan folder. If you do not know where something should be stored it is your responsibility to ask. Folders should never be left out: they should be kept in a place where unauthorised people cannot get at them.

Other information may need to be accessible to all – information for visitors, policies or health and safety information, for example. So it is important to use the most appropriate method which has been agreed by the home.

Information held on a computer should be backed up on disk and the disk stored away from the computer. This will prevent information being lost if the computer crashes.

Communicating information should always be carried out within the requirements of the rules of confidentiality as described in Chapter 1.

Good practice points – managing aggression

- Staff should not attempt to manage an incident of physical aggression alone. You must always call for help
- Leave the situation if you feel your own safety is in danger
- The Police should be called (dialling 999) if the senior member of staff on duty feels the person cannot be managed or they feel the safety of the staff is threatened
- All incidents of aggression should be reported to the home manager who will also report the incident to the National Care Standards Commission and complete all documentation
- The member of staff and/or the team should be offered the support of the manager and/or any other member of the senior management team
- The incident should be discussed and an action plan drawn up, as appropriate, with regard to:
  - The care needs of the resident
  - The social needs and rights of the resident
  - The needs of the staff involved (training or support)
  - The needs of the home (changes in practice or procedure)

Positive skills in response to aggression

Positive communication skills can help greatly when a care worker is faced with aggression or violence. The message you send through your words, posture, facial expression and actions can either calm a situation or inflame the person who is being aggressive.

An incident of verbal or physical aggression could involve a resident or relative or another member of staff. The principles of aggression management, as explained below, should be used in every incident.

Naturally it is better to try and avoid any incidents of aggression by anticipating that they may occur. This can be done by all staff using good communication skills between themselves and the residents.

But if you find yourself in an aggressive situation, you will need to concentrate on using all your skills to calm the situation. Think about:
- your breathing
- how frustrated/angry/upset *you* are feeling
- are you being too strict or rigid?

- do you need to hand over to another member of staff? This is good practice
- tell yourself: the outcome will be positive, this person is just expressing themselves in this way. Think about why that might be
- change your mental picture: try to see the situation in a calm way, or from the other person's point of view
- does the issue that provoked the incident have to be pursued?
- whether the problem can be solved indirectly by removing someone or something else
- think about all the training and skills you have. If you have the skills to deal with the situation, use them.

There are three stages in the management of aggression:

Calming

Nothing can be achieved until the person has calmed down. The person is in a highly aroused state and only selective information will be absorbed. Talk to them calmly – try to show that you are sympathetic to their feelings and can understand why they might have reacted the way they did. If the staff member becomes angry this will fuel the person's aggression. Therefore remain calm and be conscious of your own behaviour. The calmer the staff member remains, the less stimulus the person has for continuing the behaviour.

Relating

Once the person has calmed down, continue to try to understand the problem from the person's point of view. Adopt relaxed body language. Remain calm, and through non-verbal communication allow the person space to express their feelings.

Managing

Deal with the visible symptoms and then attempt to uncover the real cause for the person's anger. Staff who are not skilled or experienced should refer the matter to a senior member of staff. Once the reasons for the anger have been established, diplomatically explore solutions or suggestions of ways to address their concern. If the person begins to become aggressive again, return to the calming stage.

Conclusion

As we have identified in this chapter, everyone communicates differently. For some older people their method of communication or the method required by the staff member may need adjustment, depending on their needs. It may be because English is not their first language, that they have lost the skills of using English because of a disease process, they may have a hearing impairment, vision impairment, cognitive impairment or physical disability. It is very important when writing a care plan to identify the communication skills staff will need to ensure that the resident will understand them (and they the resident) and will not be put at a disadvantage because staff are not taking a person-centred approach.

Chapter 3 - Communication

ESSENCE OF CARE					
Privacy & Dignity Factors					
1	2	3	4	5	6

NMS			
10.2	10.4	37.1	37.2

NSF		
1.2.1	2.1	2.1.6

TOPSS									
Induction									
1.2.1	1.2.2	1.2.3	1.3.1						
3.2.1	3.2.2	3.2.3	3.2.7						
Foundation									
2.1.1	2.2.1	2.2.2	2.3.1	2.3.2	2.4.1	2.4.2	2.4.3	2.5.1	2.5.2

NVQ 2 CARE

CL1.1
All Performance Criteria, Range and Knowledge
CL1.2
All Performance Criteria, Range and Knowledge
CU5.1
1 All Performance Criteria, Range and Knowledge
CU5.2
1 All Performance Criteria, Range and Knowledge

Compiled by Adrian Muir

CHAPTER 4

Health and safety in a care environment

Katrina Levett, Jane Hall & Lynne Phair

• Promoting safety and security • Assessing risks • Identifying hazards
• Record keeping • Moving and handling people and objects • Control of
hazardous substances • Fire safety • Infection control • First aid

Health and safety is about taking the right precautions to prevent people being harmed at work. Because it is so important, there are laws which have to be obeyed in order not to put anyone in danger. They are also there to protect the public from workplace dangers.

The laws of health and safety apply to everyone. Employers have a responsibility to ensure the requirements are met, and employees have a responsibility to ensure the requirements are carried out and to report any concerns to the manager. It is also a legal requirement that every member of staff and every volunteer has training in health and safety, moving and handling and fire safety. Once again it is the employer's duty to supply the training but it is a legal requirement of the employee to attend and carry out what has been taught.

Every organisation which employs more than five people must have a health and safety policy which tells staff what to do in different situations. They must also ensure risk assessments are carried out and recorded in order to reduce the chance of accidents. Every organisation must display a poster telling staff what they should know about health and safety.

The health and safety laws

The main law for Health and Safety is the Health and Safety at Work Act 1974. This contains numerous regulations which govern different parts of the Act and different aspects of work safety. For example, the Management of Health and Safety at Work regulations (1999) governs risk assessments, and the Manual Handling Operations Regulations (1992) govern moving and handling.

You do not have to know all the details of the law, but it is important to understand how the health and safety regulations affect you and the way you work.

This chapter introduces you to key aspects of health, safety and security that affect your work.

Security in a care environment

The dictionary defines security as 'a secure condition or feeling'. Your care setting is the residents' home, and security is very important to them. To help people feel secure is a fundamental aspect of a person-centred approach to care. Many care settings are kept locked at night and some are locked at all times. However, it is necessary to strike a balance between the individual's right to freedom, to have a choice, and their right to be secure.

Visitors

It should not be taken for granted that because a visitor has arrived, a resident wants to see them. It is a good idea to ask the resident if they would like to receive the visitor, rather than just directing that person to the resident's room. With very frail or confused people, the family may identify unwelcome visitors and this should be recorded in the care plan.

Intruders

The care setting may keep the doors locked and have a buzzer entry system or key pad. The use of badges can also help to identify staff. Staff should greet anyone they do not recognise, ask whether they need help and, if the person is on official business, politely request identification. Having a book to sign in and out serves two purposes: it helps identify visitors and complies with fire regulations.

The care home may have a policy regarding the opening of windows, especially at ground level, perhaps ensuring they are closed at night. There may be a checklist to help remind staff what to do to make the premises secure at night.

Property

You should always complete a property list when a person is admitted to a care setting. If the resident is especial-ly frail or confused, this can be done with a responsible family member. Every resident has the right to be given a key to their room and this should be offered to them. If the person cannot manage to look after a key, other arrangements should be made and a record kept in the care plan. Every room should have a lockable drawer for the safekeeping of valuables and medicines.

The security of the belongings of a confused resident can be a real challenge as they may put objects down in the most unusual places and then not be able to find them again. Diligent carers can help in these situations, but it may be necessary to take special measures if a resident keeps misplacing an object of value. However, the resident's family should be fully involved in deciding what to do.

Promoting safety

Hazards can be found in all areas where people work and live. Care settings are full of people, equipment and materials, all of which could be hazardous and affect safety. Some hazards are more obvious than others. (See table opposite: *Examples of hazards.*)

One of the most important ways of maintaining a safe environment is for staff to be constantly aware of potential hazards. This is not as hard as it sounds, as much is common sense. Imagine your own home and how you maintain a safe environment there without really thinking about it; it is the same when you are at work. Sometimes potential problems may be overlooked because everyone assumes somebody else has noticed the hazard and done something about it.

If you see a hazard, always report it.

Examples of hazards

Environment
Worn carpets
Edges of rugs
Wet or slippery floors
Cluttered halls and doorways
Cramped bedrooms/bathrooms
Electrical flexes

Materials
Cleaning fluids
Oxygen
Medications
Food and drink
Incorrectly labelled substances
Poor waste disposal
Leaking substance containers

Equipment
Broken wheelchairs
Broken or worn mobility aids
Worn or incorrectly-used hoists and slings
Brakes – broken or not used: on beds,
wheelchairs, hoists and commodes
Vacuum cleaners
Worn or faulty gas or electrical
appliances
Poorly stocked First Aid facilities

People
Aggressive and violent behaviour
Staff not following safe working methods
Unwelcome visitors
Intruders
Staff suffering stress and fatigue

RISK ASSESSMENTS

The Management of Health and Safety at Work Regulations (1999) require all workplaces to make risk assessments. This involves analysing all the tasks carried out in the care home and looking specifically at hazards, risks and control measures.

What are risk assessments?

Every day all of us, mostly without thinking, make several risk assessments. For example, when you want to cross a road, you look to see if the road is clear and then you decide whether or not you can make it across the road before encountering any traffic. All the while you are taking account of the size of the road, the traffic flow, the weather conditions, how many people are trying to cross the road with you, and whether you need to find a safer place to cross.

Formal risk assessments at work are usually undertaken by trained, competent persons who are familiar with the areas to be assessed. Staff who carry out the tasks also need to be involved in the assessment in order to identify all potential risks.

What is a hazard?

A hazard is anything that has the potential to cause harm, such as: chemicals, slippery floors, rugs or mats.

What is a risk?

A risk is the likelihood or chance a hazard has of causing harm or damage.

What are control measures?

Control measures are preventive items or actions taken to try to reduce the risk or to remove the risk altogether.

Risk assessment is a proactive approach to try to prevent an accident. This means dealing with a problem before an accident can occur rather than after something has happened.

Making a risk assessment

There are five steps in making an assessment:

1. Identify the hazards

Some hazards are apparent, such as wet floors; some are not so obvious, such as faulty electric plugs. It may be easier to look for hazards under different headings. For example:

- *fire* – blocked fire exits, smoking, naked flames
- *electricity* – trailing cables, faulty plugs, damaged cables
- *biological* – blood, clinical waste, bodily fluids, soiled linen
- *manual handling* – handling heavy or awkward loads
- *environmental* – noise, poor ventilation, poor lighting
- *chemical* – hazardous substances.

2. Ask who is at risk and how

Depending on the location of the hazard, you must decide who is at risk. If the hazard is in a resident's room it may be the resident and the staff who enter the room. However, if it is a fire hazard, it may present a risk to the entire home. Think about other people who may be at risk, such as visitors, contractors, domestic staff, volunteers, young people, or new and expectant mothers.

3. Ask if control measures are adequate

Look at the hazards and the risks and decide whether the control measures in place are adequate. If you decide they are not, what needs to be done to reduce or remove the risk?

Think about the following:

- Can a safer, less risky method be used? This could mean taking a few potatoes out of a sack at a time rather than trying to move the whole sack.

- Is it possible to prevent people getting near to the hazard? For instance, using red bags for soiled linen means the laundry staff do not need to come into contact with this hazard.

- Can you organise your work to avoid or reduce exposure to the hazard? This may involve sharing tasks such as cleaning or handling
- Can Personal Protective Equipment (PPE) be provided? However, PPE is always a last resort. The above methods must be considered before considering PPE as a control measure.

You are now in a position to decide whether the risk is high, medium or low.

4. Record your findings

According to the law, if it isn't written down, it didn't happen. It is a legal requirement that all risk assessments must be recorded. This means writing down all significant hazards and results from the assessment. Employees must be informed of the findings.

5. Review and revise

Risk assessments must be reviewed and, if necessary, revised. This is especially important in the care setting because the risk of hazards can quickly change.

Examples of risk assessment

Low risk

When adequate control measures are in place
A cleaning chemical labelled 'irritant' is locked away in the correct storage cupboard and only authorised persons are key holders. These people have had special COSHH training (see pp48-50). They know how to use the product safely and with which protective clothing.

In this case, the controls in place are adequate and the risk low.

High risk

When further controls are necessary

The same irritant cleaning chemical has been left in a communal bathroom which is is regularly used by vulnerable people. The lid on the container is loose and the label has been worn away. Because of its pink colour, the chemical could easily be mistaken for bubble bath.

This is a high risk scenario and immediate action should be taken to ensure the safety of the residents. Staff and managers should be informed of the findings and appropriate training given.

Balancing health and safety in a care home

The care home is the resident's home and you should be aware that risk assessments can bring to light some sensitive issues. For instance, the rug you have decided is too hazardous to be in a resident's room may be the rug their mother had made for them (which is therefore very precious). In this situation, you may consider moving the rug to a less hazardous area of their room rather than removing it altogether.

However, you must discuss the situation and the risks with the person (and/or their family) before taking any action, and only take action with their agreement. If a person is mentally able to understand the risks, and only they are affected, they must be able to make the decision to live with that risk. Only when risks affect others can a manager insist on making changes that have not been agreed with the older person.

Risk assessments and care-giving

The principles of risk assessment apply to every aspect of life in a care setting – whether in the kitchen, the garden or in a resident's room. They also apply when care is being delivered. The most common types of risk assessment are: moving and handling; pressure sores; and falls. Every aspect of a person's care should be considered using the five steps of risk assessment, and the centre of that assessment should always be the person, using a person-centred approach.

Other risks which should be assessed are those that affect independent living. Can the person bath alone? Are they able to judge the temperature of water? Can they get out alone?

Risk assessment must be undertaken around every aspect of care and life, not to stop people from living the way they want to, but to reduce the chance of accidents and enable the person to live the way they want to, safely.

Health and safety records

Records are a part of the health and safety law. They are essential in order to demonstrate that appropriate safety measures are in place. These records include information on fridge temperature, water temperature, equipment checks, fire safety tests, hazardous substance records and risk assessments. The law regards written records as proof that safety checks are carried out. If a record is not made, it is considered that the work was not done. Many staff are involved in keeping these records and everyone must make sure they are completed accurately.

Reporting accidents and incidents

If an accident or incident happens at work, an accident or incident form must be completed. The record must be accurate: it must say exactly what happened. It must also be readable and it must be complete (all the sections filled in). If you witness an accident you are asked to complete a witness form. This is a legal document and has to be stored by the organisation in case there are difficulties at a later date.

All serious accidents have to be reported to the RIDDOR (Reporting of Injuries, Diseases and Dangerous Occurrences Regulations 1995) reporting office in Cardiff. RIDDOR is the legislation which governs the reporting of accidents. If an accident is serious it may be investigated by a representative of the Health and Safety Executive or by an Environmental Health Officer. The official will expect to see that appropriate first aid was carried out and that proper health and safety assessment and procedures were followed.

Every care setting has its own system of recording accidents. You should ask your manager to explain your system as you may be required to fill in a form if you help at an accident or witness one in the workplace.

MOVING AND HANDLING PEOPLE AND OBJECTS

It is an unfortunate fact of life that accidents do happen at work and result in staff being injured. Nearly a third of all workplace accidents reported to the Health and Safety Executive involve manual handling. In the health services this figure increases to more than a half. Some studies have shown that nearly a quarter of nurses suffer back pain every year and that care assistants are at even greater risk of suffering a back problem.

Moving and handling does not just involve lifting. It includes pushing, pulling, putting down, carrying or moving by hand or bodily force.

There are laws in place designed to protect us from manual handling injuries; they include the Health and Safety at Work Act 1974 and, more recently, the Manual Handling Operations Regulations 1992. You don't need to know these laws in detail, but it is essential you have some understanding of them to help you work in a safe manner. It is a legal requirement that all staff attend moving and handling training and that their knowledge is updated annually and/or when something changes.

Understanding why moving and handling regulations are so rigid will help you to see the importance of using good techniques.

The legislation

The law governing moving and handling is the Manual Handling Operations Regulations 1992. It states that both employers and employees have responsibilities regarding manual handling.

Employers must:
- ensure staff avoid all manual handling wherever possible
- carry out a risk assessment if the manual handling is unavoidable
- provide information on the weight of each load
- ensure the risk assessments are kept up to date
- provide suitable equipment and ensure it is in good working order
- provide information and training for new staff, whenever there is an important change, and give regular updates
- maintain a safe working environment.

Assessing risk in manual handling

If you cannot avoid manual handling, you need to assess the risks. The five principles of assessing the risk are the same as for any risk assessment. But you should assess these risks looking at the four aspects of a moving and handling procedure, set out in the box above/right) An easy way to remember the four points in assessing this procedure is to think of the word **LITE**

You need to document the assessment and ensure the care plan describes exactly how a person or object should be moved in the different situations, for example from bed to chair, on to the toilet, and into the bath.

The needs of older people vary a lot from day to day and sometimes even from hour to hour. This can be seen in their handling needs. A resident who is able to stand and walk by themselves during the day may well need to be hoisted onto the bed at night.

The needs of residents with mental health problems may vary from hour to hour depending on their level of confusion. This underlines the need for different approaches to manual handling.

Ensure the plan is regularly reviewed in accordance with the risk assessment and amend it as necessary.

Reducing the risks

• When you have assessed the risk of injury, you should reduce it as far as is possible. You can use LITE to help:

Load
Can it be made smaller? Can you grasp it more easily using a handling belt?

Individual capability
Train staff in how to use the equipment.

Task
Does it need to be done? Can it be done in a different way? Can you use equipment?

Environment
Create enough space. Ensure the floor is not slippery.

Employees must:
• take reasonable care for their own

LITE

Load
What is being moved? Is it heavy, bulky, unwieldy, difficult to grasp, unstable or unpredictable?

Individual
What is the capability of the worker/s involved? Has the person been trained? Is a certain strength or height of person required? Does the task create risks for those who are pregnant or have health problems? Is special information or training required?

Task
What you are doing? Does it involve twisting, stooping, reaching, excessive lifting, lowering or carrying? If the load is a resident, is their behaviour predictable? Or will they move suddenly? Is there frequent or prolonged physical effort or insufficient rest/recovery periods?

Environment
Where do you have to do it? Is there enough space? Are the floors uneven or slippery? Is there good lighting? Is the temperature appropriate?

health and safety and for that of others who may be affected by their actions
• co-operate with their employer.
• Use the appropriate equipment provided for them in the way they have ben instructed
• Follow the written policies and procedures for maual handling – eg in the care plans
• Ensure that they carry out their work in the way they have been trained. If they are unsure how to use equipment they must ask
• Report anything potentially dangerous, eg faulty equipment, unsafe systems of work.

Preventing back injury

Your spine is made up of 26 bones. Each is called a vertebra, or, in the plural, they are called vertebrae. A pad of cartilage called a disc separates each. The bones are held together by ligaments which prevent excess movement.

Your spine can move because it is surrounded by muscles. The neck and the lower back have the most movement and are therefore most at risk from injury. The thoracic spine in the middle is attached to the ribs and does not move as much. The spinal cord and nerves are also closely associated with the spine. The natural shape of our spine is not straight but has slight curves, forming an S shape.

Damage can occur to any of the structures in the back. It is most likely to happen when the spine is not in its natural S shape. Lifting incorrectly or picking up loads that are too heavy can damage the spine but so can poor posture. How often do you find yourself bending, twisting, reaching, pushing, pulling or maintaining an awkward posture for a long time while at work? It is this cumulative effect on the spine that can be far more damaging than a one-off lift. You may be putting your back at risk at home as well as work: think about what you do while gardening, doing the housework and laundry, and how you sit when relaxing.

Other factors which can contribute to back problems include being overweight, smoking, not taking enough exercise, having poor posture, getting older, or using a poor mattress.

Principles of safe handling

The safe moving of a person will be different in every circumstance. It is not possible to describe all of the ways of moving a person. You must combine the knowledge of good handling techniques with the way equipment should be used to decide the best way to move a person or object. Remember all of this information and use it every time you move someone.

Always think through the following before helping a person to move.
- Is the lift or manoeuvre absolutely necessary?
- Can you use a piece of equipment instead?
- Think LITE before you do anything: Load, Individual capability, Task, Environment.
- Are you wearing appropriate clothing (loose) and footwear (flat)?
- Encourage the resident to do as much as they can themself.
- Have you been trained to use this equipment?

If the lift or move is necessary then consider the following **every time** you move someone.
- Check the care plan
- Clear the area so there are no obstacles
- Get the help of another carer if necessary
- Make sure all the carers and resident are aware of what they are about to do
- Stand with your feet hip width apart so you have good balance
- Stand with your leading foot facing in the direction of the movement
- If necessary bend your knees – not your back
- Keep the load (or person) as close to you as possible – this may require wearing protective clothing
- Make sure you have a firm grasp
- Keep your spine as close to its natural S shape as possible
- Appoint one person to give the commands for the movement

- Agree on the commands to be used and ensure everyone understands. It is better to say Ready, steady, stand! than One, two, three, as it is clearer when to do the actual movement
- Never *lift* a resident, no matter how many carers there are
- Carry out the move in several small stages, not one big movement
- Do not twist your body.

Moving and handling techniques

The Royal College of Nursing in association with the National Back Pain Association publishes a book called *The Guide To The Handling Of Patients*. It is an excellent resource and covers all aspects of manual handling. One section in this covers unsafe lifting practices and describes lifts and handling techniques that are dangerous to carry out, most of which were routinely used in the past. Ideally every care home should have a copy of this book for staff to refer to.

Handling aids

There is a wide variety of handling aids on the market. Each piece of equipment will come with an instruction sheet or manual. This should be kept in a convenient place so it can be referred to whenever necessary. Remember you should never use a piece of equipment you have not been trained in the use of. Likewise, if you have had training but remain unsure or if you have forgotten how to use it – it may have been some time since you last did so – never use the equipment, instead ask for help. The more common handling aids include:

Hoists

There are three main types, those that:

1) lift people totally

These are used to transfer residents in and out of bed, between chairs and toilets or to lift residents from the floor. They can be mobile or fixed to tracks in the ceiling.

2) help people to stand

These are used to transfer residents between chairs and toilets and can be very useful for helping a resident to dress or go to the toilet. They can be used to sit a resident on the side of the bed but cannot lift someone on to the bed or off the bed from a lying position. To stand in the hoist the resident has to be able to put weight through their legs and hold onto the hoist handles. Some standing hoists can be adapted to lift if a resident is unable to put weight through their legs, but can still only transfer a resident from one sitting position to another.

3) lift people in and out of the bath

These are designed specifically to get a resident in and out of the bath and usually are attached to the side of the bath.

Some newer types of hoist are multipurpose. This means they can be used to help with lifting, standing or even walking. You may need to change the boom arm to suit the task so it is essential that everyone is trained in using the different attachments. Some hoists also have a weighing mechanism built into the boom. This is very useful for those residents who are unable to sit on a weighing chair.

All hoists have a 'safe working load' – the SWL. This is the maximum weight the hoist can lift. It is therefore essential a resident's weight is recorded regularly and written in the care plan to ensure the appropriate hoist is used. Different hoists have different SWLs.

Slings for hoists

It is essential that you use the correct sling with the correct hoist. Not all slings are interchangeable between hoists and it is highly dangerous to use the wrong one. Therefore, always follow the manufacturer's instructions. Some companies do make slings that can fit more than one type of hoist, so check the list given in the instructions.

There are also different slings for different uses. General slings tend to be larger, cover more of the resident and are good for most transfers. Some have extensions for the neck, for residents who have poor head control. There are also toileting slings. These are cut away to allow easier access to clothing, however because the leg straps are often narrower, some residents find them uncomfortable. Padded versions may be available. The slings used in the standing hoists are often just a strap you place around the chest. For residents for whom standing is more difficult, some slings have leg pieces. These enable you to lift the person in a sitting position.

It is also vital that you use the correct size of sling for the resident. Some slings are colour-coded for size but each has the size written on them. Each also has its SWL printed on it. It is important that care plans include the size of sling to be used for each resident.

Profiling beds

These are essentially electric beds and can come in various designs. Some are described as three-section or four-section – this just describes how many sections of the bed are capable of moving. They can sit people up, raise a resident's legs, convert into a chair position (ie head up, middle section flat and foot section down). Some beds have a mechanism that turns the resident from one side to another over a certain amount of time. These beds are an essential piece of equipment for very dependent residents. And, for those who can use the controls, they can also give some residents the luxury of independence as they may be able to use them to sit themselves up and get out of bed – something they couldn't do in a normal bed.

Sliding/slide sheets

As the name suggests, you use these to move people by sliding them. They are not to be used as lifting sheets! Two layers of fabric slide over each other with very little friction. You can use them to reposition a resident in bed (to turn them or move them up the bed) or in a chair. The sheets can also be used to help insert slings for a hoist; and with the slide boards (see next). Some residents may be able to move themselves up the bed by sitting on a slide sheet. Note: most slides require two carers.

Slide boards

You use these to transfer residents in a sitting position between chairs, the toilet or the edge of the bed. It is essential the resident is able to sit unsupported and has reasonable arm strength as they use their arms to slide across the board. These boards are not to be used for those residents unable to move themselves: carers should not be doing the sliding action. The boards are usually made of wood or plastic and can be straight, curved (like a banana) or an S shape.

Hand blocks

Residents use these to move themselves around the bed. They look like large plastic handles with a flat base and when held in each hand they effectively lengthen the arms. This means when someone attempts to lift their bottom off the bed, the blocks give better clearance.

Bed ladder

This helps people who have a reasonable amount of arm strength to sit themselves up in bed. It is a rope ladder with wooden or plastic handles at one end. The end without the handles is looped over the bottom leg of the bed and the ladder lays down the middle of the bed, on the resident's stomach. The resident can then pull themselves into sitting by working their hands down the ladder.

Bed pole

Residents with good arm strength can use these to move themselves around in the bed. The poles are attached to the back of the bed and hang over the top part. A handle is attached to the pole and hangs down, usually at about shoulder level.

Turn discs

You use these during standing transfers to allow the feet to rotate. They are useful when a person has difficulty stepping. However they should not be used if the person requires significant help to stand up (in other words, if the carers would have to take most of the weight).

They are circular discs with two layers that rotate on each other with very little friction. They can be made of hard plastic or of material. In the past they have been used widely with handling belts to transfer people with very little standing ability. However, today hoists should be used. Turn discs can be used in conjunction with a slide board.

Handling belts

These are useful for assisting a person to stand and walk and during some chair to chair transfers. They are designed to give good hand grips for carers when helping residents to move. They are especially popular with residents who have very delicate skin. They come in a variety of styles. They are often criticised for riding up the chest during the transfers, however, if this is happening it is because the carers are lifting too much, hence the upward movement. If used correctly they will stay in place. Note that they are called handling belts not lifting belts.

Raises for chairs and beds

Simply raising the height of a chair by two or three inches may make the difference between a resident being dependent and independent. Raises are attachments you place on the legs of chairs and beds to make them higher. There are different styles for different furniture, to fit under castors, square or round legs for example.

Raised toilet seats

These are very useful for taller residents and those who have arthritis in the hips and knees. They are thick plastic seats that sit on top of the toilet and, like the chair raises, simply increase the height.

Raiser-recliner chairs

Residents who may need to be hoisted from a normal chair or wheelchair may be able to use one of these to stand up. (Very often older people find it very difficult to stand up but once they are up they are able to walk independently, though usually with some sort of assistance device.) These chairs are armchairs that recline backwards but also rise. As the seat height increases the chair tips forwards slightly.

Moving and handling residents with dementia

The manual handling care plan may include strategies for working with residents who have dementia and who do not understand why they are being moved. This includes strategies learned as part of a person-centred approach; in other words, looking at the situation from the person's point of view – trying to understand how it might feel to them – rather than just viewing it as a task you have to get done.

Good practice

• Never lift a resident

• Always encourage the resident to assist him- or herself as much as possible during any transfer. Beware PIP – pyjama induced paralysis! (This will be covered in detail in chapter 9)

• It is essential that you use appropriate equipment and not yourselves in moving and handling.

Moving objects

It is not just people that staff have to move but objects, too. This may include laundry, pushing beds and wheelchairs, moving furniture or rubbish bags, or undertaking kitchen duties.

The same rules apply both for objects and people: you should avoid manual handling if possible, and when you can't, you should carry out a risk assessment and follow the appropriate procedures.

THE CONTROL OF SUBSTANCES HAZARDOUS TO HEALTH REGULATIONS 1999 (COSHH)

The regulations which control hazardous substances are known as The Control of Substances Hazardous to Health Regulations 1999. To comply, the employer must:

• makes an assessment of all hazardous substances used in the care home in order to prevent exposure to staff or residents

• introduce control measures or proce-

Hazardous substances – The COSHH requirements

A hazardous substance is described in the COSHH regulations as: "Any substance or material that has the potential to cause harm either by injury or illness." Such substances fall into four categories:

• **Irritant** These can cause inflammation of the skin, eyes or respiratory tract.

• **Corrosive** These will attack, and can destroy, parts of the body they come in contact with.

• **Toxic** These are poisonous to the body. They can affect certain organs and interfere with normal functioning.

• **Flammable** – These have the potential to burst into flames or to burn quickly.

Hazardous substances/material in the care setting include: some cleaning chemicals; clinical waste, such as needles/sharps; blood; soiled dressings; soiled laundry.

It is important to ensure residents and staff are protected from exposure to such hazardous substances. For example, a substance stored in an inappropriate container can easily be mistaken for a drink, and the consequences could be fatal.

dures to remove or reduce risk of exposure
- ensure all staff are aware of these procedures, and attend COSHH training
- record the assessments and the findings
- review and revise the assessment.

Hazardous substances can find their
way into the body by a number of different paths, such as: breathing in vapours
or mists (inhalation); swallowing the substance (ingestion); touching the skin
(contact); through broken skin (injection) or through the eyes. Therefore, it is
important that safe procedures are followed to protect everyone from the possibility of hazardous substances entering
their body.

There is an order (or hierarchy) of
measures to consider and follow:
- Elimination – do you need to use the
substance?
- Substitution – can you use a less hazardous option?
- Isolation – can you move the hazardous process to another area?
- Ventilation – can you reduce the hazard by opening a window?
- Good housekeeping – can you avoid
creating a hazard by reducing spillages,
or getting rid of dust, etc?
- Reduction of exposure – can you
reduce the amount of time you spend
dealing with the substance?
- Training – is training available?
- Using personal protective equipment –
can you use gloves, goggles, aprons, etc?
- Provision of welfare facilities – are
there areas in which to wash?

Hazard data sheets
All organisations that use hazardous
substances must keep records on the
substances they use. These are called
hazard data sheets.

Manufacturers have a legal duty to
supply these details and these sheets

Good practice tips: hazardous substances
- **Always** use the correct personal pro-
tective equipment
- Always make sure the product is only
used for the task it was intended for
- Always ensure defects in containers
are reported immediately
- Always store chemicals in a secure area.
- Always dispose of used needles in the
sharps box
- Dispose of clinical waste regularly
- Use red bags to dispose of soiled linen
to prevent exposure to other staff
- Report any indication of ill health
immediately
- Always wash your hands after dealing
with any hazardous substance
- Read your home's health and safety
policy and COSHH assessments to
identify safe methods for dealing with
hazardous substances and materials
- Be aware that people who have
breathing difficulties may not be able
tolerate scented chemicals. (Always
ask the person what they prefer to be
used in their room)
- Always ventilate the room when using
a hazardous substance

- **Never** mix chemicals. Substances
that may not appear to be particularly
dangerous on their own, may emit
extremely hazardous fumes when
mixed with others. Some residents
may like to keep their own toilet
cleaners. This should be indicated in
a risk assessment and care must be
taken to flush the toilet before it is
cleaned
- Never put chemicals into containers
that have been used for food or drink.
- Never use chemicals you have not
been trained to use
- Never use chemicals that are not
labelled.

give the information on which to base a COSHH assessment. The sheets provide the following information:
• product name
• hazard identification – whether it is an irritant, or a corrosive, etc
• fire fighting measures
• handling – what you need to wear or use to protect you
• storage
• exposure controls and personal protection
• disposal considerations
• first aid measures
• toxicological information
• accidental release measures.

As previously said, this information is used to undertake COSHH assessments. It is stored in a COSHH file which should be available to all staff and must contain details of all hazardous substances used.

Safe handling and storage

The hazard data sheets and COSHH assessments tell you whether you need to use gloves, an apron or a mask, when dealing with a particular substance. All substances should be stored in their original container and labelled. If they are decanted into a smaller container, the new container must also be labelled and printed with the same risk phrases, for example, 'avoid contact with skin'. Storage cupboards or lockers must be locked to ensure there is no unauthorised use of the substance.

When a substance is spilt or needs to be disposed of, you must always follow your home's health and safety policy, the data sheets and COSHH assessments.

Emergency procedures

In the event of accidental exposure to a particular hazardous substance, it is important you look at the data sheet for first aid information.

If someone has to be taken to the doctor or to hospital following an accident involving hazardous substances, you must take the data sheet, the substance itself, or both, with you to help the hospital staff give the correct treatment.

FIRE SAFETY

The most common cause of fires is not buildings or materials, but people. Fires are not usually started intentionally but are mainly caused through carelessness or ignorance.

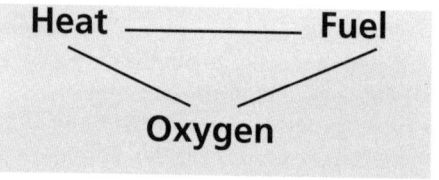

The fire triangle

To understand how fires start, it is important to know the three elements vital to the structure of fire. These are:

Fuel

Fuel can come in the form of gas, such as domestic gas; a liquid, such as petrol; or a solid, such as wood, coal, paper or fabric.

Lighter forms of fuel catch fire more easily. It is considerably more difficult to set fire to a large plank of wood with a match than wood shavings or paper.

Heat

This may come from naked flames, smoking, friction from working parts of a machine, hot surfaces, or open fires.

Oxygen

Oxygen is present in the air we breathe, hence this is a little more difficult to control.

Depending on the proportions, the three elements of the triangle will start a fire. To try to put a fire out, you must try to take away one of the sides of the triangle. To achieve this, you must starve the fire of fuel, limit the oxygen by smothering it, or cool it by taking away the heat.

Causes of fires and ways to prevent them

Here are typical causes of fires and suggestions for ways to try to reduce the risk.

• Cause: Electricity

Electricity can create a dangerous level of heat, and therefore you must be aware of the importance of not overloading plugs, and ensuring that items not in use are unplugged – this is especially relevant at night.

Prevention
Electric fires must not be placed too close to items such as blankets or clothes. Flammable items must also be kept at a safe distance from any form of electricity.

You need to take special care with electric blankets: disconnect them before the resident goes to bed. All electrical appliances must be tested annually by a qualified electrician.

• Cause: Waste materials

A build-up of household waste in communal areas or in residents' rooms will act as fuel to a fire.

Prevention
Waste bins must be emptied regularly.

Good practice: fire safety

- **Always** read and follow the fire procedure in your home
- Make sure you know what your fire alarm sounds like
- Familiarise yourself with the fire exits, location of fire extinguishers and the assembly point for your care home
- Attend regular fire training
- Keep fire doors closed – they provide vital protection for up to 30 minutes
- Be prepared to be involved in at least two fire drills a year
- Remember, once a fire has started, it can get out of control very quickly Therefore, fire prevention is very important. This is why fire risk assessments should be undertaken in your home.

- **Never** tackle a fire if you are not trained to do so
- Never use a lift in the event of a fire – you may become trapped
- Never prop fire doors open, especially with a fire extinguisher
- Never return to a fire. Once you are out, remain out until the fire services say you may go in.

• Cause: Smoking

Prevention
If staff are permitted to smoke at work, they should be given an area in which to do so. The area must be away from flammable substances. Ashtrays and metal waste bins must be provided.

It is unfair to prevent residents from smoking – and doing so may encourage secretive smoking, which is a fire hazard.

Designated smoking areas should be provided. Encourage the use of sturdy pedestal ashtrays rather than the plac-

The different fire extinguishers

Extinguisher	Colour	Used on	Action
Water	Red	Paper, wood Cloth, etc.	Cools fire
Dry powder	Blue	Oil, fats Electrical fires	Starves fire of oxygen
CO_2 (carbon dioxide)	Black	Electrical fires	Starves fire of oxygen
Foam	Cream	Petrol, oils, fats	Smothers fire
Fire blanket	Red cover	Oils and fats in small containers, people	Starves fire of oxygen

ing of an ashtray precariously on the arm of a chair where it can be easily knocked off. Smoking rooms will need to be monitored regularly, especially last thing at night. Residents must be warned that it is dangerous to smoke in bed.

Danger areas

• Corridors

Prevention
Corridors act as an escape route in the event of a fire. Therefore, they should be kept free from clutter and combustible items, such as furniture.

• Kitchens and laundries

Prevention
These are naturally hot areas especially if they contain items such as ovens, fryers, toasters and irons. Such appliances should not be left unattended and must be maintained regularly.

What to do if you discover a fire

1. Raise the alarm before you do anything else
2. Ring the fire brigade. Even if your care home has a link to the fire station, always ring 999 because this number will always be answered. Do not ring the local fire station. Always give your telephone number and your full address, including the postcode. You may also be asked for directions
3. Follow your home's fire procedures to ensure you make a safe exit from the building.

Different types of fire extinguishers

All public buildings must have fire extinguishers. There are different types to tackle different types of fire (see above). You should never tackle a fire with an extinguisher unless you have been trained to do so because a delay to read instructions could be dangerous. All extinguishers are now red with a band of the appropriate colour to identify the type.

PREVENTING ACCIDENTS

It is vital to identify and monitor potential risks as this will help prevent the risk turning into an accident. Every employer has a duty to monitor and investigate accidents and take the necessary measures to prevent further accidents happening. Identifying and monitoring the risk of an accident, rather than the accident itself, is even more effective as it puts safe systems of work into place that should prevent the accident occurring.

By constantly monitoring the way we work, and the risks involved, we help prevent accidents.

Risk assessments for people with mental health problems

Residents who have mental health problems can present a challenge to staff who are undertaking a risk assessment because providing care for that person may, at times, require very skilled intervention. If their safety awareness and judgement is severely impaired, they may not be able to recognise potential risks to themselves. They may not be able to speak or express themselves. They may not be able to understand what you are saying to them and therefore be unable to answer questions or follow instructions.

Some such residents may be disoriented, while others may express their frustration through aggressive and uncoopera-tive behaviour. It may be very difficult to help them understand your point of view or why you are asking them to do something. Therefore a risk assessment for a person with mental health problems may need to be much more in-depth and involve a larger number of people than for other residents.

For example, Mr B is normally independently mobile throughout the unit but has suffered two falls in the past 36 hours. He is unable to tell staff if he feels unwell or is in pain. He is not worried about his mobility, continually tries to move and becomes aggressive when prevented from doing so. The risk assessment needs to include:

1) baseline observations – temperature, pulse, etc, to see if Mr B is suffering any underlying infection;
2) a review of his current medication to see if this is contributing to his falls;
3) a check-up to find out if he is in pain or has problems with his joints;
4) an assessment of his balance to find out if he needs a mobility aid;
5) a check on the timing and place at which the falls happened to see if there is a pattern;
6) an assessment of his general health and well-being.

This example shows how many different people – nurse, doctor, carers, physiotherapist – may need to be consulted to carry out a full assessment.

UNIVERSAL INFECTION CONTROL PROCEDURES

Preventing the spread of infection in any care setting should be something all staff in every department work towards.

All care environments will have a policy which describes the basic rules of preventing the spread of infection. These rules are called the universal infection control procedures.

The rules are very simple, but ignoring them puts residents and staff at risk. Staff should always assume all body fluids have germs in them and therefore should treat them as potentially infectious.

The term *germ* is used to describe organisms such as bacteria and viruses which are contained in the environment. The body can become immune to some germs, but older people are vulnerable to infections and illness caused by germs.

There are simple rules to follow about a few key aspects of care.

Universal precautions – hand washing

A report by the National Audit Office published in 2000 concluded that the main cause of cross-infection was poor hand washing and poor hand washing techniques.

Hand washing is the single most important factor in infection control. You may carry out this procedure without thinking about it, but do you always complete the task correctly?

Hands can become contaminated by germs without your realising it. You can transmit germs by touch to other staff, visitors or other older people, and from inanimate objects, such as door handles, curtains or equipment. As you cannot see the germs, it is easy to forget they are present and are using you as their transport system. Therefore it is important to wash your hands before and after giving any care or treatment:
- before – to protect the resident, and
- afterwards
  – to protect you,
  – to protect others by preventing the possibility of spreading germs.

The five factors affecting good hand washing technique

1. The condition of the skin

It is important to look after your skin because if it becomes dry, sore or chapped, it stops being waterproof and can let in bacteria. This can lead to an inflammation of the skin, such as dermatitis, or a skin infection. Skin becomes damaged if it is washed too often, the water is too hot, the soap is not washed off properly, there is not enough softener in the soap or if there is too much alcohol in the skin cleanser. Hands also become damaged if they are not dried properly and are not moisturised.

To prevent dry skin, simply do the opposite of the causes of damage: use mild soaps, rinse and dry your hands properly, and use a good moisturiser.

However, it is also important to ensure the soap and moisturiser work together as some moisturising cream prevents antibacterial soap from working

2. The facilities available

Be sure to use water which is running freely. Check that the soap available is the most appropriate for the task.

Some situations require alcohol-based cleansers. These may be good to use when your hands look clean but there may be micro-organisms present. Soap or washing lotions should be used when a procedure has been carried out or when you can see dirt on the skin.

Alcohol-based cleansers do sanitise the hands and so are useful before carrying out clinical procedures. However, just allowing water to run over your skin does not remove any germs.

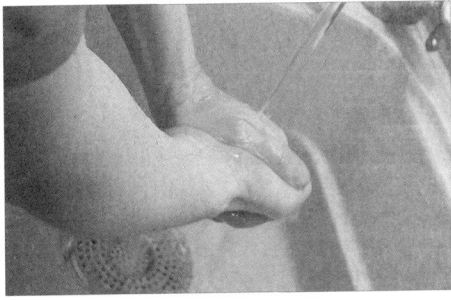

3. Clothing and jewellery
You should never wear jewellery, apart from a wedding band, while working in a care home. If you wear a wedding band, you should remove it while washing your hands. A good hand washing technique may mean you need to wash up to your elbows, which might involve removing some clothing.

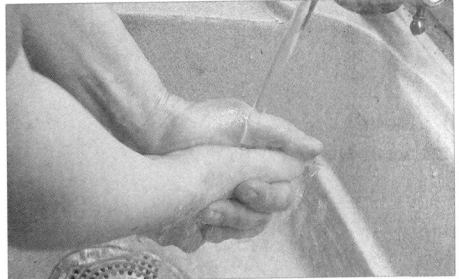

4. Time
Handwashing should not take long but it must be an automatic part of any activity.

5. The technique (illustrated, right)
How you wash your hands is as important as what you wash them with:
- Wet your hands with warm water and apply soap in the palm
- Rub your hands together, palm to palm
- Using one hand, rub the back of the other, not forgetting to clean between your fingers, around your knuckles, your fingertips and fingernails
- Repeat this with the other hand.
- Clench your fists and squelch the soap in them
- Rub your thumbs and the skin between your thumb and forefingers on both hands
- Rub your palms with your fingers
- Rinse your hands thoroughly
- Dry your hands thoroughly
- Moisturise them.

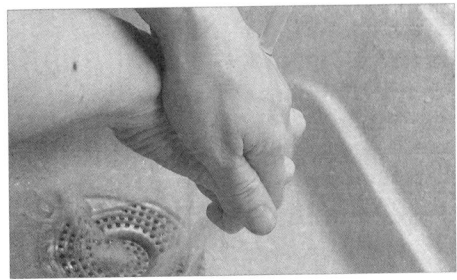

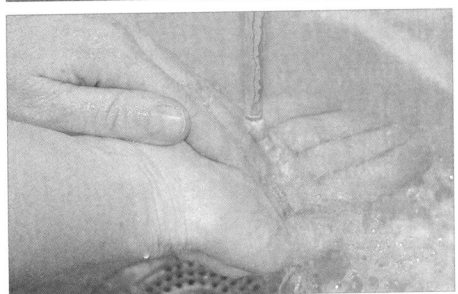

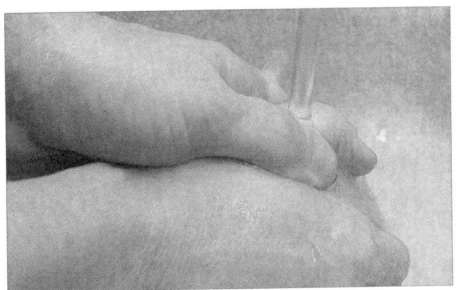

LESLEY DANN

If you are right-handed, this (dominant) hand will make a better job of cleaning than your inferior (in this case, left) hand.

Therefore you need to make extra effort with your left hand; and vice versa if you are left-handed. The back of the hand and the palm are areas most frequently missed.

Protective clothing and infection control

Protective clothing is governed by the Personal Protective Equipment at Work Regulations 1992. It is your responsibility to wear the appropriate protective equipment for the situation you are dealing with.

You must always wear an apron when you are caring for a person, because you cannot see any germs they may have on them. Some companies will have a uniform while other care environments do not. However, it is important to acknowledge that a uniform is a method of identification, it is not an infection control system.

Germs will live on anything so even if you wear a uniform, you should also wear a plastic apron and gloves, and change them before moving on to another resident.

Different coloured aprons should be used for different activities. This makes it easy to check that a person who has just helped someone out of the bath, is not now serving food.

You should wear gloves whenever you are handling body fluids; but this does not stop the need for hand washing. It is important to check to see if you are allergic to latex. If you are, your employer should provide non-latex gloves to prevent a reaction. Some people become allergic to latex due to over-exposure, so if possible, always use non-latex gloves.

Cleaning of equipment and soiled linen

Although it may sound obvious, it does not occur to everyone to ensure that everything should be cleaned properly. Beds should be washed between patients and linen should not be put on the floor when the bed is being changed – it must go in a linen basket. Likewise, soiled linen should be put straight into a red alginate bag to ensure nobody else touches it and contaminates themselves.

At the laundry, the soiled linen is washed on a special sluice cycle at a temperature of 70°C for at least 10 minutes.

Toilet aids, including urinal bottles, commode pans and raised toilet seats must be regularly put through the bed-pan washer to avoid contamination.

A person's room should be cleaned thoroughly when they vacate it, with all surfaces being washed. If the person has had an infection of any type, then everything, including the curtains, should be thoroughly washed.

Disposal of waste

If you are asked to assist with clinical procedures, the universal precautions apply, and you should place the soiled dressing in the yellow clinical waste bag. You should put needles in the sharps container and follow the instructions for its disposal.

Every care environment should have clear instructions about the local arrangements for the disposal of different types of waste, and you should follow these at all times.

If a person has any particular type of infection or bacteria, including MRSA (methicillin-resistant staphylococcus aureas), the universal infection control procedures are the fundamental approach to preventing it spreading.

FIRST AID

Under the Health and Safety (First Aid) Regulations 1981, every employer has a duty to make first aid provision available in the workplace.

Your employer should also be able to identify who the qualified first aider is on duty at any time.

In a nursing environment, this may be the registered nurse, but only if he or she has undergone first aid training and is competent.

There are two first aid qualifications:
• an appointed person who undertakes a one-day course, and
• a qualified first aider who completes a four-day course and an exam.

This section offers an introduction to first aid techniques and should become useful background knowledge. It also offers some tips on emergency first aid practice.

Courses can be costly but most approved first aid training organisations offer two-hour Save a Life courses which give training in cardiopulmonary resuscitation (CPR) or mouth-to-mouth rescuscitation, and are free.

You should not be expected to be considered a first aider in your work environment unless you have completed either course. You have a right to refuse to take on that responsibility if you do not have those qualifications. However, it is important that you know the procedure for dealing with an emergency in case you are asked to assist at an accident:
• Ensure you know the emergency procedure for summoning medical or paramedic assistance (999 or internal call number)
• Ensure you know where the first aid box is, and, if they are available, where the oxygen and suction equipment are kept
• Ensure you know how to work the emergency call bell system
• Ensure you know the procedure for calling for senior staff assistance.

Having some basic skills can always help in an emergency situation.

The aim of first aid is to:
• preserve life
• limit the effects of the condition
• promote recovery.

As an unqualified person your role will be to:
• assess the situation
• make the area safe
• call for help (who you call and how, depends on your work place)
• give emergency aid if possible.

Whatever the accident or incident, the same procedure must always be followed:
• Assess for **Danger**. There is no point in putting your own life at risk
• Check if there is any **Response** from the casualty – by shaking their shoulders and calling into both ears
• Check the person's **Airway** (their mouth and throat) in case it is blocked
• Check if they are **Breathing** – by placing your hand over their nose and mouth to feel breath and by looking down the line of their body to see if their chest is moving
• Check if they have any **Circulation**– by looking at the colour of their skin, breathing, coughing or movement for no more than 10 seconds.

This procedure is also referred to as **DRABC**.

If you have made this initial assessment, you are in a better position to tell the emergency services, or the manager, what has happened to the casualty.

What to do if...

The person is not breathing and their heart has stopped – cardiac arrest

To be able to carry this procedure out competently it is recommended you undertake the Save a Life course.

- Check DRABC
- Call for assistance
- Check the person again
- If there is no change give two ventilations
- Check – no pulse?
- Give 15 compressions
- No change? Give two ventilations
- Continue to alternate the compressions and ventilations until the emergency services or other qualified person tells you to stop.

What to do if...

The person is breathing and has a heart beat, but is unconscious

It is important to keep the person's airway clear. If they are unconscious, they could choke, so the risk of causing more injury by moving them is secondary to the risk of them choking. They should be carefully moved into the **recovery position** (illustrated above) as follows:

- Place two fingers under the casualty's chin, one hand on the forehead and gently tilt their head back, straightening the limbs
- Talk to the person all the time
- Place the hand nearest to you ① in a native American 'How!' position: elbow bent, hand at the same level as the face, palm uppermost
- Bring the arm furthest from you ② across the casualty's chest, and place the palm, upwards, against their cheek. With your other hand, pull up the casualty's far leg ③, just above the knee
- Keeping the casualty's hand pressed to his cheek, pull on his far leg ③ to roll him towards you, onto his side
- Bend the casualty's far leg (now upper leg) ③ at the knee so it is at right angles to his body. Position the lower leg ④ as pictured
- Check the casualty's head is tilted back and their airway is open
- Summon help.

What to do if...

A person is bleeding severely

It is sometimes difficult to decide if there is a lot of blood because there is a large wound or because the blood has spread a long way. This decision is not yours to make. Always assume there is a severe wound and ensure help is obtained to assess the wound properly. Until help arrives you should:

- call for help
- remove any clothing to expose the wound
- press firmly over the wound with your hand or fingers or with a dressing, clean cloth or pad
- maintain the pressure and raise the injured part (if possible) so it is higher than the person's heart
- lay the person down and raise legs to help prevent shock, keeping the injured part raised
- keep the pressure applied until assistance arrives.

LESLEY DANN

What to do if...

A person is choking

Choking requires prompt action. The signs that a person may be choking are:
• they have difficulty in speaking
• their face becomes blue/grey
• they are in distress
• they may cough or be totally silent.

Action
• Always – call for help.
• Stand behind the person and encourage them to cough
• Give five sharp slaps to their back with the heel of your hand between their shoulder blades
• Get the casualty to cough with each slap.

If this fails:
• place your arms around their abdomen, place a fist just below the breastbone, place your other hand over your fist and pull sharply inwards and upwards (this is called the abdominal thrust)
• give five thrusts then five back slaps
• continue until the blockage is dislodged.

If the person is unconscious:
• lay them on their side and give five back slaps then turn them onto their back and give five abdominal thrusts
• continue as required, until the ambulance arrives.

It is important that anyone who has been given abdominal thrusts should go to the hospital to be reassessed.

What to do if...

Someone suffers from shock

When a person goes into shock it can be life-threatening, if there is not enough oxygen travelling around the body. This may be because of severe blood loss or a severe allergic reaction to something (anaphylactic shock).

There is difference between shock and fainting. However, a person may faint as part of the shock and therefore the treatment is the same.

If a person is in shock they may become drowsy, have fast, shallow breathing, be gasping for breath, be cold and clammy to the touch, have a rapid pulse and be restless and disorientated.

The treatment is:
• DRABC
• lay them down and raise their legs
• call for help
• reassure them.

What to do if...

A person suffers a burn or a scald

The treatment is the same whether the injury is a burn or a scald:
• Place the affected area under cold running water for at least 10 minutes (20 minutes for chemical burns).
• Remove any constricting objects eg rings or watches.
• Treat for shock
• Cover with a clean, dry dressing or a plastic bag
• Seek professional help.

• DO NOT touch the burned area
• DO NOT apply cream or butter
• DO NOT burst blisters
• DO NOT remove stuck clothing
• DO NOT use cotton wool.

What to do if...

A person suffers an electric shock

- Do not touch the casualty while they are in contact with the power supply
- Make the situation safe by turning off the power, or pushing the casualty's limbs away from the power source with a wooden broom or similar
- DRABC
- Call for help
- If the person has touched a high voltage pylon do not go any closer than 18 metres. Call the emergency services. Do not approach the casualty.

What to do if...

A person suffers a fracture

A fracture and a broken bone are the same thing.

The person may complain about pain, tenderness or swelling. If it is an older person and they have broken their hip, there may be a lump at the hip site, it may feel warm and the broken leg will be shorter than the other; the foot may also appear to be rotated outwards. However, some people do not show these signs.

The treatment

- DRABC
- Support and immobilise the limb
- Treat for shock
- Do not move the casualty
- Do not give the person anything to eat or drink
- Call for help.

What to do if...

A person has an epileptic fit

The person may fall to the ground, become rigid, then begin shaking and convulsing. They may go blue around the lips and stop breathing. When the shaking stops they will then start breathing again, but they may be unconscious for a few minutes. They may also be incontinent.

- If you see someone falling, make a space around him or her
- Loosen any clothing around their neck
- When the convulsions cease, and the person is still, place them in the recovery position
- Stay with them until they are conscious.

What to do if...

Someone takes in some poison

People do sometimes swallow substances by mistake, and if not treated these can act as a poison. This is why liquids should never be kept in unlabelled bottles.

If the person is unconscious:

- DRABC
- Check there is nothing in their mouth
- Place the casualty in the recovery position
- Call for help and tell the person what the poison is (if you know)
- If the person is conscious and their mouth is burning, give them sips of water of milk.
- DO NOT try to make them vomit.

THE GOLDEN RULES OF HEALTH AND SAFETY

A care setting is not only a home for people but is a work place, too. The responsibility for achieving a safe working environment is shared by employers and employees.

So remember...

As an employee, you should:

1) remain vigilant and observant regarding the residents' safety at all times – in other words, keep a constant lookout for potential hazards
2) deal with any health and safety risks you see, yourself if you can. This may be as simple as clearing a hallway or mopping up a small spill of juice. If you are unable to deal with it, inform the appropriate person, be it your manager, housekeeping or maintenance. You will need to warn people of the hazard. This may involve placing a wet floor sign in the affected area; attaching a note to a broken hoist; or removing a worn out sliding sheet so it will no longer be used
3) follow your home's health and safety policy and COSHH file
4) be fire safety-conscious at all times and make sure you attend fire training regularly
5) follow your home's manual handling policy and attend training updates
6) dress appropriately for your work
7) encourage your co-workers to work in a safe manner.

Sometimes situations arise where you are complying with all the health and safety guidelines but someone you are working with does not. For example, how many times has someone tried to persuade you not to go to 'the bother' of getting the hoist, as it will be 'quicker just to lift him'. By doing this, the co-worker is not only putting him- or herself at risk, but also you and the resident. In this situation you should not agree to the lift. Instead you should carry out the movement as specified in the care plan. You are in a position to lead by example and can encourage your fellow workers to work with you in promoting a safe working environment for you all. It is important they understand that their actions can have a detrimental affect on others.

8) remember: risk assessments apply to everything from using equipment, to enabling a person to remain independent, and carry them out.

Employers should:

1) maintain a safe environment for residents, staff and others
2) regularly service and maintain all equipment that is in use
3) offer the facility for risk assessments in all departments
4) offer fire safety, manual handling, first aid and health and safety training, to all employees
5) adhere to government legislation – the Health and Safety at Work Act 1974, and other relevant legislation.

Further reading

Five steps to risk assessment from the Health and Safety Executive gives details on how to assess workplace risks.

Tullett S (1996) *Health and Safety in Care Homes – A practical guide.* Age Concern, London.

National Back Pain Association (1999) *The guide to handling of patients. 4th Edition.* NBPA (now called BackCare), London.

Mohun J, John K (2002) *First Aid Manual* 8th edition. Dorling Kindersley, London.

Chapter 4 - Health and safety

ESSENCE OF CARE

Safety

1	2	3	4	5	6

NMS

19.1	19.3	19.4	19.5					
26.1	26.2	26.3	26.4	26.5	26.6	26.7	26.8	26.9
38.1	38.4	38.6						

NSF

6.11	6.12	6.36

TOPSS

Induction

4.1.1	4.1.2	4.1.3	4.1.4	4.1.5	4.2.1	4.2.2	4.2.3	4.2.4	4.2.5	4.3.1
4.4.1	4.4.2	4.4.3	4.6.1	4.6.2	4.6.3	4.6.4	4.6.5	4.6.6		

NVQ 2 CARE

CU1.1

All Performance Criteria	All range	All knowledge

CU1.2

All Performance Criteria	All range	All knowledge

CU1.3

All Performance Criteria	All range	All knowledge

Z7.2

Range 2A	2B	2C	Performance criteria 4

Z7.1

2A,2B,2C	Performance Criteria 8,9

Compiled by Adrian Muir

CHAPTER 5

Promoting well-being and preventing abuse

Buz Loveday

Types of abuse : physical, sexual, psychological, financial, neglect and isolation • How abuse arises • Rights, responsibilities and risk • The dangers of routine • The signs of abuse • Responding to allegations • Criminal abuse

George was an older man with a learning disability. He had lived for a number of years in a supported housing scheme with three other people and assistance from a support worker. He managed to do much for himself, including going out to the local shops and the pub. He was happy and enjoyed life. But things changed for George when a new tenant moved into the scheme.

Although this was George's home, he had not been told that a new person was moving into the house and, moreover, he did not get on with the new tenant. He became quite distressed, and acted this out through his behaviour. As the situation deteriorated, the managers of the housing scheme decided that George was no longer a suitable tenant. He was moved, without his consent, into a care home for older people.

The staff in the care home did not understand George's needs. He was unhappy in the home and frequently asked to go back to his house. He also wanted to go out to the shops and the pub, but he was not allowed to do this. Although George was quite particular about what he liked to eat, his favourite foods were not available in the home, and George hardly ate at all. He became frail and depressed. He would not co-operate with staff and was sometimes verbally abusive to them.

One particular member of staff began hitting George as a way of controlling him. Although George tried to tell people about this, he was not believed. Over the next few weeks, George became frailer and his injuries became more serious. He had to be admitted to hospital. Shortly afterwards he died.

Sadly, this is a true story.

I'm sure that most care staff will feel sickened at reading about what happened to George. But, while George's story is extreme, it is important to recognise that abuse can and does occur. The more aware we are about how abuse can happen, the more attention we can pay to ensuring that our own practice does not degenerate into abuse. There are many care homes where practice is far from abusive, and this is achieved through a high level of awareness about residents' needs and an understanding of the impact that all staff have on the lives of residents in their care.

Types of abuse

Clearly George was abused in a number of ways. He was hit, and anyone would recognise that this is abuse. But the denial of George's needs, feelings and choice also constituted abuse: abuse of a psychological nature. Abuse can take a number of forms:

- physical
- sexual
- psychological
- financial
- neglect
- isolation.

Any of these forms of abuse, whether or not it has been carried out on purpose, causes harm or distress to an older person. The effects of abuse may be temporary or long-lasting. George's abuse actually led to his death. But even if the effects of abuse are not so dramatic, there are many ways in which an older person can be harmed. Imagine how the resident might be affected in each of these examples:

1a. A care assistant says to Irene: 'Come on, cheer up – your daughter won't want to visit you any more if you always look so miserable.'

2a. Mumtaz is sitting in the lounge, calling out. Following a stroke her speech is not clear, but she sounds frightened. A care assistant walks through the lounge, gathers some cups and then leaves the room, without paying any attention at all to Mumtaz.

3a. Mr Omwole has always been a busy, active person and in the care home he feels bored and useless. He has dementia and is not able to say clearly to staff that he wants something to do, wants to feel involved. He spends much of his time walking around and often goes into the office and picks things up. Staff frequently tell Mr Omwole to 'sit down, there's a good boy' or to 'stop fiddling and annoying people'.

4a. Mohammed is a Muslim man who has always prayed five times a day. He has a disability and is not able to go independently to his own room when he needs to pray. A care assistant, finding him kneeling down in the lounge, says 'Oh, what's happened – come on, up you get. If you want to sing, why don't we all have a sing-song?'

5a. Marie is unable to eat independently and needs to be fed. She chews slowly and if she is offered another forkful while there is still food in her mouth, she will refuse it until she has swallowed. However, when she refuses the forkful of food, the care assistant believes that she is full up and removes the plate of food, only half eaten.

6a. Miss Fernandez is able to go to the toilet without help, but needs assistance to stand up afterwards. The care assistant leaves the toilet door wide open and tells Miss Fernandez to 'give me a shout when you've finished'.

7a. When Jack is asked what he wants to wear, he looks blank. So the care assistant chooses something for him.

8a. Rosa has severe dementia and does not respond to much of what goes on around her. So when care assistants are attending to her personal care they do not talk directly to her, but instead chat to each other.

9a. Mrs Abraham has been very agitated lately. She cannot seem to sit still and paces around; unfortunately, because she has Parkinson's disease, she is very unsteady and has had a number of falls. If staff try to stop her she becomes physically aggressive. So the doctor is called in and Mrs Abraham is put on a tranquilliser.

10a. Donald, who has dementia, has walked into the kitchen while staff are preparing the residents' lunch. A member of the kitchen staff shouts: 'Get out of the kitchen – you're not allowed in here!'

How abuse arises

Undoubtedly the way they have been treated will affect each of these residents. Their rights have been over-ridden; their needs neglected; their feelings dismissed. Some older people may react to these types of abuse by becoming withdrawn and depressed. Some may become angry and resentful. And unfortunately, the residents' reactions will often be misunderstood and the person becomes labelled as 'a problem'. If the person does not appear to react, it is probably because their self-esteem and self-respect have sunk so low that they no longer believe they have any rights.

In the above examples, the abuse has quite possibly been unintentional. The care assistants have not meant any harm. But maybe they do not understand the resident's needs; do not have information about the resident's abilities and difficulties; do not have insight into the perspective of the resident; or do not have the skills needed to work with the resident in a more helpful way.

Maybe factors outside the care assistant's control – such as the routines of the care home – have contributed to the abuse. Maybe staff are working with high levels of stress. Caring for vulnerable people with high dependency needs, who may behave in challenging ways or have problems communicating, is an emotionally and physically demanding area of work. Staff need good supervision and support and if this is not available, abusive practice can easily occur.

Anyone, from a close family member to a complete stranger, can be an abuser. A paid staff member can abuse, and so can another resident. Sometimes the abuser knows they are causing harm, and sometimes not. Even organisations can be abusive. The challenge is to notice that abuse is taking place and do something about it.

Rights

All human beings have rights, and these rights remain when an older person moves into a care home. In addition, once in the home, the older person has the right to a certain standard of care. A key aspect of the care process is empowerment. This means that the older person is enabled to use their remaining abilities, and assistance is given to compensate for their difficulties, the result being that the person feels in control of their own life and has a sense of well-being. Some important rights are:

• to be recognised and cared for as an individual, who has an individual personality, life history, preferences, needs, beliefs, abilities and disabilities
• to be enabled to make choices
• to be given the best possible opportunity of understanding all aspects of the care they are being given
• to be treated with respect for their privacy and dignity and in accordance with their cultural needs
• to have their physical and psychological needs addressed in the course of daily care
• to be as independent as possible and to do things at their own pace
• to be safe and secure
• to have freedom of movement.

Some rights of older people are set out in *No Longer Afraid* – a set of guidelines published by the government. Upholding the rights of a resident empowers them.

Let us think again about the previous examples of abuse and consider how the resident's rights could be upheld:

1b. The care assistant could say to Irene, 'Irene, you look sad. What's wrong? Is there anything I can do to help?'
2b. The care assistant could prioritise Mumtaz over the need to collect cups.

They could approach Mumtaz and kneel or sit down in a position where Mumtaz can clearly see them. They could speak clearly and gently, trying to draw Mumtaz out. They could listen carefully and observe Mumtaz's non-verbal signals to try to ascertain what she is frightened about.

3b. Staff need to find out what Mr Omwole would gain pleasure and satisfaction from doing. Perhaps they could involve him in helping out in various ways around the home, and thank him for his help. Perhaps they could find other activities which he would enjoy, which make best use of his remaining strengths.

4b. Mohammed has the right to practice his religion. He needs help to access private space in which to pray and he needs a prayer mat. Perhaps there is a local mosque he could attend.

5b. Marie needs all staff to be aware of the time it takes her to eat and to make sure that she is given enough time to eat all she wants.

6b. Miss Fernandez is entitled to go to the toilet with the same degree of privacy we would want for ourselves. The door should be firmly closed; perhaps the care assistant could say 'I'll be right outside – just let me know when I should come in'.

7b. If Jack is unable to understand a wide open choice such as 'What do you want to wear?', then he needs more assistance to enable him to choose. Perhaps he would be able to choose if he was shown what was available. If a full wardrobe of clothes was too overwhelming for Jack, he may still be able to choose if a limited range of choices were shown to him.

8b. No-one knows for sure exactly what Rosa understands. Her level of understanding may vary considerably at different times. Staff should always speak to Rosa, explaining exactly what they are doing in as clear a manner as possible, and pay close attention to Rosa's responses which may indicate her needs. They should try to find any possible way of making contact with Rosa: perhaps she would like it if they talked to her about her past; perhaps listening to music would help her relax; perhaps holding Rosa's hand and establishing eye contact would help her to feel safe.

9b. Staff may feel that both Mrs Abraham and they were at risk from her behaviour, but the tranquilliser is effectively restraining her. They should have looked at ways of enabling her to move around safely (eg by using walking aids and by removing hazards from the environment) and, importantly, they should work to discover the reasons for her agitation. Is she in pain? Is she upset about something? Whatever the reason, it needs to be addressed constructively.

10b. There is a reason why Donald has come into the kitchen – and the staff need to ascertain what this reason is. It could be that Donald has lost his bearings and is looking for a different room. It could be that he is lonely and wanting company. Perhaps he is bored and wants something to do. Maybe he used to be a keen chef and would like to do some cooking himself. Whatever Donald's reason, it involves some needs which staff should meet in order to help Donald achieve a sense of well-being.

Responsibility and risk

Even though many staff in care homes do not feel that they are in positions of power within their organisation, in fact, anyone who has face-to-face contact with residents has an awful lot of power over their well-being. In all the examples above, staff have used their power – negatively in the first set of examples and positively in the second.

It is important to recognise the impact

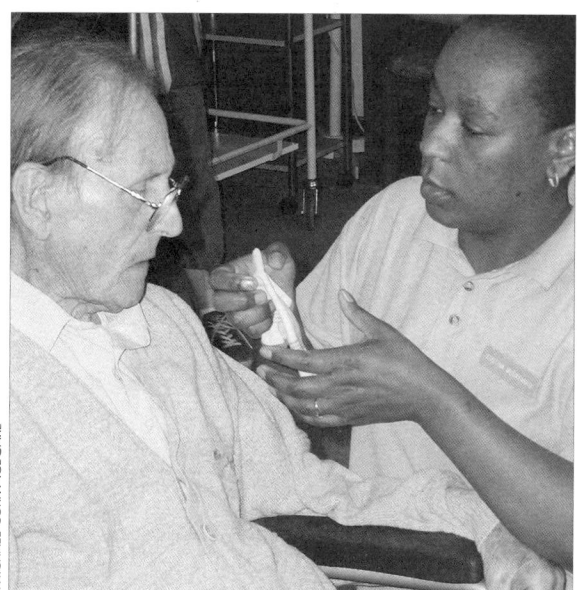

Michael corp/AgeCare

Following an individual's care plan helps to empower them and minimise the possibility of abuse.

of the person's psychological, cultural or social needs.

Life always involves some element of risk-taking. In our own lives, we constantly assess whether a risk is 'reasonable', and worth taking. Care home residents have as much right to do this as we do. There may be steps we need to take to minimize the risk or address the needs it indicates (for example with Mrs Abraham in example 9b above) in order to maintain the resident's well-being.

Each resident's care plan should include details about how to meet their emotional, cultural, religious and psychological needs; how to give them an opportunity to utilise their abilities; how to compensate for their difficulties; how to enable them to make choices; how best to communicate to enable them to understand; how to work towards understanding them. Following an individual's care plan helps to empower them and minimise the possibility of abuse. Care practice with all residents should focus on upholding their rights.

Dangers of routine

Earlier on, I mentioned that the routines of a care home can contribute to abuse. Let's look more at this. Consider Elsie, a resident with dementia who needs some help with dressing and washing. There is much she can do for herself, given the necessary prompts and assistance. She can wash herself if the care assistant points out the basin, flannel and soap. She can choose what she wants to wear if the care assistant shows her what's in her wardrobe. She can put on one item of clothing at a time if the care assistant hands it to her.

that all interactions and care interventions (or lack of them) can have on the lives of residents in a care home. For example, being shouted at to 'get out of the kitchen – you're not allowed in here' could give Donald a deep sense of sadness, a feeling of rejection, of not belonging.

Staff need to take responsibility for how they use their power: power should always be used to have a positive, rather than negative, effect on the resident.

Sometimes there seem to be reasons why a person's rights cannot be upheld. This most commonly occurs when risk is involved. If it seems necessary to over-ride the rights of a resident, a starting point in making this decision should be to ask ourselves a question: is it genuinely in the resident's best interests or is it more for the convenience or peace of mind of others?

Consideration of the resident's well-being is important in determining what their best interests are; we cannot consider only physical safety at the expense

But all of this help takes time, and in the care home where Elsie lives each care assistant has one hour to help four residents get ready for breakfast. So the care assistant washes Elsie, chooses what she will wear and dresses her, and the job is done in fifteen minutes. Elsie feels childlike, powerless and incompetent. In a few weeks or months, Elsie will no longer be able to wash herself or put on her own clothes, because her abilities will rapidly dwindle if she does not get a chance to use them. But the care assistant can move on to her next resident and everybody will be ready in time for breakfast at 9 o'clock. And her next resident is Bill, who, when he lived at home, always liked to lie in till 10 o'clock. But here in the care home he's up and dressed by 9, too.

The rigid routines of this care home mean that residents are not treated as individuals. Both residents and care assistants are disempowered. 'Care' of a kind is being provided, but the setting is not a 'home', if we consider what we really mean by 'home'. Our own home is more than a building. It's a place where we can be ourselves, where we have some control over what goes on, where we feel secure.

When a care home has rigid routines, it may in some ways make working practices easier. Staff know what they have to do and when they have to do it. But working in such an organisation is often unfulfilling, too, because there is no room for initiative, imagination or flexibility. If such a care home can be frustrating to work in, imagine what it must be like to live in: not really a 'home' at all. By the very nature of a routine-driven care home, residents are being abused because they cannot live their lives in the way they choose, their individual needs cannot be properly addressed, their independence is undermined, their choices are denied.

Sometimes routines can develop which make the work easier but which erode the rights of residents. Consider these two examples of abusive practice:

• In Ivy Lodge, a care home for people with dementia, there have been a number of occasions when residents have taken out their false teeth and hidden or lost them. Now residents are not given their false teeth in the morning. Pureeing all the food means they are still able to eat, but staff do not have to waste time hunting for lost teeth.

• In Oakhill House, residents are all toileted at regular times. Those who pass urine or faeces outside the set times are put in incontinence pads.

Some aspects of a home's routines are in the power of the manager; others may be controlled by the larger organisation, through policies, procedures and resources. But care assistants also often develop their own routines, as a way of making their work easier.

Had time constraints not been placed on Elsie's care assistant in the above scenario, it is clear that by giving Elsie a little assistance, the care assistant could enable her to wash and dress with a fair degree of independence. Even with the time constraints, the care assistant might be able to use her time more creatively: eg having pointed out Elsie's basin, flannel and soap, she could leave the room for a while and go in to her next resident.

But if the care assistant then gave exactly the same help to Bill, it might not be enough assistance to meet his needs, or it might be too much help, if Bill is a more able resident. So in order not to be abusive, care assistants need to be flexible in order to tailor the help they give to meet the individual needs of residents.

In all care homes there are tasks which

Sue Benson/Adamwood Nursing Home

Each resident is an individual, with individual needs, skills and interests.

must be done. Most of these centre around the basic physical needs of residents (for example, eating, hygiene and dressing) and housekeeping duties (for example, bed-making and laundry). Because these tasks have to be done, and because the results of doing these tasks are obvious, it is all too easy to focus on tasks at the expense of the residents themselves.

Perhaps, one morning, Elsie has been thinking about her mother and really needs to talk about how much she misses her. But where does this fit into a task-focused day? The truth is that Elsie's emotional needs are probably more important than anything else at that moment in time and to show interest, to encourage Elsie to talk and to empathise will possibly enable Elsie to express her emotions and feel more able to face the day. A focus on tasks rather than Elsie's emotional needs would probably leave Elsie feeling isolated and disempowered. A sensitivity to the needs of individuals is an essential part of care work.

The signs of abuse

I'd like to return to think about George's story, where this chapter started. George showed various signs of abuse. There were bruises from the beatings he got. He was withdrawn and depressed. He lost weight. He even spoke about the abuse. Indicators of abuse will not always be so obvious, and victims will not always speak up, so it is important to know how to identify the signs of abuse.

Signs of physical or sexual abuse include:
• frequent falls or injuries, without a good explanation
• bruising – perhaps in unusual places (eg inner arms or the genital area), or a covering of small bruises (from fists or poking fingers)
• burns or cuts, without a good explanation
• red marks, bruising or indentations which could indicate the use of physical restraint
• genital infections
• unusual sexual behaviour
• blood on underwear.

Criminal abuse

Some forms of abuse are criminal offences, in which case the police should become involved. If a prosecution is to be brought, the government's 'No Longer Afraid' document specifies that the vulnerable person has the right to have an independent advocate or representative to act on their behalf, if necessary. Even if the abuse is not a criminal offence, all care homes are controlled by legislation: they have to be registered with social services or with the health service and have registration and inspection units which investigate allegations of abuse and could, in extreme circumstances, close down an abusive care home. The rights of vulnerable adults are further protected by:
• the Mental Health Act 1983
• the Sexual Offences Act 1993
• the NHS and Community Care Act 1990
• the National Assistance Act 1948
• the Chronically Sick and Disabled Persons Act 1970/1986
• the Disability Discrimination Act 1995
• the Race Discrimination Act 1976
• the Sex Discrimination Act 1975
• the Care Standards Act 2000

Signs of psychological abuse include:
• changes in behaviour or mood (eg becoming anxious, withdrawn, depressed or uncooperative)
• disturbances in normal eating or sleeping pattern
• fear
• increased confusion or dependency.

Whether abuse is physical or psychological, whether it involves one dramatic incident or it is more subtle and insidious, its effects are devastating. It destroys self-esteem and self-confidence and can send the older person into a downward spiral where they become less and less able or motivated to stick up for themselves and become wide open to further abuse.

Anyone can be abused – not just older people. But people who are dependent on others for at least some aspects of their daily living are particularly at risk. The greater the level of dependency, the higher the risk of abuse. Those who are unable to communicate clearly, or whose mental functioning is impaired, are particularly vulnerable. Some types of abuse are less likely to occur in a care home because there are more people around and involved, although other types of abuse, as outlined above, may be more likely.

Responding to allegations

If a resident makes an allegation of abuse, it is essential to respond with sensitivity, listen carefully and calmly and believe what the person is telling you. Reassure the person that they have done the right thing by telling you and that it is not their fault. Don't ask any leading questions (such as 'did she do anything else to hurt you?'). The person may ask you to promise that you will not tell anyone, but of course you cannot make this promise – do, though, reassure the person that you will only tell your manager

and that people who don't need to know won't find out. Do not try to talk to the alleged abuser or anyone else involved – this will be the job of whoever carries out an investigation.

Staff who are told about or who witness abuse often feel that they are in a very difficult situation. They may well feel very upset about what has happened, angry about how the older person has been affected and anxious about what they should do. At least some staff in George's care home must have noticed some signs of the abuse, but nobody took action, with tragic consequences. Perhaps they did nothing because they were aware that the perpetrator was one of their colleagues and they contributed to a 'conspiracy of silence'. But 'blowing the whistle' on a colleague who is abusing is an essential thing to do. Even though other staff may have sympathy for the abuser – might perhaps know that the person is having problems at home; might be aware of what the consequences would be for the person if they lost their job – it is essential to uphold the rights of the vulnerable person who has been abused.

Whether abuse is perpetrated by another member of staff, by a visitor or by another resident and whether there is substantial evidence of abuse or just a slight suspicion, it is essential that staff should share their concerns with their manager. It is also important to write down (or tape record yourself talking about) what has happened, what you have been told or the signs you have noticed. Do this as soon as your suspicions are raised.

Many care homes will have a form on which to record details of abuse or suspected abuse. If your care home does not have such a form, make sure that you write down exactly what happened, what was said (note the exact words if you can) or what you saw, when it occurred, who was involved and whether it is similar to anything that has happened previously. Many homes will also have a policy and procedure about adult protection and how to deal with abuse; make sure you are familiar with your own organisation's procedures (for example, if it is not possible to talk to your manager about what has happened, you need to know who else you should talk to – perhaps a more senior manager or an inspector). You also need to know about the complaints procedure in your organisation.

All older people in care homes have the right to live without abuse. Good care meets individual needs, promotes well-being and upholds the rights of residents. When this is the focus of work with older people, they are empowered and enabled to thrive in the care home environment.

Reference

Department of Health (1995) No longer afraid: the safeguard of elderly people in domestic settings. HMSO, London.

Chapter 5 - Promoting well-being and preventing abuse

ESSENCE OF CARE

Privacy & dignity

1	2	3	4	5	6	7

NMS

16.1	16.2	16.3	16.4		
17.1	17.2	17.3			
18.1	18.2	18.3	18.4	18.4	18.6

NSF

1.1	1.2						
8.1	8.2	8.3	8.4	8.5	8.8	8.11	8.14

TOPSS

Induction

1.2.1	1.2.2	1.2.3
2.1.1	2.2.1	
3.2.7		

Foundation

1.4.1	1.4.2				
4.1.1	4.2.1	4.3.1	4.4.1	4.5.1	4.5.2

NVQ 2 CARE

Z1.1
All Performance Criteria, Range and Knowledge
Z1.2
All Performance Criteria, Range and Knowledge
Z1.3
1 All Performance Criteria, Range and Knowledge

Compiled by Adrian Muir

CHAPTER 6

Normal ageing

Hazel Heath

*• What is ageing? • Effects on the senses • Communication
• Memory and decison-making • Ageing and the body: the heart and lungs,
eating and digestion, elimination and continence, the skin, mobility and exercise
• The importance of relationships and sexuality*

We are all ageing all of the time, yet most of us could neither define 'normal' ageing nor describe the main changes that take place, other than in physical appearance. Ageing is a highly individual process, and not only do we vary greatly in the way we age, but the physiological systems within each person's body age at different rates.

There is a lot more variation among older people in terms of physical ability, health, social circumstances and lifestyle than is commonly believed. Nevertheless, most people age 'normally'. There is a range of identifiable changes which take place within our bodies as we grow older. The changes affect how we look, how we function in our everyday lives and particularly how illness affects us in later life.

This chapter explains:
• the main changes that occur in normal ageing and how these can affect older people's health and functioning;
• how to recognise common changes that can indicate ill-health in an older person and which need to be reported to the qualified person who has responsibility for this individual's care;
• the care you can offer to minimise the effects of disabling changes and to help the person to remain as well and as fully

functioning as possible.

Most people lead independent lives well into older age but, when illness or disability brings older people into contact with care services, the help they are offered will need to acknowledge the ageing processes they are experiencing. The more you understand about ageing, and how people can be helped to maintain the best possible health into later life, the more appropriate can be the help you offer to older people.

What is ageing?

Ageing is a process of development that begins at birth and continues throughout life. People show signs of ageing as early as in their 20s and 30s and there is no age at which we become 'elderly'. It happens naturally within our bodies and is different in each person.

How long you live depends on your individual genes but the maximum lifespan for human beings is around 115 years. Your lifestyle (whether you smoke, exercise or eat a healthy diet) and your environment (whether you breathe clean air or are exposed to pollutants or toxic substances) determine how close to your maximum lifespan you manage to live. As has been said, the different systems in our bodies can age at differ-

Sue Benson/Westminster Health Care

Generally you take into older age the personality you have had all your life.

ent rates and the rate of ageing of these systems varies from person to person.

Some ageing patterns may be partly determined early in life. For example, the amount of calcium in your diet or the amount of physical exercise you take as a child can affect the amount of bone you build during development, and this can affect the risk of osteoporosis (thinning of the bones) in older age. Other ageing patterns can be changed by your lifestyle in later life. For example, if you give up smoking or start to take adequate exercise, even if you wait until middle or older age to do so, your health and fitness will improve.

Many of the age changes described in this chapter, such as weakening of bodily systems, seem negative. In addition, it is true that older people tend to experience more illness, need more health care and take more medicines than younger people. But there are positive aspects to becoming older. People who reach old age have survived when others born at the same time have not. Scientists have identified some 'survival factors' in older people that are not found in younger people – for example a factor that protects against heart disease. This can mean that older people might respond better than younger people to some treatments for heart disease.

Also, the longer you live, the more events and challenges you encounter. These experiences can help the older person to cope with problems in later life. For example, people who lost family and friends in wars may have found ways of coping with loss that younger people have not yet discovered.

How we grow old, therefore, is not just a matter of how our bodies age but also of our life experiences and how we each deal with them.

Some general changes

There are many misunderstandings about ageing – for example that people become more stubborn when they become older. This is untrue. Generally you take into older age the personality you have had all your life.

Another misunderstanding is that illness is inevitable in older age and therefore not worth investigating. You may know the story of the older man who went to the doctor with a pain in his leg. 'It's your age,' the doctor told him. The man replied, 'But the other leg's exactly the same age and that isn't painful.'

People often ignore symptoms of illness, thinking they are due to ageing. In addition, research has shown that older people often receive less prompt or thorough treatment than younger people because it is believed they will not respond to it or that it will be too powerful for their bodies. As a result, diseases such as cancer are sometimes left to progress in older people when treatment could have cured them.

In health care, general fitness is more important than a person's chronological age. A person who is able to benefit from a treatment should not be prevented from receiving it on the grounds of age. In addition, the way in which a person is able to function in their everyday lives, for example in preparing a meal or using the toilet, can be more important than individual age changes or diseases. A person should not just be labelled as, for example, 'arthritic'. He or she should be offered the equipment and support which will help them to remain independent despite the condition.

The most obvious age changes, such as wrinkled skin, hair loss, increased body fat and some height loss, do not affect everyday functioning to the same extent as the body's internal changes, which tend to go unnoticed until a problem arises.

One major change that takes place with ageing is a gradual reduction in the body's ability to rebalance its systems when things go wrong, for example as a result of illness or taking medication. This balancing is known as *homeostasis*. Older people have a reduced ability to maintain homeostasis. As a result, if one health problem arises in someone who is very old, other systems cannot compensate and the person's health gradually deteriorates. This is known as the 'domino' effect because it works like a line of dominoes – after the first is knocked down, one after the other the rest fall.

Another important result of age changes is that older people do not always show the same symptoms of disease as younger people do. For example, a younger person with a bladder infection may complain of pain or that they are passing urine frequently. They may have a raised body temperature. An older person may just say they feel unwell or tired, or may show different symptoms. This is known as 'altered presentation of illness in older age'.

The four most common signs of illness in older age are listed below – it can be helpful to remember this as The Four 'I's.

The Four 'I's

- Immobility
- Instability
- Incontinence
- Impairment of mental function

For example, if a person seems to be more mentally confused than usual it should not be assumed it is 'just old age'. The cause could be an infection, constipation, not drinking sufficient fluid, or changes in the person's life which are upsetting them. If an older person starts to show any of The Four 'I's, you should report this to a person who is qualified to investigate.

AGEING AND THE SENSES

Age-related sensory changes affect our ability to communicate and to avoid hazards in life. They can begin while we are still in our 40s.

Hearing

As we get older, we can become less sensitive to sound. The ability to hear high frequencies is usually lost first. It can become more difficult to distinguish the different tones in sound, especially speech, and to locate where a sound is coming from. In addition, loud sound can become distorted or cause pain to an older person. Even normal speech can cause pain to someone whose hearing is affected in this way. Such age-related changes in hearing are known collectively as *presbycusis*.

Common conditions include:

• wax (cerumen) accumulating in the ears

• tinnitus – a constant ringing, buzzing or hissing in the ears. (Tinnitus is more common in older people, although it is not considered normal in old age.)

Sight

As you get older your sight deteriorates. The eye muscles weaken and it becomes more difficult to focus without the help of glasses. Peripheral vision (being able to see around the edges of the visual field) can reduce with ageing. Older people need more light than younger people to be able to see and may experience night blindness.

In addition, older people may be less able to tolerate glaring light and less able to adapt if they go from a dark to a light environment or from a dark place to a better lit area.

Together, such age-related changes are known as presbyopia.

There are three common sight problems you might experience in later life, although they are not viewed as normal ageing:

• macular degeneration – the centre of the visual field is lost

• cataracts – the lens of the eye becomes opaque and the person cannot see through it. However, the lens can be removed to restore sight

• glaucoma – pressure within the eyeball increases. It can be reduced with the regular use of eye drops.

Smell and taste

The senses of smell and taste become less sensitive in later life. Older people, particularly women, may lose their sense of smell. The size and number of taste buds in the mouth of the older person may also decrease. This, with the loss of the sense of smell, can reduce a person's enjoyment of food. The older person may use more sugar and salt on their food than they did because the taste buds most affected are those at the tip of the tongue which sense sweetness and saltiness.

The loss of sense of smell can put older people at risk. They may not so easily sense when food is deteriorating or detect the smell of gas or of something burning.

Health promotion and care

Older people should have regular sight and hearing checks. This is particularly the case for people who are unable to express their own needs. It is also important that older people wear any glasses or hearing aids prescribed and that they put drops in their eyes to control glaucoma if advised to do so. Specific problems, such as ear wax, must be treated regularly, while, as mentioned, cataracts can be surgically removed. There are organisations to help people with tinnitus.

The environment can make a difference to how much an older person is able to see and hear. They need good lighting levels without glare. They also need to be allowed time to adjust to changes in lighting levels, for example when going from a dark bedroom into a bright lounge. Notices should be in large print and displayed prominently. The layout of a person's immediate environment should not be changed without their knowledge.

Communicating

Communicating with someone who has visual or hearing impairment requires thought and skill. As discussed, any physical barriers to communication, such as ear wax, should be identified and treated. Make sure the person has all the aids they need to hand (glasses, magnifiers or hearing aids) and that these are working properly. This is particularly important for people with mental health needs. Health services can also offer information on local opticians, eye and hearing aid care and hearing centres.

Always ensure the person knows who you are and where you are. Get their attention before you speak. Try to minimise distractions. You should also find out what helps each individual, for example someone may hear more clearly on one side than the other. However, the person's attitude, approach and language can also affect the relationship. (Further details on communication are given in Chapter 3.)

Because of sensory loss, older people can be particularly affected by what is going on in their environment. They can feel isolated when unable to see and hear. When little is going on in their lives they just sit inactive for long periods which can lead to *sensory deprivation.*

However, if the environment in a hospital or care home is busy, the person may feel bombarded by what is going on and suffer *sensory overload.* This may make it difficult for older people to function to the best of their ability; they may become disorientated; they may lose concentration or they may want to withdraw.

Maintaining body temperature

Normal ageing reduces our ability to adapt to temperature change. As a result of a number of changes our bodies become less efficient in detecting temperature change and responding to it. Older people are especially at risk of hypothermia, which means they have a dangerously low body temperature. It is caused by a fall in environmental temperatures. People who are unable to heat their homes adequately or who are unable to be active, for example when they are ill, are most at risk.

Health promotion and care

If the environmental temperature drops there are ways an older person can prevent becoming cold. They can:
• wear adequate clothing and have additional clothing to hand
• wear a number of thinner layers rather than one thick one because more layers trap warmed air and are therefore more effective than just one
• wear thermal underwear
• wear a hat because this helps prevent heat loss from the head
• keep as active as possible.

AGEING, MEMORY, LEARNING AND DECISION-MAKING

There are many misunderstandings about how ageing affects mental functioning. Some people believe there is a severe decline in memory or intelligence. This is not true. There may be some slowing of thought processes, a slight decline in mental agility and minor effects on memory, but these have little effect on everyday life. In fact, about three-quarters of people retain good mental functioning, even into very old age. And, as you read earlier, if they have encountered similar situations before, these experiences can help older people to solve problems.

When older people undergo tests, they often find their memories are better than they believe them to be. However, losing confidence in your memory can affect your confidence in daily life.

Health promotion and care
Tiredness, stress, changes in your general health and specific illness, such as a tumour or head injury, can affect how well your brain works. For this reason, it is important to maintain a person's general health at the highest possible level. If you notice any change in the mental functioning of a resident, it should be investigated.

Older people are most able to understand, learn and make decisions when information is presented in an appropriate way and though skilled communication (See Chapter 3).

AGEING IN THE HEART AND LUNGS

The heart and blood vessels (the cardiovascular system)

The heart circulates blood, oxygen and nourishment around the body through the blood vessels. As the blood flows, it picks up waste products from the body's internal processes and takes them to the organs which remove them from the body, such as the kidneys.

As you get older, fatty substances (known as atheroma) tend to be deposited within the blood vessels including the arteries. This is particularly common in the arteries which carry blood from the heart and around the body. With age, the blood vessels also tend to become hardened and this, with the atheroma, makes it more difficult for the blood to flow freely through them. (This condition is called atherosclerosis or arteriosclerosis.) This can cause an increase in blood pressure, adding to the rise in blood pressure that tends to come with old age.

An older person might have this condition if they feel faint when they stand up quickly. This happens because the hardened blood vessels may not be able to carry blood up to the brain fast enough. Sitting for a while (for example when getting out of bed), or rising more slowly when changing from a sitting to a standing position, allows the body to adjust and can help prevent the feeling of faintness.

Atherosclerosis also builds up in the arteries supplying the heart muscle – the coronary arteries. This is not 'normal' but it is common in older age. It can cause pain in the chest (angina) when the person is energetic. Arteries can also become blocked with a blood clot. If this happens it may cause a heart attack (a coronary thrombosis). Heart disease is common in later life but the symptoms are not always the same as in younger people. Older people can have a 'silent' heart attack. This means they only become aware of it when it is diagnosed following a tracing taken of the heart's electrical activity (an electrocardiograph).

Another condition that happens in later life is heart failure. When this occurs, the blood cannot easily return to the heart. Fluid tends to collect in the lower legs and, later, in other parts of the body. It is important to report if an older person's legs seem swollen, as there are medicines to reduce this. (See Chapter 7.)

Lungs

As we age, our lungs become less elastic and the blood vessels around the lungs are not so easily able to absorb the oxygen we need to breathe from the air. Shortness of breath may be one of the first indicators of age changes. This is particularly common when an older person is faced with something unusual or stressful, because the body needs more oxygen in such situations.

Also in later life, the lungs become less efficient at removing the mucus that collects. This, and the fact that the immune system does not tend to work as effectively, mean older people can easily acquire a chest infection. Other problems include dizziness, and coughing or wheezing. They may find it harder to take physical exercise.

An older person's respiratory health (ability to breathe) will, to some extent, have been determined by their previous lifestyle – their occupation, smoking habits and whether they were exposed to environmental pollutants. Many older people have smoked cigarettes or been exposed to pulmonary (lung) irritants, such as asbestos or coal, and a significant number, particularly in previously industrial areas such as the North East of England, have a condition called chronic obstructive pulmonary disease. This can be extremely disabling.

Health promotion and care

Breathlessness can be extremely distressing for the person experiencing it and for those who see it. People should be offered the best support available. Changes in breathing, shortness of breath, coughing or wheezing, should be reported as soon as they are noticed, and, if a chest infection is suspected, medical advice should be sought.

A person can reduce the symptoms of breathlessness by:

• keeping an upright body posture which allows maximum lung capacity with minimum effort; and

• deep breathing using the diaphragm (the large muscle that goes across the middle of the body under the lungs and pulls them down to open them).

People should be encouraged to try to relax and to take deep breaths, for example, six every hour.

A person who experiences breathlessness should be encouraged to drink adequate amounts of fluids, to move around, and to exercise as much as they are able without it becoming uncomfortable. Lung irritants, such as cigarette smoke or dust, should be avoided. Reducing stress can also help.

Influenza ('flu) can be dangerous in older people and there are vaccinations available to help prevent the older person catching it.

AGEING, EATING AND DIGESTION

Older people are at particular risk of undernutrition, and malnutrition has been found to be a common problem in hospitals and care homes (as well as for older people at home). There are many non-age-related reasons why a person finds it hard to eat properly. These may be:

• physiological (caused by the body). For example, a person with mobility problems or arthritic joints can find it difficult to shop for food and prepare it;

• psychological (caused by the way they are thinking). For example a person who is unhappy or worried about something may find it difficult to eat;

• or social (caused by circumstances). For example, if someone is alone they may feel it is not worth bothering to prepare a meal, or they may forget.

Many older people have lost teeth or have dentures. This is not related to age but is a consequence of what happened when they were younger. In the past, good dental care was not so readily available, there was little preventive dentistry, and dentists tended to remove teeth rather than fill them.

There are also age-related changes which may affect the older person's eating. Older people may not need to eat as much as they did. This may be partly due to a reduction in the amount of muscle in their bodies. However, they still need at least as many nutrients, particularly protein, minerals and vitamins. Therefore, if person eats less, it is vital that what they do eat should be very rich in the nutrients they need to keep healthy.

Losing the sense of smell, taste, touch and sight, can make food less enjoyable. The older person may have less saliva in their mouth, which may make chewing and swallowing more difficult.

Changes in the digestive system reduce the ability of the older person's body to absorb the nutrients in food.

Health promotion and care

The principles of good nutrition, including eating a variety of foods from all the food groups, are the same for older people as they are for younger people. However, for the reasons outlined before, special care needs to be taken to ensure that older people receive sufficient nutrients, particularly iron, calcium, vitamins C and D, and fibre. Natural sources of fibre, such as wholegrain cereals, fruit and vegetables, are preferable to bran. This is because eating bran can cause pain in the digestive system and reduce the body's ability to absorb minerals such as iron or calcium.

It is also important that the eating environment is pleasant and sociable. This is especially the case for people who are restless, distressed or easily distracted. Other aspects of eating, such as the cutlery, as well as the food itself, should be culturally acceptable. It is also important to ensure the person is able to get the food to their mouths. Therefore utensils should be appropriate for specific problems – for example, if the person has arthritic hands. The person must also be able to chew and swallow. Their food and drink intake should be monitored. (Further details are given in Chapter 7.)

AGEING, ELIMINATION AND CONTINENCE

Urinary elimination

Age-related changes can mean a person passes urine more frequently during the night they used to (this is known as *nocturia*.) The reasons are that, with ageing, the kidneys can gradually lose their ability to concentrate urine and the bladder becomes less elastic and therefore is less able to store it.

In men, the prostate gland enlarges with age (prostatic hypertrophy) and can block the outflow of urine from the bladder. Older men commonly experience difficulty in starting and stopping the flow of urine. 'Dribbling' is also common.

Infections of the urinary tract are common in later life, particularly in women. These can happen if the bladder is not completely emptied and the remaining 'pool' of urine is invaded by bacteria. Although these are age-related changes, they are not an aspect of normal ageing.

Urgency – the person needs to get to the toilet urgently or the bladder will empty – can also occur. Unlike in younger people, who sense their bladder needs emptying when it gets to about half full, older people may not feel this urge until the bladder is nearly full, by which time they need to use the toilet immediately.

Age-related changes in kidney function can become significant when people are ill or start to take medication.

Some older people experience continence problems but incontinence is *not* an inevitable consequence of ageing. Perhaps the toilets are difficult to reach; or changes in eyesight make it difficult to find them. The person may have reduced mobility making it difficult to get there; arthritic hands, which means he or she cannot remove clothing quickly; or mental health problems which makes it difficult for them to recognise the toilet or remember how to use it.

Continence problems can be made worse by constipation, bladder infections and some types of medication.

Health promotion and care

It is easier to help a person keep control of their bladder if the older person can reach the lavatory and remove clothing easily. Health teaching can also help. This may include teaching the person pelvic floor exercises – squeezing the muscles around the genitals and anus to keep the muscles in these areas toned.

If there are continence problems, a comprehensive assessment should be offered and the person referred for specialist advice or equipment, if necessary. Any underlying problem, such as an enlarged prostate or a urinary tract infection, needs to be diagnosed and treated.

Elimination of faeces

Constipation commonly occurs in older age. There are several reasons for this.

As you get older, the nerves and muscles of the digestive tract become less active and food passes more slowly through the system. Exercise stimulates the digestion process, therefore older people who are not able to move around are at particularly high risk of constipation.

Also, the inside walls of the gut become less efficient at absorbing food. Other contributing factors may be general weakness, insufficient fluid intake, insufficient fibre in the diet or taking certain medicines.

Problems around the anus, such as

haemorrhoids (piles), can make it difficult to pass faeces, particularly if the faeces are hard. If a person has regularly used laxatives, he or she may need to continue to use them to maintain adequate bowel movement.

Health promotion and care
To maintain a regular bowel action it is recommended you drink at least eight full cups of liquid a day and eat enough natural dietary fibre. Exercise plays a part, too, because it stimulates the activity of the muscles of the digestive system and can help strengthen them. However, it is also important that toilets should offer privacy and comfort so the user can relax and empty their bowels properly. (Further details are given in Chapter 8.)

AGEING AND THE SKIN

Often the first signs of ageing are changes in the skin and the hair. Such changes affect how we feel about ourselves but do not usually affect functioning. The skin loses some of its supporting structure (collagen and fat) particularly immediately under the surface, and becomes less elastic. Hair loses its colour and becomes grey or white. Hair thinning or hair loss is common, particularly in men.

The skin becomes more dry as the skin cells produce less natural oil. In addition, the blood supply to the skin is reduced and the blood vessels tear more easily, making older people more prone to bruising. The healing process can also take longer as damaged cells are replaced more slowly.

It is important to know that the older we become, the more easily our skin can be damaged. The most common cause is trauma (eg direct blows to the skin), but it can also be the result of shearing forces (as the skin is dragged).

Health promotion and care
Maintaining a healthy skin is important for comfort and self-esteem and to prevent problems such as breaks in the skin.

Aged skin should be washed gently and not over-washed. The water should not be too hot and the skin should be patted dry rather than rubbed. Particular attention should be paid to the areas between skin folds (e.g. under the breasts) and fingers and toes.

If the skin is dry, emollients such as a soft skin wash or moisturising cleansing lotion are better than soap, and moisturisers can help maintain skin texture. It is best not to use strongly perfumed products.

Sitting in direct sun, particularly without protection, is not advisable. Nails may need professional attention, especially if the person has poor circulation.

Preventing skin breakdown due to pressure is vital. Encouraging appropriate movement, eating and drinking properly can help. It is essential to move and handle someone carefully and according to policies. Appropriate pressure-relieving devices and strategies, as prescribed by a professional person, should be used.

Incontinence should be prevented as it increases the risk of skin breakdown, especially if someone is doubly incontinent (of urine and faeces).

Any changes in skin condition must be reported immediately. This includes skin rashes caused by irritation or which are a reaction to a medicine the person is taking.

AGEING, MOBILITY AND EXERCISE

Many of the major changes in how older people function are associated with age-related changes in the muscles, joints and bones. Ageing alone does not necessarily restrict an individual's movement, but age-related changes tend to affect an individual's strength, speed, posture, body image, independence and safety.

The older person may experience a decrease in general strength and flexibility; have a more limited range of motion in the joints and a mild reduction in physical endurance (how long they can keep going without tiring).

Changes also occur in the way the older person walks – their gait. They tend to develop a narrower standing base (they keep their legs closer together), take shorter steps and have a wider sway when walking. This means they are generally less stable and less able to control their own posture which in turn affects their balance. Not being able to see or hear as well, and taking certain medicines, can also affect stability.

Osteoporosis (thinning of the bones) is also common in later life, although this is not classed as normal ageing.

If older people become inactive they can experience a whole range of direct complications, including a decrease in muscle strength, increased stiffness, muscle wasting and chest infections.

Health promotion and care

Older people are at particular risk of falling. Most falls result from a combination of physical changes, hazards in the environment and older people wanting to continue to do the things they have always done but perhaps have become less able to do, due to physical changes. Many falls can be prevented by recognising when a person is not well, for example if they feel dizzy when rising to stand or feel their legs are weak; and by removing environmental hazards, such as rugs, loose wiring or slippery surfaces.

A slogan relevant to ageing is, 'use it or lose it'. People should be encouraged to move around as much as possible, and maintain natural body posture and positions. Regular exercise of all muscle groups by older people can improve muscle strength and this can help to maintain or re-establish personal independence. Therefore older people should be encouraged to keep active, to continue with the activities of daily life: to move around the home, to shop and continue with sport and hobbies where they are able.

Good footwear and podiatry advice and treatment are also important.

Furniture, such as chairs of the correct height, can assist considerably and there should be space to move around. Moving and handling policies must be followed.

AGEING AND RELATIONSHIPS

Relationships are as important in later life as at any other time. In fact they may be much more so because the need to share, to feel cared about and to be close to others can become much greater at times of difficulty, change and loss or illness.

The older we become, the more we experience the death of loved ones and friends. Any such loss can be devastating for older people who might have shared so much with the person who has died.

Relationships maintained over decades can be particularly rich because the mutual understandings have developed over a lifetime of caring and sharing. Within such quality long-term relationships individuals may talk in a kind of shorthand, which can be incomprehensible to others, and sometimes, because the mutual bond of understanding is to strong, no words are necessary because each understands the other's experience and viewpoint.

The loss of a partner, wife, husband or closest friend can be particularly devastating. Older individuals may appear to come to terms with such loss, but many continue to feel the grief at the deepest level and in their innermost thoughts.

This is not always the case, though. Some older people will have stayed with partners even when they were unhappy because they were born within a culture which dictated that marriage was for life. For these people, the death of a partner brings feelings of liberation or freedom.

Growing older can affect relationships in a number of ways. In contrast to patterns of family living in the early 20th century, the past 50 years or so have seen young people moving away from where they grew up. If older family members remain with their roots, this can leave both generations geographically isolated.

Maintaining relationships is made even harder if hearing loss makes it difficult to use the telephone or sight loss makes it difficult to read and write letters.

Seeking new friendships in later life may not be easy, particularly if a person cannot walk for long distances, if local transport is not good and if there are no local places where people gather. If someone wants to seek close or intimate relationships, this can be even more difficult. As their appearance changes, or as they experience illness or disability, the older person may think they are less attractive than when they were younger. These changes are made more distressing by the images around us which suggest that falling in love and having sex are not appropriate in later life or are not for people with less-than-perfect bodies.

Physical age changes not only affect how we feel about ourselves and our relationships, they affect our sexual functioning. If a person feels they have a problem, the services offering health care to older people should be able to advise where they can get expert help.

At a time in our lives which can easily become dominated by illness, disability and loss; caring and loving relationships, intimacy and sexual sharing can be a powerful confirmation we are still attractive and lovable as individuals. It can help us to feel wanted, desired, valued and enjoyed.

Health promotion and care
Studies have found that the more people are able to remain socially active, the more healthy they remain. Research also shows that many older people still want intimacy and to be able to express them-

Relationships maintained over decades can be particularly rich, with mutual understandings developed over a lifetime of caring and sharing.

selves sexually. It is, however, important to appreciate that each person will make individual choices. Some will not want another relationship after the loss of a lifelong partner. Others will seek new and different relationships. Some will find love, intimacy and fulfilment with a person of the same gender or someone much younger. Some will want to remain celibate.

Everyone who works with older people brings to that situation their own experiences, knowledge, values and opinions. It is important to acknowledge these and, if they seem at odds with the situations in which you work, to share them with colleagues and supervisors who could help to reconcile the different perspectives.

Older people deserve to be given respect, dignity and as much privacy as is possible. For example, before going into a person's bedroom, you should knock and await permission to enter.

Trying to remain open-minded, non-judgmental, and sensitive in your approach to the whole area of relationships and sexuality can make a great deal of difference to the quality of the care older people experience. It is important to respect older people for who they are, regardless of their lifestyle. After all, isn't this how you would like to be treated?

People are now generally living longer and staying healthier into older age. This is a cause for celebration. Our task now is to help those older people for whom we care to adapt to the changes they are experiencing and to enjoy real quality of life, on their terms.

Recommended reading

Alison Clarke, Les Bright and Chris Greenwood (August 2002) *Sex and relationships: A guide for care homes.* Counsel and Care, London.

Anne Roberts (April 2001) *Better Health in Retirement.* Age Concern Books, London

Chapter 6 - Normal ageing

ESSENCE OF CARE

Self care

1	4	7	9

Privacy & dignity

1	2	3	4	5	6	7

NMS

None

NSF

1.3
2.1

8.1	8.2

TOPSS

Induction

1.1.1	1.3.1

3.2.8
4.1.4

Foundation

1.1.1	1.1.2	1.2.1
2.1.1	2.2.1	2.4.1

5.2.4

NVQ 2 CARE

Z6.1

Range:	1a	1b		
Performance criteria:		2	6	7

CL1.1

Range:	1a	1b	1c	2b
Performance Criteria:		1	2	4

CL1.2 Range

1a	1b	1c	2b
Performance criteria:	1	2	4

O1.1

Performance criteria: 1

O1.2

Range: 1a,1b

Compiled by Adrian Muir

CHAPTER 7

Chronic health problems

Jane Slack

*Chronic ill health • Parkinson's disease • Stroke • Dementia
• Coronary heart disease: heart attack, angina, heart failure
• Care and support during a chronic illness*

Chapter six explored normal ageing. It is not inevitable that when a person gets older they will become ill and frail. However, there are some major disorders which may affect older people, and research does show that if an older person has to move into a care environment, they are likely to be affected by at least four different forms of health problem or disability.

This chapter will look at a few of the most common chronic diseases that may be found in a care setting. A chronic disease is one where the person may suffer from the signs and symptoms of the illness or the effects of the illness for a very long time, if not for the rest of their life. So chronic ill health is very different from an acute illness which can often be cured and the ill effect remedied.

PARKINSON'S DISEASE

Parkinson's disease (often known as PD) is a disorder of the central nervous system. It is one of the most common neurological problems affecting older people; however, one in seven people diagnosed is under the age of 40. It is not known what causes Parkinson's disease. It is a slow, progressive, degenerative disorder, which attacks the cells in the part of the brain that influences how movement is initiated, planned and carried out.

Signs, symptoms and effects
The disorder affects both movement and speech. The person affected may find it increasingly difficult to speak clearly, manipulate the hands or walk. They know what they want to do, but the muscles will not respond to their wishes. The three main physical symptoms most often seen in people with this disease are:
• Tremor, typically of the hands and arms
• Rigidity – stiffness of the muscles
• Slowness of movement and difficulty in initiating movement

Difficulties
The most challenging effect faced by many people with PD is that there can be an enormous fluctuation in their

ability to carry out activities. This is often called 'on/off syndrome', and is usually the side effect of the long-term drug therapy.

This fluctuation can be very disabling: they may be able to cook a meal for themselves, but by the time they are ready to eat it, they may have 'frozen' or be in an off period, unable to initiate any movement. For some individuals this period of fluctuation can be predicted, which can lead to them carrying out activities at abnormal times of the day – perhaps ironing or preparing food at 3am as they know they will have 'switched off' at 8am.

Communication can also be difficult for a person with PD, as their voice can often become very quiet and the speech can sound slurred. The disease also affects how the persons expresses or shows emotions, as the facial muscles are affected in the same way as those in the rest of the body. This can give a person with PD a 'mask-like' expression. To a carer, the absence of any clues as to whether the person is happy or sad, combined with an absence of body language or non-verbal cues, can make communication difficult. The person's handwriting can become very cramped, small and illegible.

Due to the effect of the disease on their muscles, they may find it difficult to eat, turn over in bed, or manipulate the fingers to carry out fine movements such as fasten buttons or a tie.

Hallucinations can be another very distressing symptom of PD.

Abilities

Parkinson's disease alone does not normally affect intelligence. A person with this condition is just as alert and mentally agile as anyone else of his or her age. The individual can still make decisions about what they want to do, and how they want to do it. The most important point to remember about caring for a person with PD is that whatever activity or task they wish to undertake, plenty of time needs to be allowed for them to complete it and something they can manage today may be impossible next time.

Supporting independence

Care staff can help by enabling the individual to carry out activities when their body will allow them to – for example allowing a person to wash their own laundry, make a drink or tidy their room – even if it is at a different time than other residents may choose to do these tasks.

It helps to understand that a resident may begin to undertake a task and then 'freeze' and allow them to complete that task themselves later on. The timing of any medication for treating the symptoms of Parkinson's disease can be critical for maintaining independence. The care assistant must report to the manager any concerns they may have regarding difficulties with medication.

Care staff must remember above all that if the ability of a person with PD to care for themself varies at different times, it is the condition which causes this. It is not the person being difficult or demanding.

STROKE

The medical term used to describe a stroke is a *cerebral vascular accident* (CVA). This describes what happens when a part of the brain is suddenly cut off from its normal blood supply and is permanently damaged as a result. The impact of this 'accident' depends on which area of the brain has been damaged and how large that area is.

There are two ways in which a stroke may occur:

● when the blood supply to a part of the brain is interrupted either by a blood clot or a piece of debris causing a blockage

● when a person suffers from high blood pressure causing one of the smaller blood vessels in the brain to burst.

Signs, symptoms and effects

The effects of a stroke and the signs and symptoms are often the same. When a person has a stroke they may become unconscious, or they may just suddenly find they cannot move or speak the way they were able to before.

The most common effect is limb weakness. Limb weakness down one side of the body can be of varying severity. Some individuals are not able to move either their leg or arm without assistance, while others can still carry out such activities. Movement can sometimes return to the affected limb if the person has the benefit of rehabilitation and exercise. This should be managed by a specialist nurse or a physiotherapist. Care staff can carry out simple exercises to help the person once instruction has been given.

The other common effect is the loss of the ability to speak. In old age, the most common language disorder is loss of ability to use language normally; this is called *aphasia*. There are two main ways

in which this affects people who have had a stroke.

Receptive aphasia means that the person cannot understand language. It is as if they are in a foreign land, though they may recognise objects and their uses.

Expressive aphasia means that the person affected can understand verbal and written communication but cannot organise concepts into words or meaningful phrases.

A stroke can also affect a person's ability to control their emotions. This is called *labile moods* – emotions may swing between happiness to despair, without control.

Other changes will depend on which part of the brain has been affected, and the severity of the disability will depend on the density (or severity) of the stroke.

Difficulties

In common with an individual with Parkinson's disease, a person who has had a stroke can find it difficult to communicate with others or express themselves in the way they would wish to. They may find it difficult to dress or wash themselves without assistance from others due to their limb weakness. They may find it difficult to eat or drink in the way that they feel is socially acceptable and may become embarrassed at eating with other people. A person who has had a stroke often experiences pain in their affected limbs, and needs regular medication. Some people who have experienced a stroke find it difficult to use their bowels and bladder, and will require assistance in the form of special aids. The resident should be assessed by a registered nurse to determine the correct aids required.

Some people also have difficulty in

Risks that may cause a person to have a stroke

There are various factors that can increase the risk of a person having a stroke. In order to help prevent people either having a stroke for the first time, or having another stroke, care staff should be aware of these risks, so that they can advise residents if appropriate. The risks are:

• Untreated high blood pressure (hypertension)

• Irregular heart beat which can increase the risk of blood clots forming in the heart and moving into the brain

• Diabetes – a side effect can be high blood pressure and atherosclerosis (fatty deposits in the blood vessel walls)

• Smoking can raise blood pressure

• Regular heavy drinking, which again raises blood pressure

• A high salt and fat diet, which causes furring and narrowing of the arteries

• Age – strokes are more common over the age of 55

• Gender – men are more at risk than women

• A family history of stroke

• Ethnic background – Asians Africans or Afro-Caribbeans are at greater risk

• Certain types of contraceptive pill.

Transient Ischaemic Attack (TIA)

A TIA, sometimes called a mini stroke, occurs when the blood supply to a part of the brain is interrupted. The symptoms may be the same as for a stroke, with the person losing sensation or consciousness for a short time.

Alternatively the person may just feel some tingling or numbness, or even just feel very unwell and nauseous, but not be able to describe why.

Unlike a stroke, the effects will wear off usually within a few hours, but definitely within 24 hours, and the effects are usually short lived. The causes are the same as for a stroke, and are often seen by doctors as warning signs that the person may be at a very high risk of having a full stroke.

If a person experiences a TIA the doctor must be informed as soon as possible, to investigate why it has happened and possibly put the person on some treatment to prevent a TIA recurring.

More information can be obtained from the Stroke Association about caring for people with a Stroke and TIA.

registering their affected side. This means that their brain no longer remembers they have two sides to their body. This means that the person has difficulty in many aspects of their life because their brain has 'forgotten' half of their body. This may be spotted in some people who never turn to look towards their affected side or register if a person is sitting and talking there. It may also be noticed when a person is eating. If a person has this deficit, they may only eat half the food on their plate, leaving the half which is on their affected side simply because the brain does not register it.

Some people lose the sensation of eating and swallowing. They may then have difficulty in eating meals, and may pouch food in their mouths. This can be dangerous if they are unaware of this and continue to put food into their mouths. It can also cause oral problems if unnoticed as food can sit in the mouth for a long time causing ulcers or dental problems.

Supporting independence

The most important aspect of supporting a person who has had a stroke is to understand their difficulties and be patient when caring for them.

When helping a person to dress, the care assistant should encourage them to do as much as they can for themselves, but the arm or leg on the affected side should be put into the item of clothing first, and should be carefully lifted as it will be heavy and may be painful.

All other aspects of care must be based on the needs of the individual, as a stroke can cause so many different effects. However, using adapted equipment or aids of daily living can often mean that the person who has had a stroke can carry out any activities that they would otherwise not manage. The key role of the care assistant is to work with the person and then find ways of helping them to help themself, only undertaking the task if the person cannot manage to do so.

Supporting the person emotionally and showing understanding through good communication is most important. It will be very hard for a person to learn new ways of doing things, and sometimes they will have to come to terms with the fact that they may never be able to do a certain activity again.

DEMENTIA

Dementia is not primarily an emotional or psychological disorder. It is caused by physical changes in the structure of the brain. These changes lead to problems with memory, thinking and actions. It is not a part of the normal ageing process. There are a number of causes that can lead a person to experience dementia. Alzheimer's disease is the most common, but people who have had a number of strokes, or who suffer from very severe Parkinson's disease can also experience dementia. At the moment there is no cure for Alzheimer's disease, nor most of the other types of dementia.

Signs, symptoms and effects
Dementia is associated with changes in behaviour, motivation and personality. It is more than just forgetfulness. The person with dementia may have problems in remembering; may sometimes find it hard to find the right words; have difficulty in understanding what people are saying; have problems recognising people; find it more difficult to solve problems and complete tasks; or find it harder to concentrate. The different types of dementia will cause different changes in the brain, and so cause slightly different problems, but the effect is broadly similar.

However, each person with dementia remains the individual they always were, and will be affected in an individual way. The effects of the disease will depend on the person's personality and character, their way of life, other illnesses that they have, how they have lived in the past, and – crucially – how they are looked after now. So, to a much greater extent than with other diseases, the way people around them react and relate to them, as well as their past life and character, can have an enormous effect on the person's well-being and behaviour.

Difficulties
People with dementia can experience a range of difficulties with many daily living activities such as getting dressed, managing personal care, and eating. It will vary from one person to another and will also vary depending on how the dementia is progressing, and how well they are being cared for.

People with dementia may find it difficult to say exactly what they want in a way the care assistant can understand, especially when that involves feelings of pain, cold, hunger, anxiety or fear. They may often find it difficult to adjust to changes in staff or environment, due to their short term memory loss, so will need more time and support than perhaps another resident in adapting to new surroundings or to a change in routine.

People with dementia may forget that they have just eaten a meal, or forget that they have not eaten. Refusing food is a common problem which can lead to weight loss. Weight loss can lead to increased problems with muscle weakness, immobility and pressure sores.

Abilities

The most important aspect of caring for a person with dementia is to assume they are still able to undertake various aspects of their life until it is established that they can't.

If a person with dementia is left to have everything done for them, the skills they still have will be lost and the person will become even more dependent on others.

It is also important to ensure that they are always included in all aspects of decision making about their life, and can express their likes and dislikes. Enabling a person with dementia to choose their food from the menu, what clothes to wear, or what activities to participate in are very important in maintaining the older person's self esteem, dignity and independence.

People with dementia will be able to sense the atmosphere, regardless of how severe the effects of the disease, and they will be able to understand the tone of voice or the way things are said to them. So it is vitally important that person-centred care is central to all aspects of helping the person manage their lives.

Supporting independence

Good dementia care is person-centred. This way of thinking and working is set out in detail in chapter two, and followed through in every chapter of this book. Good dementia care is demonstrated when the staff make every effort to live and work in a person-centred way, seeing first not the disease or disability but the individual person who needs help and support.

Staff have to accept that many problems which arise when caring for people with dementia are because the staff have not considered their actions before carrying out care, or talked to the person first.

Common difficulties occur when a person is prevented from doing something or going somewhere. Although there are risks to be assessed, staff must ask themselves why a person should not walk down a certain corridor, or sit in a certain place? Often friction and frustration occurs because staff are only thinking of the 'rules' of the home and not of the needs of the person. Safety must be paramount, but blanket rules are not good care.

Whatever aspect of physical care a person requires, staff must always think about how they communicate with and support the person with dementia, always referring to the principles of person centred care and communication (see chapters 2 and 3).

Good physical care is not the only type of care required, and other problems often occur when the person is bored. Research has shown that people will continuously walk, shout, bang tables and be disruptive because they are just trying to occupy themselves: they have nothing to do and are bored. So activity and conversation are vital aspects of good dementia care, and should be planned with the same level of importance as any aspect of physical care.

Some difficulties occur because the person cannot find their way around the care setting. The environment is therefore very important, with good visual cues to show people where to go, warm friendly colour and seating areas so that people have a choice and points where they can rest. Everything learned in this book applies to good care of people with dementia, just as it does to every other older person.

CORONARY HEART DISEASE (CHD)

Estimates suggest that one out of every two people aged 60 years and over has some severe narrowing of the coronary arteries, but only half of these will show any symptoms of coronary heart disease (CHD). The most common symptoms experienced by a person with CHD are heart attacks (myocardial infarction); angina; heart failure.

Heart attack

A heart attack happens when a coronary artery (blood vessel) becomes blocked with a clot of blood or fat. The person will experience chest pain, may feel sick and may become cold and clammy. Typically the pain will radiate down the left arm and will often last for longer than 15 minutes. A heart attack can happen at any time and is not necessarily associated with exercise.

Care and support

Prompt treatment must be organised by a doctor, and if a heart attack is suspected the person must be taken to hospital as soon as possible. It is important then to reassure and support the person until the ambulance arrives.

Angina

The word *angina* means pain. Narrowing of the blood vessels in the heart means that when the person is carrying out physical activity such as walking up stairs, the heart is unable to receive enough oxygen and nutrients for the muscles to work. This results in the pain experienced by patient.

Care and support

Many people wrongly think that severe angina is a mini-heart attack and that each time they have an attack their heart is wearing out. It is extremely frightening to experience an angina attack. Heart attacks and angina are very unpleasant, and even a minor episode of angina can trigger unpleasant memories, provoking feelings of anxiety. Stress can often provoke an episode of angina, and many sufferers learn to avoid things that cause stress, which can be brought on by anxiety, fear, anger and frustration.

If a resident complains of any of the symptoms of angina – pain in their chest, arm or jaw, feeling of tightness around their chest, breathlessness, sweating – the first thing the care assistant must do is remain calm and reassuring. As angina attacks usually occur when the resident is undertaking some form of physical activity, sit them down. Encourage them to take slow deep breaths. Many sufferers will have been taught relaxation techniques to use at this time, if so the care assistant can help them with these

If the pain does not stop within one minute, they may need to take one of their prescribed medications for use when an angina attack occurs. This can be in the form of a small tablet that dissolves when put under their tongue or a small spray (rather like a mouth freshener) that again is placed under the tongue. Usually, once the medication has been administered and the resident has rested for a few moments, the pain will subside. Sometimes, during a more severe attack, the resident will need more than one tablet or spray. They can take as many as they need to in order to take the pain away. However, if the pain has not subsided after 20 minutes, a doctor will need to be called.

The care assistant can play a very important role in caring for people with angina by ensuring that if they have prescribed medication for their angina, they carry it with them at all times. Some people have a number of bottles or sprays so that they can keep one in every handbag or pocket.

Heart failure

As medical treatment of CHD improves and more people survive after experiencing heart attacks, many individuals develop heart failure later in life. Heart failure is a condition that is the long-term consequence of a damaged heart, and affects not just the heart but eventually all other organs in the body. Heart failure can cause the person to experience breathlessness, fatigue, swelling of the lower limbs (oedema) and reduced ability to tolerate exercise. Some older people may also have a persistent cough or confusion.

However the heart disease affects the older person, the symptoms are distressing and greatly decrease quality of life.

Difficulties

For many people experiencing angina or heart failure, inability to exercise is a major problem. This does not mean they cannot go to work out in the gym – it often means that the individual cannot walk more than a few steps without experiencing pain, breathlessness or fatigue. Just getting out of bed and going to the bathroom in the morning can be a major effort, requiring them to take medication before they actually get off the bed, and resting for a time after they get there. Getting up and washed and dressed can take perhaps an hour, and then they will need to rest before having their breakfast. For many people with heart failure sleeplessness and fatigue can lead to memory loss and poor concentration. This can affect the individuals ability to manage their own medication, which is often very complicated. The health care assistant can prompt the older person and report back to the manager if medication does not appear to be taken correctly

Care and support

Although the person with heart disease may be limited physically to the activities they can manage, intellectually they are still able to make decisions about their care, about what they feel is important to them and what they want to do.

By working with the resident, the care assistant can ensure that the physical layout of the environment makes it as easy as possible for them to carry out daily activities with the least amount of physical effort. Make sure that things are within reach, such as by laying out their clothes in the morning.

Many patients with heart failure are taking medication (diuretics) which helps the kidneys work more efficiently to remove extra fluid from the body in the form of urine, so as to relieve the heart. This medication is usually given in the morning and has a very rapid effect for a few hours. The person will need ready access to toilet facilities during this time to avoid distressing and embarrassing incontinence. The resident's activities may need to be adjusted to take account of this side effect of their medication.

Most importantly, discuss with the resident what activities in the day are the most important for them, and help them conserve their energy level so that they can complete these activities. This might be that they want to go and play bridge in the afternoon, so they will stay in bed longer in the morning. They may want to walk into the dining room to greet their visitors, but might be too tired to walk back and so will need assistance.

CARE AND SUPPORT DURING A CHRONIC ILLNESS

Physical health

The expert in knowing how to keep a person with a chronic illness as healthy as possible is usually the person themself. After all, they are the one who has been living with the disease, often for many years. All the symptoms of the chronic illnesses discussed in this chapter will become worse if there are other health problems, such as a chest or urine infection. The principles of a healthy lifestyle and good nutrition are even more important for a resident with a chronic illness.

This is more difficult for many residents: because of the physical changes in their body and, often, the results of medication, they are unable to exercise as they would like to, and their appetite may be reduced. Loss of appetite is a particular problem for people with PD and heart failure.

Identifying activities that a resident can enjoy – such as movement to music, swimming, gardening with raised flower beds – is extremely important. Helping a resident walk to the dining room can be therapeutic, as long as there is plenty of time both for the walk and for the resident to recover before commencing their meal.

Be alert to changes in the physical status of the resident, such as constipation or confusion. These are important signs that need to be reported to the manager of the home so that appropriate action is taken.

Social well-being

For many people with a chronic illness, maintaining their social well-being is increasingly difficult as their symptoms become worse over time. It is difficult to maintain friendships when you are not able to go and visit people, having to rely on them to visit you. Attending regular activities such as being on a committee, attending a church or going to night school becomes impossible for some people as the unpredictability and variability of their symptoms means that they cannot guarantee they will be well enough to attend. For many people, moving into a care setting is an opportunity to re-engage in social activities – but they may need time to adjust. The care assistant can support the older person with a chronic illness by helping to find activities that can be undertaken at the times when the resident is able to participate.

Psychological and spiritual well-being

Communication for many people with a chronic illness can be difficult. Think of the number of times a day you stop to have a quick chat with a friend, perhaps text messaging someone close to you or giving someone a smile, or a hug. All of these things can be difficult for a person suffering from chronic illness. Giving people time and showing understanding of their difficulties are fundamental principles of support.

After a stroke, or the onset of dementia, a person may not be able to speak the 'correct' words or understand them. In Parkinson's disease the muscles in the face are affected in the same way as muscles in the arms and legs, which can mean it is difficult for the person to show whether they are happy or upset (the typical mask-like face). A person with angina or heart failure may be too breathless or in pain to be able to hold a conversation. Any of these factors can cause the person to feel frightened, angry, frustrated, or depressed – often a combination of all of them.

Anxiety or stress can make the symptoms of many chronic illnesses worse, and those discussed in this chapter are particularly sensitive. If an individual is feeling stressed or anxious, for example by feeling they have no time to complete an activity, their physical and mental ability will be reduced in many cases.

Depression in a person suffering from a chronic illness is very common, but it is

Further information

This chapter can only act as an introduction to the care and support needed by people who have these chronic conditions. A number of voluntary organisations offer support, education and advice to individuals, their families and staff working with older people with these conditions. More information about aspects of caring should be obtained and used to promote good care (see Useful Resources p173).

often not always recognised by health professionals who come into contact with the individual. The care assistant can play a very important part in helping to identify changes in the resident's behaviour that might indicate depression. Knowing about the resident's past and finding out about their lifestyle before they became a resident in your home are important steps in meeting their psychological and spiritual well-being.

Chapter 7 - Special needs

ESSENCE OF CARE						
Principles of self care						
2	4	5	6	7	8	9

NMS				
7.1	7.2	7.3	7.4	7.5
8.1	8.2			
12.2				

NSF							
5.2	5.5	5.10	5.23	5.27			
7.8	7.14	7.15	7.16	7.17	7.32	7.36	7.37	7.39
5.24	5.3	5.14					

TOPSS							
Induction							
3.1.1	3.1.2	3.2.2	3.2.3	3.2.5	3.2.7	3.2.8	3.2.9
Foundation							
1.1.1	1.1.2	1.2.1					
2.2.1	2.2.2						

NVQ 2 CARE
None

Compiled by Adrian Muir

CHAPTER 8

Helping residents to eat and drink

Jane Slack & Lynne Phair

• Food, culture and well-being • Nutrition and health • Fluid intake
• A person-centred approach – choice and individual tastes
• The eating environment and food presentation • Food safety
• Eating and swallowing difficulties • Challenging issues
• Assessing nutritional needs • Assistance and aids to eating
• Medically prescribed diets • Alcohol and food

Food is more than just a necessity, it is an important part of every culture throughout the world. Graham Kerr, a television chef, once said, 'The last tribal meeting place of our culture is the dining room table. Food is entrenched in our culture; every season, every public holiday, every religious festival involves food, either growing, preparing, eating or enjoying.'

When a person lives in a care setting they lose some control over what they eat, when they eat and the quality of the food they eat. It is the responsibility of everyone involved in the preparation of food to serve meals that are part of a social occasion that people can look forward to. There have been many reports highlighting the problems of malnutrition in care settings for older people, both in hospitals and care homes. A hundred years ago Florence Nightingale warned of neglect that could lead people 'to starve in the midst of plenty'. The care assistant is a key member of the team which can ensure a person receives the food and drink in a way they can manage.

In order to survive, body cells need energy to power their activities, raw materials for renewal and growth, and a variety of supplementary substances that play small but crucial roles in cellular processes. These needs are met by the nutrients we absorb from food. Cells require nutrients all the time, not just when we happen to eat. A constant supply is maintained by the control systems that regulate our intake of food, and by hormones that regulate the use and storage of nutrients within the body between meals. Food is made up of the same constituents as any living thing:
• carbohydrates
• minerals
• electrolytes
• proteins
• fats
• water
• other organic molecules
   (including vitamins).

Nutritional status can be defined as the state of health produced by the balance between requirement and intake of nutrients. Good nutrition helps to maximise significantly the functional capacity, well-being and independence of older people. Ill health can be avoided or managed more effectively if the older person has a well-balanced diet. Most adults who live in our society and are able to eat a varied diet with enough calories, will consume sufficient amounts of essential nutrients. This does not always happen with older people. Many eat less food because they are less physically active or have a lowered metabolic rate. This means that the amount of food eaten is less than adequate to meet their needs. In addition many older adults need increased amounts of calcium and vitamin A.

Fluid intake

The average person consists of around 60 per cent water. Dissolved in the water are many substances including glucose and electrolytes. The volume of water in the body and its distribution between cells and tissues affects many processes, especially the circulation of blood. The balance normally maintained by the healthy body between fluid intake and output can be disturbed by certain medical conditions. This might include a person with heart failure who is retaining fluid or someone who has had a stroke and is not able to swallow liquids safely.

Water and electrolytes are gained in food and drink and lost in body fluids such as sweat and urine. Adequate fluid intake is as important to total nutrition as food. Under normal circumstances a healthy adult needs 1.5 litres of oral fluids or 8 glasses of fluid a day. Older people are vulnerable to fluid and electrolyte imbalances due to changes in how the kidneys work. This means that an older person cannot cope with fluid deprivation as well as someone younger. This also means that the clearance of drugs from the body is affected, and that drug doses that are safe in younger people can be toxic in an older person. Many older people living in a care setting are taking a significant number of tablets, and therefore need to be able to drink regular amounts of fluid throughout the day. Drinks containing caffeine – such as tea, coffee and cola – can make people pass more urine, so it is important to offer plenty of water and/or fruit drinks as well. A lack of fluids can cause other complications including constipation and confusion, so the type of drink the person prefers should be offered and encouraged throughout their waking day.

A person-centred approach

Everyone has different likes and dislikes with respect to food and drink. A person's preferences will be shaped by their culture, religion and life experiences. Obviously simple likes and dislikes and allergies will also affect their preferences. Imagine what it must be like to be offered or fed food that you do not like and to have no control over what you eat every day and when you eat it. A person-centred approach to food must be based on meeting the person's needs by understanding their dietary experiences and preferences.

When a person is first admitted to any care setting they should be asked about their dietary requirements. An assessment of what food and drink they like and dislike should be noted, as well as simple information, for example, such as whether they take sugar in their tea. This is just as important as finding out information about their physical needs. It is a very common problem that a person stops drinking or eating simply because they do not like what they are offered and either don't want to tell anyone, are unable to tell anyone or, occasionally, are too scared to tell anyone.

Within any care setting the meals are

often served at set times. The organisation of meals and ensuring they are served properly does mean that it is difficult to offer complete freedom to a person as to when they want to eat. However, it is important to offer some flexibility to the person so that they can eat at times to suit them. Everyone has different patterns of eating. Often this is affected by the job a person did or their cultural or religious needs. For example, if a person has always had breakfast at 6am because they used to get up for work at that time and they want to continue this practice, the home must find ways of ensuring the person's wishes can be met. If a 'person-centred approach' is taken, the issue is not 'This person is being difficult', but 'How can we help this person to have breakfast early?'.

We all enjoy some food simply because we like it. Often these 'comfort foods' are enjoyed while watching the television or reading a book. When a person lives in a care environment they do not necessarily have the opportunity to have their favourite comfort foods around. A good person-centred approach will mean that the staff find ways of ensuring that a person can have a supply of their own comfort foods, either by asking relatives to bring them in, or perhaps asking the volunteers' shop to ensure it has a supply. Other types of comfort foods can be supplied by the care setting when a person does not want to eat properly because of illness.

For example, one woman who was terminally ill only wanted bananas and ice cream, while another man craved a boiled egg.

Working together with the catering staff, and informing them of the reasons why some people are making specific requests, will mean that a person can eat something because it is just what they fancy. Every care setting, even on a restricted food budget, should ensure that the catering arrangements meet the needs of the people it is caring for.

A simple checklist, similar to the one in the box, can be used to decide whether the care setting is person-centred and also as a development plan, working together with the chef and hotel services team.

It is interesting to ask these questions of different people – care staff, catering staff, managers and the resident – all of whom may have different perceptions of what happens and what the resident is entitled to have.

The menu, and how it is planned, is also an area where a person-centred approach should be taken. Wherever possible the chef should ask the residents what the content of the menu

A quality assurance checklist – choice in food

- is there an advertised choice of meals for both lunch and supper?
- is the choice complementary in taste, texture and style?
- is there a soft diet alternative (not just pureed)?
- is there a planned vegetarian alternative? Is there a planned menu for people with special cultural or religious needs?
- is there a choice of dessert?
- is there fruit available and readily accessible?
- are hot and cold drinks accessible and available all day?
- is there food available after 8pm and is it advertised?
- are people offered a night drink at a time of their choice?
- do people decide what time they want their breakfast and where?
- do people decide what time they want their early morning drink?

should be. This can be done to suit the menu planning process of the care setting, but in some care homes it is now carried out on a weekly basis with a different group of staff and residents. The chef guides the process and ensures that there is variety and a well-balanced diet. Individual needs should also be catered for wherever possible.

The eating environment

The condition and location of the place where meals are taken within the care home, must be suitable and encourage people to want to eat. The condition of any café or restaurant we visit will affect us and, generally, will influence how we enjoy the food. The dining room should be clean and have a fresh smell. It should be tidy and inviting. This may be difficult if care is being delivered in an old or run-down care setting, but small things can make a difference; for example, table-cloths and the tables laid appropriately with place mats and correct cutlery, condiment sets and, perhaps, a small vase of flowers or a plant. Some care settings place a menu on the table to encourage interest and social interaction. A glass and water or other drinks should also be readily available. Napkins if at all possible should be cloth.

For people who need help with eating and drinking, the type of bib that is tied around the neck should be avoided if at all possible. These are demeaning and lower the self-respect of the person. Finding other ways of offering protection would be more positive.

The level of noise in the dining room can also affect how a person enjoys their food – people should be asked if they want to have music or the TV on, or not. And staff should ensure that they do not use the mealtime as an opportunity to gossip about their own lives or their work. The meal is a social event for the older

If a person chooses to eat in their own room, the food should be well-presented.

people and this should be respected.

A person may wish to eat in their bedroom and not want to eat in public at all. This is a dilemma for the staff as there are many advantages in encouraging a person to eat in the company of others. The reasons why a person wants to eat alone should be explored. Research evidence has shown that people who have disabilities which affect their ability to eat do feel very embarrassed that perhaps they dribble or have other difficulties. If this is the reason, the team should look at ways that perhaps the person can eat in the dining room but on a separate table, perhaps being kept company by a staff member eating their own lunch. Equally, some people who do not have eating difficulties feel uncomfortable or are put off their food by others who do have problems. It is important that the arrangements for eating meet everyone's needs, while still encouraging the social aspect that the mealtime offers.

Presentation

An important aspect of encouraging a person to eat and drink a good diet is to ensure that the food is presented in a way that is appealing. The table and dining room have been prepared; it is also important to think about how the food looks on the plate. Some simple checks can be made to ensure the food and drink appeals to the person who has to eat it.

For example, some people:

- are put off their meals simply because there is too much on the plate. Ensure the person is asked what size portion they would like
- will not eat food that has gravy on, or sandwiches that have had mayonnaise put in them
- cannot eat food that is hard to chew but can manage softer food. If they are just given liquidised food they may not eat it at all
- will not eat food that has just been piled up on the plate
- cannot see the different types of food on the plate because of visual problems
- will not eat food if it looks bland and unappetising
- will not eat food that has gone cold, which may happen because they eat slowly
- will not drink out of plastic cups and beakers because it changes the taste.

Good practice when presenting and serving food and drink should always be to:

- ask a person what they want to be put on their plate
- ask a person if they want gravy and other sauces
- ask the chef to ensure that the choice of vegetables complements the food and gives colour and variety

- ask the manager if plates can be purchased that have a coloured rim so as to give guidance to people who are visually impaired
- ensure that the food is at the correct temperature for the person and offer to reheat if it is needed
- ensure that the cups and beakers are made of a substance that the person will drink from.

Food safety

Food safety is vital to everyone, both to food handlers and people who eat the food. It is so important that there are legal obligations for keeping, preparing and serving food. The catering department will have very particular rules and regulations to follow. They have to have an Assured Safe Catering Policy, which states how they will store, check, and record the safety of the food. All staff who handle and prepare food must also pass the Basic Food Hygiene Certificate. For care staff who serve food and assist with eating, these basic principles should be followed:

- when handling food the universal infection control procedures (described in chapter four) must be followed
- food must be stored at the correct temperature, and labelled when in the fridge
- food should never be left uncovered
- water jugs should be changed daily
- food should not be used if it has passed its use-by date
- rooms should be checked for food that may be old, which should then be disposed of. It is important of course to discuss the health risk and reasons for this practice with the resident
- all equipment must be cleaned thoroughly following the cleaning instructions
- food waste must be disposed of correctly to avoid food pests.

DIFFICULTIES WITH EATING AND SWALLOWING

The desire to eat depends on the smell and taste of food as well as the changing levels of nutrients in the blood. The number of taste buds and the ability to smell decreases in older age, which can lead to a loss of some of the sensations contributing to the pleasure of eating. Personal beliefs, lack of appetite due to depression, illness, boredom, drug therapy or a large intake of alcohol can all adversely affect the ability to take an adequate amount of food and fluids. A number of other physical factors can affect the residents' ability to eat drink and swallow effectively. These include:

- a stroke or cataracts in the eyes can impair eyesight, which means the resident cannot see the plate properly
- mouth infection (thrush) or poorly fitting dentures can mean the resident cannot bite, suck, chew or swallow effectively
- arthritis causing joint pain, a stroke causing muscle paralysis, or Parkinson's disease causing muscles to freeze or move uncontrollably can make it difficult for the resident to cut up food, load it onto a fork, or lift a cup up to the mouth
- some medicines will affect the person's desire to eat by decreasing or increasing their appetite, while other drugs affect the absorption of some nutrients from the food. There are some drugs which cannot be taken with certain foods, so the leaflet which is supplied with the medicines should always be read by the person who is managing them.

Dementia

A person who has dementia may not have any difficulties with their diet at all. They may be able to choose their food and manage independently. However, for some people the effects of dementia may cause specific difficulties. As the condition progresses, the person may lose the ability to eat appropriately. This may lead to weight loss through loss of the physical ability to eat or loss of the intention to eat.

For others, weight loss is due to the amount of energy they use because they are constantly walking about and doing things, so they use a lot of calories. Some people may lose the ability to understand how to use a knife and fork, or not register that the things in front of them are food.

The menu should reflect this, and a special diet of food that the person can eat with their fingers could be offered. As long as the person is able to achieve the nutritional balance required, how they receive it should be looked at, and the food should be prepared and presented in a suitable manner. Finger foods are literally food that can be picked up: nuggets, chips, baby boiled potatoes, carrot sticks, fruit loaf, pizza slices, fruit kebabs, chapatis and bhajias are just a few examples.

Antisocial behaviour

Sometimes when a person with dementia is placed in a dining room they may exhibit behaviour such as refusing to eat, refusing to open their mouth, turning their head away, spitting, refusing to swallow or leaving their mouth open. Staff must try to find out why the person is doing this and not just assume it is part of the person's dementia. There may be a number of reasons, both medical and social, and all of them should be explored.

A person-centred approach is demonstrated by staff enabling the person to eat when and where they want. If the person cannot concentrate for

 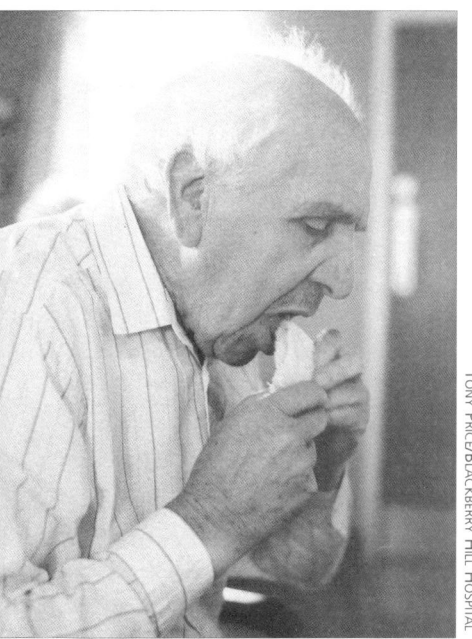

TONY PRICE/BLACKBERRY HILL HOSPITAL

A menu of 'finger foods' can be planned to ensure that an individual receives all the nutrients they need in this form.

long enough to sit at the table, it may be useful to offer a small amount of food every couple of hours.

Working with the chef, a menu can be planned that ensures the person receives all the nutrients they need but in a different way. Even so, the person will never eat the food if they do not like it.

Difficulty chewing

A soft diet is different from a liquidised or puréed diet. Soft diets are designed for people who have difficulty chewing rather than difficulty in swallowing, or for those who do not have teeth. Food should be soft enough to be mashed with a fork but should not be sticky or crumbly or have tough skins. The consistency should be uniform. For example, a person should not be given minestrone soup as it has both fluid and solid particles in it. White bread can cause problems as it becomes sticky when in the mouth; wholemeal bread is easier to eat.

Ingredients of a soft diet could include porridge, cod in cheese sauce, fruit yoghurt, baked egg, cottage pie and mashed swede.

Difficulty swallowing

Swallowing is something we all tend to take for granted. However, some people experience swallowing difficulties due to their medical condition. This is called dysphagia. Dysphagia is not a disease itself, it is a symptom. It occurs when the complex process of swallowing is affected either through the muscles of the mouth, tongue and throat not working properly, or because of damage to the brain. When a person has dysphagia there is a serious risk of choking; they may lose weight because they do not eat, or because of the length of time it takes to eat; and it is embarrassing for the person, who may cough a lot during meals. They are often offered a very bland diet, and the traditional method of puréeing food and mixing it all together is both undignified and unappetising. Adding a lot of fluid to the food to liquidise it also increases the bulk. This means that a person who finds eating difficult will have to eat more food to gain the same amount of nutrients.

The consistency of the food and its thickness are important. The thinner the food, the easier for it to go into the lungs of the person and choke them. Food should be thickened so that the person has more opportunity to feel the food or fluid in their mouth; the brain may then automatically implement the swallow reflex.

Whenever possible advice should be obtained from a qualified dietitian or speech and language therapist. This person will be able to give advice about how best to help a person with dysphagia.

However, there are some good practice guidelines which can be followed using products that can be purchased from any chemist. All food and fluids should be thickened for people who have swallowing difficulties. The British Dietetic Association produces guidelines on the management of dysphagia, which recommend that different foods should be puréed to different thickness depending on the difficulties the person has. Products are now available that can be added to puréed foods, then the food can be put into moulds and frozen. When it is served it is reheated in the microwave and resembles normal food. This is much more appetising for the older person and the volume of food is manageable. Helping someone with dysphagia to eat should be the same as helping anyone else who needs assistance.

Sample screening assessment

	Score if YES	Score
Ask the person:		
❏ Do you often have difficulty with eating or chewing food?	2	
❏ At mealtimes do you often have a drink instead of eating food?	4	
❏ Do you often feel full very quickly when you first start eating?	2	
❏ Has your appetite decreased over the past few months?	1	
❏ Do you often feel as though you are going to be sick?	4	
❏ Has your clothing recently started to feel loose?	1	
❏ Do you need help with cooking?	2	
Observe/find out:		
❏ Does the patient look thin?	6	
❏ Has the patient had any involuntary weight loss during the last three months?	4	
Weight		
BMS		
TOTAL		

Table of risk

0-6	Little or no risk	No immediate action required, reassess regularly.
7-16	Probable risk	Consider prescribing nutritional supplements; reassess regularly. Complete full assessment.
17+	Patient malnourished	Prescribe nutritional supplements and refer to a dietitian immediately.

How to assess nutritional needs

The aim of an assessment is to find out if the resident is eating, if an interest in eating is shown, and whether a suitable range of foods is being eaten. When a resident is admitted into a care setting ask them about their normal habits and food intake. Asking the resident whether they have been eating less than usual can often be very revealing. A regular, accurate recording of the resident's weight is very important (although weight recording alone is not enough to assess nutritional status). It is vital that any changes in a resident's weight are reported to the person in charge.

The second part of assessment involves keeping an accurate record of exactly what the person is eating or has eaten recently. A food chart needs to show the date, time, an accurate description of food and fluid intake before a meal, and an accurate description of the portion of food. Other questions that can be asked of the resident are:

- what are their likes and dislikes about food?
- have they followed any special types of diet?
- do they find eating and drinking difficult?
- what is their normal pattern of eating?

The example of a screening assessment shown in the box opposite can be used to give a guide to the level of risk a person may be at because of malnutrition.

Note that this is an assessment of nutritional risk only and is not a substitute for a full nutritional assessment by a state registered dietitian.

Assisting with eating and drinking

The information gained in the assessment of the resident's nutritional status will help the care assistant in assisting the resident to eat and drink. Where a resident is unable to express their dietary preferences, reference to their care plan should ensure that the type of drink or food a person prefers is offered, rather than one that is disliked and therefore will be refused.

Do not make assumptions about the type of food that people eat. The individual lifestyle will have an enormous impact on their dietary preferences; for example, the older person in a care setting may have lived for many years in the Far East and developed a taste for very hot spicy food, in preference to cottage pie! Many individuals who require assistance to eat and drink are very embarrassed about it, and may prefer to eat apart from other residents. This needs to be discussed with them. Some basic rules when assisting a resident to eat and drink are:

- ask them if they would like to go to the toilet and wash their hands before the meal
- the resident should made comfortable and be well supported in an upright position (use pillows if necessary)
- explain what is happening and offer the choices of food available
- ensure the table has everything needed, including a drink of the person's choice
- the care assistant must sit down in order to assist the resident to eat
- ask the person if they like to eat the food in any particular order or combination
- encourage the resident to swallow in between each mouthful of food
- synchronise breathing and swallowing

- if the resident has impaired eyesight, tell them what is on each forkful
- concentrate and talk to the person when helping them to eat and drink.

- **Never** stand up to help someone eat
- never stir all the food together
- never assist more than one person at a time
- never put more on the spoon or fork that the person can manage.

Aids to eating and drinking

It is much better for the resident to have the ability to eat independently, as they can feel vulnerable and powerless when they have to be fed by someone else. There is now a wide range of equipment and aids available to promote an individual's independence in eating and drinking. Advice on specific equipment can sometimes be obtained from specialist staff in either health or social services such as community occupational therapists, dietitians or nurses. Many voluntary societies such as the Stroke Association, Alzheimer's Society and Parkinson's Disease Society have local branches that can offer advice on eating and drinking and specific aids.

Modified crockery and cutlery (larger handles or combined fork and spoon), non-slip mats, one-way straws, flow-controlled beakers, plate guards, arm and plate supports and salt and pepper pots instead of sachets are some examples of aids that are available.

Medically prescribed diets

Sometimes a resident is on a medically prescribed or therapeutic diet. When they are prescribed this diet the doctor or dietitian will supply them with information about it. These details of what they can eat, how and when they eat, and possibly the quantities they can eat should be recorded in the care plan and be accessible by all staff.

There have been significant changes recently to many medical diets, with many of the restrictions being modified along the principles of a healthy balanced diet that is suitable for all adults. Moderation in all things is a maxim that applies equally well to diets as to other aspects in life. An occasional bar of chocolate for a person with diabetes is not going to cause any harm, and can bring a great deal of comfort. Eating chocolate to the exclusion of a balanced diet, however, will do harm to any individual, not just someone with diabetes.

Diabetes

The risk of diabetes increases with age and older people represent almost half of the diabetic population. Diabetes in older people is usually not their only health problem, and many experience problems with eyesight or foot ulceration.

Nutritional guidance for older people with diabetes is similar to that for the general population. However, many older people with diabetes are overweight, and a restriction on the amount of fat is necessary. People with diabetes are advised to eat carbohydrates such as potatoes rather than sugar, as these are digested more slowly. This ensures that glucose (sugar) enters the bloodstream at a steady rate, and the peaks and troughs that can cause a person with diabetes to become potentially very unwell are avoided.

If a resident is taking insulin to help manage their diabetes, the timing of when they eat their food is extremely important. The care plan must include details of when the resident takes their insulin, and how soon after they must eat food. Many people with diabetes require additional snacks throughout the day to ensure their blood sugar level is maintained. Ideally these should be pieces of either fruit or vegetable.

Coeliac disease

People with coeliac disease cannot digest certain grains called gluten. if they eat food with gluten in, they will experience pain, vomiting and diarrhoea. Gluten is the main component found in wheat, and this means that any food with wheat such as bread, cake or pastry cannot be eaten by a person with coeliac disease. They have to have gluten free foods. Some of these are prescribed by the doctor - such as tinned bread. It is possible to buy gluten free products from shops to replace in ordinary recipes such as xmas cake, however they can be expensive.

Inflammatory bowel disease (IBS) or Crohn's disease

Both of these disorders occur as a result of long-standing inflammation of the intestinal tract, which affects how the bowel can absorb nutrients. Diarrhoea is a major symptom of these conditions. Dietary treatment is aimed at reducing the bowel actions and replacing fluid and nutrients. Extra fluids are required to prevent dehydration and a diet high in proteins, calories and vitamins is required.

People who need a low fat diet

Coronary heart disease is a major health problem for many of us living in the western world. The current research indicates that there is a link between the amount of saturated fats and a low intake of dietary fibre taken in our diet. Reducing the amount of saturated fats can reduce the risk of heart disease and the many other com-

plications that can arise. A person who is significantly overweight or obese can also benefit from reducing their intake of saturated fats. People who have experienced problems with their gall bladder can also benefit from a low fat diet.

Diet and medication

Many residents who take medication whether prescribed by a doctor or bought over the counter are vulnerable to drug-nutrient interactions. For example, regular use of antacids may lower vitamin B12 levels, and grapefruit juice can interact with several drugs. Foods such as mature cheese or marmite must not be eaten with certain medication as they can cause a fatal rise in blood pressure. The care assistant needs to be aware of any restrictions to a patient's diet due to the medication they are taking.

Other care issues

A balanced diet is a vital part of any person's care. When a person has a specific problem, their diet can have an even more important role to play in their care and recovery. The chef should be asked to help by preparing food that the person is happy to eat and enjoy, which will aid their recovery or help to prevent further problems.

Residents who have experienced recent illnesses, such as a chest infection or have undergone recent surgery, need extra nutrients to promote healing. A person who is at high risk of falling may be encouraged to have a diet high in calcium and potassium – milk and bananas are good sources of these. A person who has a leg ulcer may be encouraged to have a higher protein diet to help aid skin repair, while a person who is lacking motivation and has poor mobility may be given food which has more caffeine and carbohydrate in it. Whatever the condition, the chef should be asked to be involved in the total care and support of the person.

Alcohol and food

A person who lives in a care setting should have access to any type of drink they want whenever they want it, although they may have to fund the purchase themselves. Some care settings use alcohol in a therapeutic way, with the agreement of the doctor. Sherry could be offered as an appetite enhancer, Guinness or stout will help with iron deficiency and whisky is often taken as a 'nightcap' to aid sleep. If alcohol has been part of a person's life and there are no medical reasons to restrict it, everyone should have access to it if it is what they want.

Further reading

Chartered Institute of Environmental Health (1998) – *Food safety First Principles.*

Voices (1998) *Eating well for people with dementia: a good practice guide for residential and nursing homes and others involved in caring for older people with dementia.* VOICES, Potters Bar, Herts .

Chapter 8 - Eating and drinking

ESSENCE OF CARE								
Food & nutrition								
1	2	3	4	5	6	8	9	10
NMS								
15.1	15.2	15.3	15.4	15.5	15.6	15.7	15.8	15.9
Food hygiene								
38.2								
NSF								
8.9	8.10	8.11	8.12					
TOPSS								
Induction								
1.1.1								
3.2.1	3.2.2	3.2.7	3.2.8	3.2.9				
4.5.1	4.5.2							
NVQ 2 CARE								
NC12.1								
All Performance Criteria		All range		All knowledge				
NC12.2								
All Performance Criteria		All range		All knowledge				
NC13.2								
All Performance Criteria		All range		All knowledge				

Compiled by Adrian Muir

CHAPTER 9
Personal hygiene and continence care
Tracy Packer

*• Individual assessment • Bathing, washing, showers • Use of hoists
• Care of hair, nails, mouth, feet and toes • Shaving • Helping people to dress
• The little things that make the difference • Elimination of urine and faeces
• Helping people to use the toilet • Promoting continence • Catheter care*

Try to imagine how frightening and, at times, annoying it must feel to have your control over something as intimate as washing and dressing taken away from you.

Some people like to have a bath or wash every day; others feel one bath a week is more than enough. Some people may simply dislike baths for practical or cultural reasons; others enjoy them but are frightened of being left alone in the water.

There is a subtle but vital difference between taking over and doing everything for a resident, and helping out or working with somebody to achieve a goal. By working with someone, we allow them to have control over what is happening. We can also promote what independence they have, and ultimately the whole experience is much more satisfying and less stressful for all concerned.

It is important (though not always easy) to find an individual routine that works for each person and, if you possibly can, make the organisational routine work around that. In one care setting,

the night staff assist one man to take a bath every night after everyone else has gone to bed. He enjoys the more restful, less rushed environment and it helps him to get a good night's sleep. This makes everybody happier in the long run.

Individual assessment

It is surprising how much information can be gained about a person's hygiene needs and habits long before they enter a bathroom. Skilled and sensitive gathering of such information can help identify potential misunderstandings before they could happen. Ask the resident and, if necessary, their family:

- what was their routine at home before they first experienced difficulties?
- later on, who helped them and how much could they do for themselves?
- how do they feel about male or female staff assisting them? Often this doesn't matter if it is undertaken sensitively, but being sure of this can prevent misunderstandings at a later stage.

• are there any obvious factors which may affect how good or bad the experience may be for them? For instance:
  – do they have pain in their joints?
  – do they have sore feet or toes?
  – do they suffer from breathlessness?
  – is their eyesight or hearing impaired at all?
  – are their gums sore? Do their dentures fit?
  – do they have sensitive skin/scalp?
  – do they have any wounds, sores or scars?
  – are they worried about any disfigurements?
  – what are their continence needs?
  – how good is their balance and co-ordination?

The assessment must always include the assessment of risks including:

• the person's ability for self care
• equipment needed for all circumstances
• risks of the person being left alone
• manual handling
• number of staff required to carry out personal care.

The needs, requirements and wishes of the resident should then be documented in the care plan, and this should be the guide about how the care is delivered.

Bathing

Most of the time, people are only too happy to wash or bathe, and this can often be the most pleasurable time of the day for them, particularly if they need assistance when they can enjoy your undivided attention. Whatever their needs, the principles of washing and bathing are the same wherever they take place, be it in the bed, at the bedside, in a bathroom at a sink, or in a bath or shower.

Take time assisting the resident to gather toiletries, towels, clothes, hair accessories etc, always using the person's own, and encouraging them to help. This is a good time to involve them as much as possible and ensure that they have everything that they are likely to need, so that it is all in the wash/bathing area before you start.

Imagine what it would feel like to be sitting in a bath, or half naked by your bedside, when the person you rely on for help keeps disappearing for five minutes at a time to find something.

The area should be warm and draught free, as well as private. This means no intrusions! If there is a lock on the door, use it. Actively discourage colleagues from interrupting once you have begun, or barging unannounced through closed doors.

It always helps to have a small bin nearby so that tissues and disposable cloths can be discarded hygienically. Try to make the whole event as friendly and relaxed as possible. Some people will feel very uneasy about exposing certain parts of their body, particularly the genital and breast areas. You need to be discreet and sensitive about this.

Washing and bathing times should be friendly occasions, with a great deal of sociable conversation. However, there is a danger that they can become mere tasks to be completed, with little or no involvement of the person concerned, if the care assistant does not take a person-centred approach.

Remember that washing and bathing:
• provide you with the perfect opportunity to assess exactly what a person can do, and where they need guidance or assistance
• offer a good chance of building up a trusting, friendly relationship with the

person you are helping. This in turn can help you find out more about the important details of a resident's life and personality

- provide a perfect opportunity for sensory stimulation, with the different textures and smells of the toiletries. A gentle hand or scalp massage could also be given at this time
- enable you to make a good all-over assessment of skin and joint conditions, and look for early signs of injury, rashes or soreness
- can influence the mood of a person some considerable time after it is over. A rushed, sloppy wash may result in a person feeling uncomfortable, disorientated and distressed
- should trigger detailed record keeping of skin condition and key hygiene needs in the resident's care plan. Any significant changes should also be reported to senior staff.

Having a bath or shower

Always ask the person you are helping whether they wish to use the toilet before you begin. Often the sound of running water from the bath triggers off the need to use the toilet. By meeting this need before you begin, you will avoid potential embarrassment and disruption later on.

While you are both getting ready you can check that the bath is clean and start running the water. (You can always do this beforehand, but take care not to leave it too long as the water will very quickly go cold.) Most places should now have mixer taps and temperature controls for the water used in bathing. If not, you should always put the cold water in the bath first and then add the hot water. People have been badly burned through getting into a half full bath that only had hot water in it. Always test the temperature of the water with

Preparation of the bathroom environment

- Ensure that the bathroom is warm and draught free. Ensure that the window blind is drawn closed in order that the resident's privacy is maintained.
- Run the bath water ensuring that the bath thermometer is in the water and registers between 38°C and 40°C (these temperatures are usually considered both comfortable and safe). Water temperature can be altered later at the client's request.
- If the bath seat/hoist is to be used, check that the seat is clean and dry as residual water can cause a surface to be slippery and cold. Check that the bathroom floor is also dry.
- Ensure the area is well lit, and that privacy can be maintained through shutting the bathroom door.
- If the resident wishes to use bubble bath or bath oil, go to their room and, with their guidance, select all the toiletries they may require.
- If the resident wishes to get dressed in the bathroom after their bath, ask them to select the clothes and shoes they would like.
- Ensure that any prescribed continence aids are discreetly available in the bath area, as well as a disposal bag for any soiled products.
- Lastly, check the prepared bath area, equipment, toiletries, wash cloths, towels, clothes, etc to ensure that you have all you need at hand. Remember that the resident should never be left unattended in the bath, unless it is their wish and a risk assessment has been completed. Therefore it is essential that the preparation you do before the resident enters the bath area is complete.

Good practice tips when helping a person have a bath

- Before a resident is helped to have a bath, care staff should establish how much assistance the person requires, as well as their personal preferences and their established hygiene routine. A risk assessment should be undertaken and recorded in the care plan. This information should be written in the care plan by senior staff. A professional relationship based on sensitivity and trust should be established between the caregiver and the resident.
- The resident's mobility should be assessed, and any aids should be used as indicated in the care plan. This will ensure the resident's comfort and confidence as well as their safety.
- When the resident requests a bath, they should receive a full explanation of the bath procedure, as well as information on any moving and handling equipment that may be used. The resident should be approached with great sensitivity, as assistance in this area may well cause them embarrassment.

your elbow or forearm (not your hands) before letting the person use it.

Be aware that the quality of sound is different in bathrooms, and communicating over the noise of the running water may be more difficult. The resident can get undressed with your assistance if necessary but try not to leave it too long between helping them to undress and getting in the bath, as the person could become very cold. The resident may be able to get into the bath with very little assistance, but always use a non-slip mat in the bath if you have one. On many occasions you may have to use a hoist. Do not ever attempt to lift a resident. Always use the equipment provided.

Hoists

Hoists can be very frightening. Be sure to explain what you are going to do before you do it and, if possible, wrap a large towel around the resident's shoulders while they are in the hoist. Imagine how exposed and frightened you would feel if you were sitting naked in mid air, in an apparently fragile moving chair, perhaps not knowing what is happening?

Keep talking to the resident as you move the hoist into position, and tell them when you are beginning to lower the chair. Don't forget to use the brakes

at this time. You can still add more hot or cold water at this stage if you want, because the resident will be able to tell you if the temperature is right for them or not by dipping their feet in it. Just before they enter the water you can remove the towel and the chair arms if appropriate, before gently lowering them right down into the bath.

Good practice tips for assisting with showering

- preparation of all equipment required for a person having a shower should be undertaken in the same way that it is for a bath
- ensure there is a good comfortable shower seat in position before bringing the resident in
- ensure the shower room is warm enough to avoid the resident feeling chilled either before or after the shower
- ensure the temperature of the shower water is correct before placing the resident underneath the shower, and wash the resident with the same care and attention as for the bathing procedure
- dry and support and dress the resident in the same manner that is described in the bathing procedure.

Assisting the resident in the bathroom

- Be sensitive to the resident's needs and preference at all times. Residents may feel embarrassed about being bathed, so chat to them and try to put them at ease while assisting them with their bath. If two carers are involved in the bath procedure, they should never talk 'over' the resident. Keep towels over the resident's shoulders and genital area while manoeuvring them over the bath in the hoist seat. Explain everything that you do to the resident at all times. Ask the resident to test whether the water temperature is to their liking when their toes touch the water.
- Always ask the resident if they would like to wash themselves if they can. This is particularly important when considering their face and genital area. Where they are not able to assist themselves, the dignity of the resident should always be maintained.
- Differentiate between the 'face' cloth and the 'body' flannel. This is very important so as to avoid cross-infection. Always assist the resident starting from their face, before changing flannels to wash their trunk, legs and lastly the genital then anal areas.
- Ask the resident whether they wish to have soap on their face flannel, or if they wish to use other specific cosmetic products. Wash the neck and around the resident's ears, rinse and dry.
- Wash the resident's chest and back. Pay attention to the area under the breasts in a female resident, in stomach folds and under arms. Rinse thoroughly.
- Wash the resident's legs, feet and lastly the genital area. Ensure in a male resident that the penile area is clean, and observe for soreness. Rinse soap away thoroughly. Raise the bath seat to above the water level to enable you to wash under the resident's bottom. Ensure you have covered their shoulders with a warm towel while doing this.
- Clean the bath area and ensure all equipment is put away.

The same principles apply when taking the person out of the bath on the hoist. When they are ready, let the water out of the bath first and place the large bath towel over their shoulders as soon as you can without getting it wet. This will help to prevent them getting cold on the way back to their wheelchair or chair.

Showering

Not every area has showers available, but they can be extremely useful and some people prefer them. Again, always take care to check the temperature of the water, and if you are using a shower chair with wheels, always use the brakes. Make sure that you do not spray the water directly into the resident's face, as this can be distressing and painful.

Washing by the basin or bedside

If at all possible, hygiene needs should be met away from the bedside. This is not usually a problem if the resident is mobile; if they are not, then you can take them in a wheelchair to the washroom area.

Again, always offer the resident the opportunity to use the toilet before they begin. Check that the sink or bowl that is being used is clean before they start, and be sure to change the water when it becomes too dirty or cold.

You will also require separate flannels for the face/body and the sacral/genital areas. If the person requires assistance, only ever expose the parts of the body that are currently being washed, and ensure that they are completely dry before

Assisting a resident to wash at a basin

- Ensure there is a comfortable chair by the basin so that the resident can sit down if they are not already positioned in a wheelchair.
- Try to ensure there is a mirror at a height that a person can see in from a chair.
- Ensure that all equipment is ready as described under the procedure for bathing. Follow the procedures for a general bath ensuring the water is the correct temperature and the correct flannels are used for the correct parts of the body.
- Ensure that the person is treated with dignity and privacy and is helped to dress afterwards.
- Ensure everything is cleared away.

putting clean clothes back on.

If the skin is at all damp, this can make dressing much more difficult, especially for those residents who have restricted joint movement or dementia; dressing could become a real dilemma for them.

Giving a bed bath

If a resident is very ill, or completely confined to bed, they may require a bed bath. This is far more extensive than a simple wash and is not something that one carer can carry out alone. The procedure should be completed as quickly as possible while still ensuring thoroughness and

Assisting a resident with a bed bath

- begin by explaining the procedure to the resident. Ask if he or she requires access to the toilet beforehand. The resident must consent to being bed bathed
- ensure that the environment is prepared. You will need to collect together all the items that you require in advance. This includes the necessary equipment; a deep bowl of water; two flannels; three towels; soap and additional cosmetics. Disposable wipes and disposal bags should be available for soiled linen and wipes
- ensure that the resident is comfortable. Remove their clothing and cover them with two warmed towels. Lying flat on their back may be the easiest position for many people for bed bathing, but ensure that someone who is breathless or has a chest condition is propped upright on pillows
- fill the washbowl full with hot water (38°- 40°C). Ask the resident to check the water temperature with their hand, if possible
- ask the resident if they would like soap on their face and whether they would like to wash their own face with a prepared flannel. If not, wash the face, ears and neck area for the resident, rinse and dry with the third towel. Assist the resident with oral hygiene and offer to brush their hair for them. If the resident is male, you would assist them with a shave at this stage (see page 116)
- change to the body flannel and wash the resident's upper body and arms, making sure you expose them as little as possible and so avoid chilling. Remember to soap, rinse and dry each area in turn. Damp skin can easily become sore skin. Particular attention should be paid to under the arms and under the breasts. Ensure the resident's nails are clean
- as you wash each area, always check the condition of the person's skin. Look for any changes: for example areas of redness or soreness, rashes, bruises or marks on the skin. Report these to a senior member of staff immediately after the bath

comfort. Privacy must be maintained at all times. This is done either by ensuring that the bedroom door is closed, or the bed screens are drawn. The room should be draught free with all windows closed to avoid chilling. During this procedure you should be aware of the resident's well-being and comfort at all times.

Use of toiletries

Talcum powder can be very pleasant, but it is no substitute for thorough drying. Take care under arms, breasts and in the groin area. Too much powder, especially if the skin is not well dried, will form clumps and cause soreness; and inhaling clouds of talc is not a pleasant experience for the resident or the care worker.

Aerosol deodorants can be very cold and quite a shock if the resident is not warned before their use. Again take care that the person does not breathe it in.

Skincare creams are very soothing, but again need to be used in small amounts and gently massaged in. The more you 'slap on' the less effective they are.

Preventing cross-infection

Whichever type of wash you give, be sure to wash your own hands thoroughly between each resident, and change your apron. Aprons help to keep you dry, and protect the resident from any infections you may be carrying on your clothes.

Always take care of your own appearance and personal hygiene. If you smell of cigarette smoke or have body odour, then the person you assist will not find it a pleasant experience, and may refuse the next time you offer to help them.

- ensure the bath temperature remains constant at the level specified, so as to avoid the resident becoming cold
- change the water after completing washing the upper body
- ensuring that the upper torso is warmly covered, progress to washing each leg in turn. Only wash and expose one leg at a time, always ensuring the groin area is covered to protect the resident's privacy
- wash each foot in turn paying attention to the area between each toe. Ensure that the skin is dry between the toes. Check that the skin on the person's heels is not red or broken. Apply any prescribed cream or moisturising lotion according to instructions in the care plan
- put on gloves and wash the resident's genital area. Use disposable wipes, and dispose of these in the disposal bag. Dry the area thoroughly, and apply barrier cream if prescribed in the care plan. Change the water
- roll the resident over, and wash, rinse and dry their back. Lastly, wash their anal area thoroughly (with disposble wipes if soiled) and dry carefully. Ensure the resident is covered at all times. Apply a barrier cream only if prescribed. Use this opportunity to observe their pressure areas and report any redness of the skin
- change the bottom bed sheet while the resident is rolled over on their side. Roll resident in the opposite direction to pull out and tuck in the base sheet
- ensure the resident is comfortably dressed. Remember, if the resident is very ill they may not be able to speak or co-operate with you. They should always be treated with dignity, and their privacy maintained at all times
- make sure the resident's bed is remade with clean linen, and that you leave them comfortable. Clear away all equipment, and open the curtains. Enter the procedure you have completed in the resident's daily record.

Grooming
Hair care

Hair washing and styling can either be an enjoyable and relaxing experience which can help a resident feel a lot better about themselves, or it can be very frightening and traumatic. While there will always be occasions when a professional hair appointment is made, this does not mean that hair washing and styling should only take place at such times. Ensure that the resident has been involved in the decision to have a hair wash and understands exactly what you are going to do before you start. It is best to wash hair over a basin, or with a bowl of water on a table if that is what they are used to. Be sparing with the shampoo and take great care not to pour water into the person's eyes. Make sure the shampoo has been rinsed out thoroughly, then wrap hair and head in a warm towel.

When using a hairdryer, ensure that it is not too hot, and always style hair as requested. If at all possible, get a second mirror so that you can show the finished result from the back. This can often be quite an occasion, so make sure you tell the person how lovely they look, and how much you enjoyed helping them.

Shaving

Most men will have shaved daily throughout their lives. It is important to continue to encourage this where possible, and allow them to do as much as they can for themselves. If your assistance is required, try to firmly stretch the skin taut, before making a smooth stroke in the direction the resident has indicated. Take your time, and be gentle to avoid unnecessary nicks. Whether they choose to use an electric shaver or a razor, be sure never to share these with other people, and always make sure they are clean and dry before putting them away.

Some men take enormous pride in a beard or moustache they have spent years 'cultivating' – don't shave these off unless specifically requested to do so.

Women's facial hair

Some women are prone to superfluous facial hair, which they may find embar-

---

Assisting a resident to shave with a razor

- Ask the resident if they would like to have a shave. Read the resident's care plan to establish the type of shave the resident wants to have.
- Prepare the warm water, towels, shaving mirror and shaving equipment – shaving foam, razor, after shave and flannel.
- Invite the resident to sit in a position that they are comfortable in; for example, in their own bathroom by the hand basin, or in their armchair in front of their bed table.
- Check with the individual which direction they normally shave in.
- Make a lather on the chin and cheeks either with a traditional shaving brush, or with shaving foam.
- Using a safety razor, make long strokes in the direction that the resident has indicated, making sure that you rinse the razor regularly to ensure that it does not become clogged with hair.
- Ensure that the resident can watch the procedure in the shaving mirror.
- After you have finished, use the flannel to rinse and dry the resident's skin.
- Offer after shave lotion, which you apply to your hands and then pat on the shaved area.
- Remember to ask the resident if they are happy with the outcome.
- Ensure the resident's face is dry, and that you put away all equipment once you have cleaned it.

rassing to acknowledge. This is best removed with a gentle depilatory cream and *not* a razor which will only encourage coarser re-growth. Always ask permission first, and be sensitive and discreet. This should never be done in public.

Using facial hair removing creams on a soft pad is the method of choice: razors should not be used on women's skin unless there is an expressed wish of this from the resident – and then it should be discouraged.

Local advice may be obtained from the volunteer beauty care service of the local Red Cross Society.

Mouth care

Mouth hygiene is just as important as the rest of the body, but often forgotten or neglected. Always provide the means to clean teeth and gums, and offer gentle assistance if necessary. If the resident wears dentures and cannot clean them independently, make sure that they get thoroughly cleansed as part of the daily routine. If a resident is very ill and bedbound, a mouth-wash and a quick face wash can help to make them feel much fresher.

It is also important to check the mouth and tongue for soreness, bleed-

Good practice tips for nail care

All diabetic patients must be checked and have their toenails cut by a qualified chiropodist/podiatrist.

For non diabetic residents

- When cutting the nails, ideally use professional nail nippers. If they are not available then nail scissors are acceptable as are nail clippers, so long as the clippers have a straight edge and are not rounded. Using rounded nail clippers runs the risk of leaving a spike on one or both sides of the nail. Nail files should have rounded ends to avoid inadvertently 'stabbing' the patient while filing the nails.

- It is often easier to cut the nails after bathing as the nails tend to be a bit softer. When cutting the nails care must be taken to avoid cutting the skin under the nail – this skin is sometimes attached quite a long way along the underside of the nail. The nails should be cut to the shape of the digit but must not be cut down the sides of the nail into the nail groove. The nails must be cut cleanly right through and not pulled which can result in tearing the nail; if this tearing extends down the side of the nail an ingrowing nail may result. Elderly skin is often very thin; this is a real problem as it can be easily pierced by little spikes on uneven nails. Never probe down the side of the nail into the nail groove.

- After cutting use a file to remove any sharp corners or rough edges. When filing nails the file should be used in the direction shown here (right) and not across the nail. Elderly people's nails are sometimes very thin and can split, again running the risk of ingrowing nails.

- Thick nails should be treated by a chiropodist/podiatrist as they will probably need to be thinned before cutting.

- All residents should be encouraged to see a podiatrist, if one is available.

ing or ulcers and report these immediately if noticed. Some residents may stop eating or drinking because of these, and those who have dementia may not have been able to tell you. They may also hit out in fear of being hurt if you try to clean their teeth or wash their face.

Always ensure that dentures actually fit, and that they are discreetly identified, labelled and stored in the correct container when not in use.

Nail care

Fingernails should be checked daily and kept neat and tidy at all times. Nails that have not received such care for a long time may be sore and tender or infected.

Always ask permission to assist with nail care if you think it may be required, and explain what you are going to do. If a resident has diabetes, or you are in any doubt at all, ask someone more senior to have a look.

If staff or volunteers are able to offer a good manicure this can be an excellent opportunity to get to know someone, who may feel very pampered – especially if they receive a hand massage as well.

See the best practice tips on the previous page for further nail care advice.

Feet and toes

Feet are often neglected by all of us, but there is something immensely pleasurable about soaking our feet in a bowl of warm, pleasant smelling water. This can be done at any time of the day, and allows toenails and hard skin a chance to soften up before trimming. If you are in any doubt about toe-nail cutting (for example if the person is diabetic) ask a chiropodist what you can and can't do. Be careful not to cut too close to the skin, and follow the guidance in the panel on the previous page.

Getting dressed

Residents should be encouraged to help themselves as much as possible at all times and staff should intervene at a level that is appropriate to that person's needs.

Residents should be encouraged to choose their own clothing and dress as they wish. There should be rules within the home about what people can wear at any particular time in any part of the home, provided it does not distress others or does not mean that a person is dressed indiscreetly.

If a resident is unable to make choices themselves due to cognitive impairment, the staff should help them make choices by limiting the number of options and ensuring that the options offered are in keeping with the person's social, cultural or religious needs and/or in keeping with the season and the events that are happening on that particular day.

Residents should be supported and encouraged to change their clothes when required. Staff have responsibility when dressing a person to ensure that they are dressed appropriately, that buttons are fastened correctly and that clothing is worn to a standard that the person would expect for themselves.

People should not be dressed in clothes that belong to another person and clothes should be clean, unless the resident themselves insists on continuing to wear an item and they are competent to make this decision.

Make-up and jewellery

Residents should be encouraged to wear make-up and jewellery which is in keeping with their social and cultural desires and beliefs.

Staff should encourage residents and relatives to purchase make-up if this is appropriate for that resident and meets their wishes.

Men should be encouraged to wear

after shave if this is something that they wish to do. Staff should ensure that it is available by talking to the relatives if appropriate.

Cultural or spiritual wear

Staff should ensure that they understand the cultural and spiritual needs of a resident and understand if there are any particular aspects of clothing or jewellery that have to be worn for that person to be able to fulfil their cultural or spiritual needs. This should be clearly documented on the care plan.

Glasses

Glasses should always be available if the person wears them and staff should ensure that they are cleaned regularly. Glasses should not be put on a person unless they can see out of them properly. To clean glasses, wash them in warm soapy water with a little bit of washing up liquid and dry them with a smear free soft cloth, ensuring that the lenses are not smeared.

Hearing aids

A record should be kept in the care plan of which ear a hearing aid is worn in and when the battery needs changing. The ear piece should be cleaned regularly to ensure that there is not a build up of wax.

Making a difference

It's the small things that can make a real difference to a resident. Ensuring they have access to a favourite perfume, aftershave, or moisturising lotion may raise their well-being enormously, as can the opportunity to wear a favourite lipstick or item of jewellery. Never take the importance of these things for granted; they are easily overlooked, but can have an enormous impact upon a person's self esteem.

It is important that you report any changes (good or bad) in the resident's mood, responses or abilities, to the person in charge. Remember, information that you gain will be useful to others who may care for the same person next time. By passing on what you have learned the information will become part of a written individualised care plan. This will help ensure that maintaining hygiene and grooming needs for your residents will be the pleasant experience it should always be.

Other prostheses

Any other particular aids or equipment worn or needed by a resident, such as corsets, wigs, surgical shoes or chemical harsh creams should be documented on the person's care plan and staff should be taught how to apply them.

ELIMINATION OF URINE AND FAECES

'Eliminating' the waste products of our bodies is a natural and necessary part of daily living, one that most of us take for granted. Going to the toilet, as it is more commonly understood, is also an intimate and very personal aspect of our daily lives, which many of us cannot imagine sharing with anyone else. Care staff have a vital role in ensuring that residents are able to maintain this activity with the same level of dignity and privacy as we all expect, especially if assistance is required.

How the bladder and bowel are affected by ageing is covered in chapter 6.

Everyone has their own routine and way of going to the toilet. This will have been influenced by their upbringing, their culture and sometimes their religion. For some people, there are very specific routines which have to be followed. The care assistant must always ensure that any special routines are understood and that the person is able to carry them out.

Equally, people have different phrases and language when describing going to the toilet. Language does change and staff must ensure the language they use is acceptable to the older person. Equally staff must ensure they understand phrases preferred by individual older people.

In order to help a person with their elimination there are a number of simple factors that can be monitored and encouraged. In other words these can be assessed as to how they do or do not affect the person's elimination patterns.

• Is the resident eating and drinking the right things?

Is the person drinking plenty of fluids other than tea and coffee? (See Chapter 8.) Are they eating the right things? Do they have a varied diet with plenty of roughage? (Again, see Chapter 8.)

• How mobile is the resident?

People who are bed-bound or unable to move around independently are more at risk of becoming constipated, because waste products do not travel through their system so easily.

The person may be mobile but have difficulties moving because of arthritis. Make sure that those who suffer painful joints or feet are offered painkillers and well-fitting shoes to help make walking less traumatic for them.

• Can they use the toilet easily?

Going to the toilet is a routine event for most of us, but it is easy to take for granted just how complex this apparently simple activity actually is. It can be broken down into a sequence of events:

Does the resident know when they need to 'go'?

This will seem obvious in most instances, but if the person has dementia or other cognitive impairment they may not always recognise that need. Some residents may rely on somebody else to remind them, or they may have set times when they need to 'go' in order to avoid accidents.

Can the resident actually ask someone that they need to use the toilet?

Some residents may have difficulty, or may even be too embarrassed to say exactly what they want. They may be physically disabled and unable to get out of their chair, and unable to catch the attention of the staff who may seem very busy. Residents may be worried about causing trouble.

Are the toilets clearly signposted and easy to get to?

Does the resident have the right footwear and walking aids to get there in time? It might be more reassuring and less humiliating to wheel somebody to the toilet, and encourage them to walk back, rather than risk an accident.

The route there, the entrance and the toilet area should be free of clutter. The journey may be difficult enough without making it worse.

Is the toilet area clean, tidy and warm?

Some residents will turn around and try to find another toilet, rather than sit on a soiled seat in a smelly room on an un-flushed toilet pan.

How many staff will it need to help this person on the toilet?

Some people may require two people to assist them, and perhaps the use of a hoist. This should be assessed and the correct toilet chosen so that care can be given without making the resident feel a nuisance.

Care staff should consider all the above as an essential part of any ongoing assessment of a resident's ability to get to the toilet and use it successfully. No resident should be described as incontinent until these factors have been considered, interventions made and outcomes clearly documented in their individual plan of care.

Collecting the right equipment

If you are using a communal toilet, make sure you assemble everything you need to wash and change a resident, including clean clothes, pads, and washing equipment.

Ensure you have the correct hoist (if required) and that it will fit through the door of the chosen toilet.

Removing clothing

Clothing can cause all kinds of problems. Braces are wonderful when men only want to urinate, because they don't have to try and hold their trousers up as well. However, fumbling with the extra buttons to remove their trousers before opening their bowels can prove disastrous.

Velcro on trouser and skirt fastenings can be a useful alternative for those who cannot co-ordinate their fingers, or who are fed up with fumbling around.

Impossible knots on pyjama cords, or complicated belt fastenings, can cause immense frustration and unnecessary accidents.

Wide skirts and dresses can be more easily tucked into the back of waistbands or lifted up, than tight fitting ones.

Different types of toilet facility

There are other facilities that people can be offered in order to help them go to the toilet. The equipment should be used in order to help the person, not because it is easier for the staff.

Commodes, placed in a person's bedroom, may be used if the person has great difficulty in getting to the toilet quickly or at night.

A bed pan should only be used if the person cannot leave the bed for very clear health reasons. Balancing on a bed pan in bed is not easy even for the most nimble person.

Urinals are bottles given to men to use as an easy way of passing urine. They can be very helpful, but the man may need assistance in organising himself. People with dementia may not recognise what the bottle is for, and this too can cause problems.

Whatever the toilet facility, it must be cleaned thoroughly and never be left in the bedroom when dirty.

A bulky continence pad can sometimes get in the way if a person spends time fishing it out before using the toilet. If this happens, think about whether the pad is really necessary at all.

Getting on and off the toilet
• Is the seat too high or low?
• Are there horizontal and vertical grab bars that can take the full weight of a person?
• Will their wheelchair fit in the room so that they can transfer safely?
• Does the alarm call work?
• Is the door locked?
• Is there enough toilet paper and where is it?
• Can the person turn the basin taps on and off?
• Are there enough accessible paper hand towels?

Indwelling catheters
A catheter is a tube passed through the urethra into the bladder to collect the urine that gathers there. The urine passes down the tube into a drainage bag attached at the other end.

Catheters should only be used if all other methods of continence management have failed. It is not good practice for a person to have a catheter to make things easier for the staff.

Whether collected in a catheter or not, fresh urine should be straw coloured, clear and should not be particularly offensive. If you are in doubt, or the resident has an unexplained temperature, inform the senior staff, who may require a urine sample for testing.

Pads and continence aids
Although pads have their uses, their success very much depends on the thoroughness of the assessment of need, and the skill of the practitioner using them. At worst, pads are expensive, open to misuse and uncomfortable. Residents should always be involved in any decision to use a continence pad and there should be a full assessment before pads are used.

Constipation
Constipation occurs when faeces builds up in the bowel and cannot be passed. This can happen because the person is not drinking enough or does not have enough fibre in their diet. Perhaps the person is immobile and has weak

Helping a person who has a catheter
• It is very important to keep the genital area very clean, to prevent infections travelling up the tube and into the bladder. Ensure that uncircumcised men understand the importance of cleaning under the foreskin and ensure that they always return it over the penis.
• Keep the drainage bag below the level of the bladder at all times, and never block, clamp or restrict the flow of urine through the drainage tube.
• Catheter tubes and bags may be a source of great embarrassment to those having to use them. Always ensure the resident has an opportunity to discuss any concerns they may have about using them.
• Urine bags should be emptied before they become too bulky and uncomfortable, and always keep them covered.
• Tie the straps according to the manufacturers instructions.
• Never leave the bag dangling below trouser legs or skirts – this is completely unnecessary and undignified.
• Always follow the universal infection control procedures when handling a catheter.

Using pads and continence aids

- Always ensure that you have the correct size and absorbency of pad to meet the need. (Do not be tempted to use greater absorbencies than needed so that the resident can go longer without a change.)
- Monitor the resident's skin closely, and report any redness, soreness or broken skin immediately.
- Ensure you put the pad on correctly by cupping to form a gully, with the absorbent surface facing upwards, and keep in position with net pants.
- If you do not understand how different catheters, sheaths and pouches work, then do not embarrass yourself unnecessarily. Find out from a senior member of staff as soon as you can.
- Consult your local continence adviser/nurse, so you can be sure you are using the right product in the correct manner.

abdominal muscles that cannot push the faecal matter through the bowel; or the person is scared to use the toilet, or is avoiding it because it might involve loss of privacy and dignity.

For some people who have dementia (but by no means all), and in some neurological and spinal conditions, the brain is no longer receiving messages from the bowel telling it that it is full and this can cause either constipation or incontinence.

Constipation can often be dealt with by addressing these issues. However, it can become so bad that it will result in incontinence of foul smelling, watery, lumpy faeces. It is important to remember this because often this kind of incontinence is mistaken for diarrhoea, and the unsuspecting resident may be given medication to 'bung them up', which of course only makes the problem worse.

With individualised planning and a regular routine, it may be possible to 'plan' when the bowel will be emptied. This can either be done with the use of prescribed medicines and/or suppositories. Or it can be integrated into the daily routine. Alternatively, sensitive use of suitable pads may be appropriate, but only if there is continuous reassessment of their usefulness.

Accidents

Mishaps do occur for many of the reasons previously mentioned. If someone has an accident, particularly in a communal area, try to appear calm, friendly and reassuring. If the resident is embarrassed by, or afraid of your response, this will only make the situation worse, and increase the chance of it happening again.

Sometimes you will feel disgusted; this is nothing to be ashamed of. It is important though, to conceal these feelings as much as possible at least while you are dealing with the episode of incontinence. Always clean the area following the universal infection control procedures, and use the correct cleaning material, disposing of the waste in the correct place.

A person's skin can become very red and chafed after repeated episodes of incontinence. Always keep an eye for signs of this around the groin and sacral area. Urine and faeces can cause further irritation and soreness if left on the skin for very long.

Monitoring

It is important to reflect upon why the accident happened. You may discover how to prevent it happening again. Always share this information with other staff, so it can be included in the care plan. Keep a daily record of bowel habits for each resident, noting in particular the amount and consistency of the stool. A normal bowel pattern will vary from once or twice daily up to once in three or four days. It is important to try and find out what the person's normal pattern was and use this as the gauge to decide whether the person is becoming constipated.

Care staff should always be observant when dealing with a person's waste products. A change in the colour, texture or odour can indicate a problem or illness.

Examples of changes to watch for include:

- faeces changing from soft to hard may indicate constipation
- urine becoming dark in colour may indicate dehydration
- urine becoming cloudy or smelling of fish may indicate an infection
- faeces becoming very black and tar-like may indicate that the person is bleeding internally

- if blood is seen in the either urine or faeces it may indicate an infection, haemorrhoids or another medical condition.

Disposal of urine and faeces

Care staff should always wear gloves when handling body fluids of any kind, and ensure that urine and faeces are disposed of down a toilet, or in the sluice area. Soiled pads, catheter tubing and bags should not be flushed down the toilet or placed in general refuse bins, but placed in designated clinical waste bags that will be sealed and incinerated according to the policy and procedure of the organisation in which you work. If urine or faeces needs to be measured or examined, it should be covered and discreetly taken to the sluice area so that this can be done immediately, then the specimen disposed of swiftly to avoid spillages or infection risk.

Chapter 9 - Personal hygiene

ESSENCE OF CARE											
Personal & oral hygiene											
1a	1b	2a	2b	3	4	5a	5b	6a	6b	7a	7b
Continence, bladder & bowel care											
1	2	3	4	5	6	7	9	10	11		

NMS						
21.1	21.2	21.4	21.5	21.6	21.7	21.8
10.1						

NSF					
2.1	2.4	2.7	2.8	2.10	2.51

TOPSS			
Induction			
1.1.1			
3.2.1	3.2.2	3.2.8	
4.2.1	4.6.1	4.6.4	4.6.5 4.6.6

NVQ 2 CARE

Z9.1
All PC's   All Range
Z9.2
All PC's   All Range
Z11.1
All PC's   All Range
Z11.2
All PC's   All Range
Z11.3
All PC's   All Range

Compiled by Adrian Muir

CHAPTER 10

Exercise and aids to mobility

Jane Hall & Lynne Phair

Why exercise is important • Motivation and assessment • Setting up an exercise class • Mobility and independence •Walking aids • Wheelchairs

Exercise is something often associated with young, fit people: running the London Marathon or going to the gym two or three times a week. The Oxford Dictionary definition of exercise is 'activity requiring physical effort carried out for the sake of health and fitness'. For many people of all ages, actively taking part in exercise is something they avoid. So when a person becomes older and more frail, the thought of undertaking exercise is often one that they do not wish to consider.

But any activity that involves movement and therefore uses our muscles can be described as exercise. Many people think of exercise in its extreme form – cycling in the Tour de France or swimming the channel – and this can in fact deter people from doing exercise as they see the huge effort involved and think that it is not for them. It is vital for you as care workers and the people that you look after to understand that exercise comes in many forms and does not need to be so extreme in order for a person to gain immense benefits from it.

One way of thinking about exercise is to divide it into 'formal' and 'informal'. By formal we mean specific exercise sessions or individual programmes, perhaps recommended by a physiotherapist; it also includes sports and games such as tennis, bowls and golf. Informal exercise is exercise carried out while doing something else. It can be as simple and enjoyable as going out for a walk or using the stairs instead of the lift.

Listed below are a few examples of the different types of exercise:

Formal exercise
• exercise to music sessions
• exercise in a gym
• tai chi
• tennis
• bowls
• dancing
• golf
• individual exercise programmes.

Informal exercise
• walking
• going up and down stairs
• gardening
• housework
• getting in and out of the bath
• getting dressed
• preparing meals.

Depending on our level of fitness and state of health, different degrees of exercise are going to be suitable for different people. For some residents in care homes a suitable exercise programme may involve them walking to the toilet or dining room instead of using the wheelchair, or it may be that the goal is for them to do it three times a day and use the chair on the other occasions. The amount of effort involved in washing and dressing ourselves should also not be underestimated and it may be that a suitable exercise programme for an older person is to wash and dress himself or herself each day.

Why exercise is important

Exercise is important as it helps us to stay healthy and maintain our independence for as long as possible. It plays a vital part in a healthy old age. There is a commonly held view that we expect to get weaker and less active with the advancing years, and it is true that ageing has an effect on our bodies: most of us cannot run as fast or lift as much as we could when we were younger. However, by far the most damaging effect on our bodies is the fact that most people's level of activity declines with old age. It is this inactivity that is potentially more harmful than the effects of ageing. The old adage, 'If you don't use it, you will lose it' could not be more true.

The benefits of exercise can be divided into three main areas:

Physical health
• increased muscle strength
• improved balance
• increased flexibility
• improved circulation
• improved continence
• promotes bowel regularity
• improves stiff and painful joints
• helps to protect against osteoporosis

• can help with heart disease
• helps in weight control by burning up calories.

Mental health
• increases self confidence
• helps with depression
– promotes a feeling of well-being
• helps combat insomnia.

Social well-being
• opportunity for social interaction
• opportunity to meet and make new friends.

Never underestimate the effort involved during activities of daily living (ADL). For a lot of older people, just doing them without assistance and walking instead of using a wheelchair may provide them with the appropriate amount of exercise – and a sense of achievement! Encourage residents to be more independent: it may take them longer to get washed and dressed or walk instead of being pushed, but the benefits gained should be recognised by staff.

How lack of exercise affects a person's health

Exercise is a vital part of maintaining good health at any age and is not necessarily associated with becoming fit enough to undertake extravagant physical activity. For many older people living in a long-term care environment, normal everyday exercise can often be diminished because care staff and the routines of the home replace many activities which would previously have provided a natural form of exercise for the older person.

Evidence shows that even healthy older people lose their strength at 1-2 per cent per year and their power may decline even faster, at 3-4 per cent per year. Long-term illness can make this

It is important to encourage and enable people to take exercise – perhaps a regular walk around the garden – to maintain their mobility and, often, lift their mood.

problem even worse. Without some form of exercise, muscle power and strength starts to waste away. This loss of strength can affect a person's sense of balance, making them much more likely to fall and possibly break a bone.

Muscle tension can increase and so can joint pain. Lack of exercise decreases circulation and so increases the risk of heart disease. Lack of exercise also increases constipation and can exacerbate urinary incontinence, if a person becomes stiff and unable to get out of the chair very easily. Psychologically, lack of exercise can cause a person to become drowsy and sleepy, lack confidence and become depressed.

Motivation

The best way to motivate people to participate in exercise is to remind them of the benefits and reassure them that it is within their ability. Some people are motivated by the setting and achieving of goals. For example, a goal could be that a person will be able to walk from their bedroom to the dining room after attending an exercise class twice a week for four weeks; or, if they practise walking with a member of staff daily over two weeks, they can increase the distance they are able to walk. Maintenance goals may be appropriate, eg attend exercises twice a week to maintain the ability to walk from the bedroom to the dining room. The goal of independence is a strong motivating factor for most people.

Finding an activity that an older person enjoys is also a very important motivating factor. It goes without saying that trying to persuade somebody to take part in an activity that they do not enjoy is fighting an uphill battle. Think about the sorts of activities you enjoy and those that you don't, compare them with a co-worker and you may find the lists are very different. Each individual in the care home is different, therefore a range of activities must be offered. These may include:

- exercise to music group
- tai chi
- dancing
- walking club
- gardening
- helping with meal preparation or meal set up/clearing away
- individual exercise programmes
- activities of daily living (ADL) – eg dressing, bathing, walking between destinations.

Just telling somebody to go for a walk around the garden may seem pointless and could also be seen as bad practice, as the person should always be given a choice as to whether they participate in any activities. However, if you explain the benefits to them they can make an informed choice.

By walking around the garden, for example, they will be:

- helping their heart muscles, helping their leg muscles and improving their circulation
- straightening their body which helps with their balance
- helping to improve their breathing
- burning off some calories
- helping their digestive system to work better
- helping with any problems of constipation
- helping them have a better night's sleep.

The psychological effects are:

- the stimulation of the senses from walking in the garden
- stimulation of thoughts, perhaps alleviating some depressive ones
- encouraging a more positive outlook.

The social benefits will mean that the resident has:

- something different to talk about
- an opportunity to meet others or walk in the garden with someone else.

Motivating a person to participate in formal or informal activity should be done by helping them to understand that the exercise is part of their overall care in ensuring that they remain independent for as long as possible.

Other types of activity for the less able can be explained in similar ways. A person in a wheelchair who is prone to falling may benefit from a session with a soft ball, for example. This would help with their balance, give them mental stimulation, and help with their dexterity (nimbleness of movement) and their hand-eye co-ordination. All of these factors will help reduce the risk of the person falling.

Assessing a person for exercise

As with any activity it is important to assess any risks that are associated with encouraging a person to take formal exercise. Discuss any ideas you have about a formal exercise class or encouraging a person to join an exercise class with your manager, the person's GP or a physiotherapist. They may be able to discuss with you any problems that a specific type of exercise may have in relation to someone's particular disability. The type of risks that need to be assessed include:

- whether the person has taken any exercise recently

- whether they can stand alone or need a chair to lean against or to sit in
- how long their concentration is and whether they can follow instructions
- if they cannot follow instructions, how that will possibly cause difficulties for the exercise class
- whether the person has any breathing difficulties and if this will affect any exercises.
- whether the person gets dizzy due to low blood pressure when they stand up
- whether they have any neck or back problems
- whether they have any arthritis in any particular joints that should not be overstretched.

These are just examples of the types of risks that need to be assessed before encouraging any particular type of exercise. A person who has not done exercise for a long time should not be rushed into doing rigorous exercises that may cause them more harm. The muscles will become tired and stiffen, and the extra strain on the heart may cause other complications. There are almost no diseases or disabilities that exist which do not allow a person to take some exercise. The key is that the exercise is appropriate for the person, their abilities and the conditions from which they suffer.

Psychological exercise

Exercise may not only be physical but might be mental exercise too. For people suffering from depression, anxiety or feelings of distress because of the change in their lifestyle, relaxation classes or mental exercises will be very beneficial. Similarly, for people with respiratory problems, breathing techniques can be used together with other treatments in easing discomfort. Anyone suffering from headaches or migraine may wish to use some alternative types of breathing to help ease their pain.

Setting up an exercise class

Exercise must be enjoyable; it must not become a competition to try to develop the fittest person in the care home! The person leading the exercise class should be totally committed and be very positive about the benefits that taking exercise will have. The class should not be too long – perhaps a minimum of 10 minutes and a maximum of 20 – and must be geared to the abilities of the people participating. It should also be fun. It is important that no one is made to feel that they are failing and that everybody, however limited their involvement in the class, feels that it has been an enjoyable, social event.

The exercise class itself should start with gentle warm-up exercises, followed by exercises which have been demonstrated or taken from a text with accurate descriptions of how to carry them out (and which have clear benefits for participants). The class should close with a 'cool down' period of gentler exercise and stretching so that the muscles can relax.

Exercise and independence

As technology has taken over more of our lives, most people are less active in their daily life than would have been the case in the past. One hundred years ago women would have gained a lot of exercise from normal life activity – hand-washing, using a mangle, hand brushing the stairs, carrying in coal, lifting heavy pots, walking to the shops and carrying heavy baskets of food. Slowly but surely, all these activities have disappeared, and today the remote control for the television means people do not even have to get up and walk across the room. So finding normal life activity which helps with exercise can be a little difficult, particularly in a care environment where people are perhaps helped more than they should be.

Many of today's normal life activities can be taken away from a person. For example: always taking a person in the lift, even when they are able to walk up a few stairs, or putting them in a wheelchair to take them through to another area of the care environment when perhaps they could walk at least part of the way. Laying the dinner table for the person, or pouring out their tea rather than encouraging them to do so and use the muscles in their arms, could lead to muscle wastage.

Involving people in the normal life activities of a home also helps to ensure that they remain actively involved in every aspect of the life of the environment in which they live. All humans strive to maximise the control they have over their lives and when a person moves into a care environment this control can very easily be taken away from them. A person will then learn to become dependent on the staff, not consciously, but because there is no reason to remain independent. As people become more dependent, they become more needy, and a cycle of dependence is established, increasing the person's disability and distress and the workload for staff – all because the environment and philosophy of the home is not one of positive activity.

The charity Research into Ageing has produced various useful books on exercise for healthy ageing (see the list at the end of the chapter). They give some useful tips about positive exercise and ways that normal life activity can help with exercise:

- Rather than having a shower or being washed by a carer completely, the person should sometimes be encouraged to sit down and wash using a flannel, stretching and reaching up and over their back, reaching behind their buttocks and behind their neck. This helps to increase flexibility. Again, when a person needs to be dried, encourage them to dry a little bit of themself.

- Hold a baking session where the residents are encouraged to help making the cake, using hand whisks or wooden spoons rather than electric whisks, or perhaps bread because kneading is good exercise for the hands and the arms. Perhaps they could have a coffee mill or a pepper mill and help the chef by grinding the corns. This again strengthens the hands.

- A game of marbles or rolling a golf ball between the palms, under the feet or around behind the neck without dropping it can be helpful.

- Encourage people to do exercises in bed before they get up; this helps reduce the risk of dizziness.

- If a resident is able, perhaps they could help with a little bit of dusting in their own room, folding clean clothes or helping to sort socks or stockings. These are all activities that will help stimulate mental activity, encourage muscle activity and most of all help the person feel useful and part of the life of the home.

The cycle of dependence

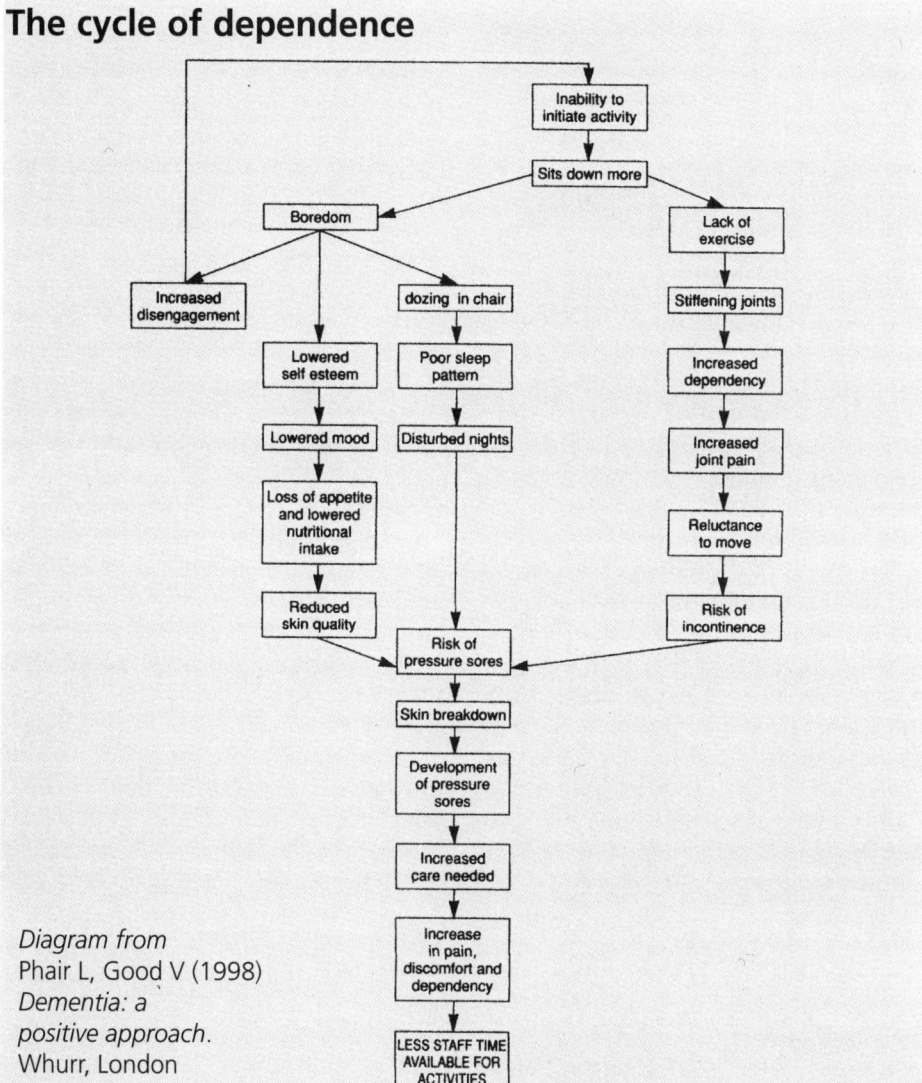

Diagram from
Phair L, Good V (1998)
*Dementia: a
positive approach.*
Whurr, London

MOBILITY AND MOBILITY AIDS

Mobility is the term given to the ability to move around. This covers activities such as:

- moving around in bed – being able to turn from side to side or sit up
- getting out of bed
- getting up and sitting down in a chair
- getting up and down from the toilet
- getting in and out of the bath or shower
- moving from one destination to another.

In other words, these are the type of activities we take for granted. Any decline in mobility means that we may have to use a mobility aid such as a stick, frame or wheelchair and/or require the help of one or more people.

Many health problems can have an effect on the ability of a person to get around. Some of the more common problems include:

- heart – shortness of breath, angina, dizziness affecting endurance and balance
- lungs – shortness of breath caused by lung disease eg asthma, bronchitis, and emphysema affecting endurance
- circulation – leg swelling or anaemia, leading to pain and decreased endurance
- joints – arthritis causing stiffness and pain
- bones – osteoporosis causing pain and poor posture
- muscles – weakness, tightness leading to pain and difficulty moving
- brain and nervous system – strokes, Parkinson's disease, dementia, making movement more difficult and often associated with pain
- skin – sores, calluses causing pain especially if on the feet
- bladder/bowels – constipation, incontinence, infections affecting general well-being
- eyes – lack of vision leading to difficulty getting around obstacles.

Mobility appliances such as walking sticks, tripods and frames can help an older person remain independent. It is important that you understand how they are used and that you know how to teach the person how to use them.

There are many reasons why a person will use a mobility appliance. They may have pain in one or both legs, making it difficult to put all their weight on them. They may have poor balance or they may simply lack confidence when walking because of a previous fall. Whatever the reason, it is essential that they use the device properly in order to stay safe.

Not only is it important that a person using a mobility aid has the correct technique but also that they are confident walking over the various levels and types of surfaces they are likely to encounter. Inside buildings this may include carpet, lino, wood floors and stepping over thresholds and, when appropriate, negotiating stairs or lifts. Outside, garden paths, grass, pavements and kerbs need to be practised as well as slopes.

Walking sticks

These come in two main types, wooden or metal. The metal ones are usually adjustable. Walking sticks come with many types of handle from the standard hook shape to those designed specifically for people with arthritis of the hands. Some people use 'ornamental' sticks – more designed for style than function – and they may not have a handle as such, sometimes just a round ball; these sticks are best left for decoration.

Of all the mobility aids, sticks give the least support but allow the most natural walking pattern. Sticks can be used on their own or in pairs although co-ordination of two sticks can be quite tricky.

When someone starts using a stick it is important that the height is correct: if it is too low the person will have to stoop, if too high it will not provide enough support, and they also risk hurting their arm.

Measuring a person for a stick

With the person standing and their arms hanging down by their sides, the top of the handle should be approximately level with the wrist crease of the hand they will be holding the stick in. When holding the stick their hand should be level with the top of their thigh, the elbow should be very slightly bent and the shoulders level. Ask the resident to walk with the stick to see how it feels, as they must be happy with it.

To adjust metal sticks, the two little buttons are pushed through the holes and then the inner part slides up or down. The two metal buttons must click back through the holes to make the stick safe to use.

Wooden sticks need to be cut using a saw. The correct height for the stick can be determined using a metal one if one is available, otherwise you will need to use a tape measure.

Which hand to hold the stick in?

This depends on why the stick is needed. If the person has a problem with one leg, eg arthritis of the hip or knee, then the stick should be held in the **opposite** hand – ie someone with a painful or weak *right* leg should hold the stick in their *left* hand.

If both legs are about the same and the mobility problem is more general, the stick should be held in the hand that feels most comfortable to the resident. Some people feel more confident holding it in their dominant hand (ie their right hand if they are right-handed) while others may prefer to leave their dominant hand free.

The stick or the leg first?

There are generally two ways to walk with a stick; the best way for an individual depends on how much support they need.

People who need quite a lot of support should do the following:
• stick is moved forward and slightly out to the side
• the opposite (and weaker) leg is then moved so that it is level with the stick
• lastly the leg on the same side as the stick (stronger leg) is moved forwards to just beyond the level of the stick
• the stick is then moved again to repeat the sequence.

For people who need less support from the stick, the following pattern can be used:
• stick and opposite leg are moved forward together
• leg on the stick side then moved forward to just past the stick.

There can be a tendency for the person to carry the stick – this should be discouraged! There should always be at least two points of contact on the floor.

Tripods and quadrapods

Tripods and quadrapods are similar to sticks in that they are held in one hand; however they are more stable and provide extra support because of the extra feet.

As the name suggests, a tripod has three feet of varying sizes, giving different bases of support.

A quadropod has four feet and therefore is even more stable than the tripod.

These types of sticks are often used by people who have had strokes and lost the use of one arm, which means they are unable to use a walking frame.

Height of tripods and quadrapods.

These are measured in the same way as sticks. These types of mobility device are always height adjustable. The walking pattern is the same as for the single stick.

Walking frames

Of all the mobility devices, walking frames are probably among the most common in care homes. Walking frames come in many styles now but basically they can be divided into two main groups – those without wheels and those with wheels.

Without wheels

These have four feet, each with a rubber ferrule on the end giving good grip on floor surfaces.

The walking pattern with a non-wheeled frame is similar to that of the stick: the frame is advanced first until the arms are almost at full stretch but not completely straight. Next the weaker leg is advanced, followed by the stronger leg. As with sticks there is sometimes a tendency for people to carry the frame; again this must be discouraged as it can easily put someone off balance and can cause shoulder and arm discomfort.

If a person is seen regularly carrying their frame, they may not need it any more. This should be reviewed carefully: if having it available 'just in case' gives the person confidence, this should be an important consideration.

With wheels

Wheeled frames can come with two, three or four wheels and provide variable amounts of stability.

Two-wheeled frames, the most common type, have two wheels at the front and rubber feet at the back. These cannot be pushed quickly as the rubber ferrules drag on the floor. They have to be lifted to turn as the wheels do not pivot.

Three-wheeled frames usually have three wheels that all pivot, making them very easy to manoeuvre. They can be turned in quite a tight circle. However, this extra manoeuvrability means that they are less stable and can easily run away from someone who has balance or memory problems. These frames usually have brakes on the handles but quite a degree of dexterity is required to use them. Also, older people often have difficulty with co-ordinating the brakes, as their reaction times can be slowed.

Four-wheeled frames are more stable than the three-wheeled ones but less than the two-wheeled. Usually all four wheels pivot and like the three-wheeled versions they generally come with brakes. The braking mechanism can be on the handles or sometimes is activated by pushing down on the two back wheels; again a significant amount of co-ordination is required. Some of the four-wheeled versions come with built-in seats, allowing someone to rest during their walk. Again, however, a reasonable amount of co-ordination is required to use it properly.

Wheeled frames allow a more natural walking pattern than those without wheels.

Height of frames

As with sticks, the handle of the frame should be level with the wrist creases when standing with the arms hanging by the side. If the frame is too low there is a tendency for the person to be hunched forward; if the frame is too high the shoulders appear to be up by the person's ears.

Assisting a person using a mobility appliance

When using a mobility appliance with an older person it is useful to demonstrate the correct method of walking as well as explaining it. It is vital that the explanation is in a manner and at a level and pace that they can understand. They should be given appropriate feedback, encouragement and reinforcement.

Sometimes, in addition to using the

mobility aid, a person may need some physical support. In order to assist someone who is walking, the carer should usually position themself behind the resident with one hand on each side of their pelvis. This may feel a slightly odd position as most of us like to face someone when we are walking and talking with them, so that we make eye contact; in this situation however it is better to be positioned slightly behind for your own and the resident's safety. Depending on the mobility aid being used and the needs of the resident, different methods of assistance may be required. If in doubt, advice should be sought from a physiotherapist.

You should not be taking most of a person's body weight when they are walking, and if someone falls you are not expected to catch them.

It is essential that residents who are not using their mobility aids correctly are told and helped to use them in the right way. If you have any concerns that the aid may not be suitable then you must report it to the appropriate person.

Think about the environment the aids are being used in. A person walking with a stick can obviously pass between two chairs with relative ease; however, someone using a frame may find the gap too narrow. The environment must be kept as clutter-free as possible and any potential hazards on the floor removed or reported to maintenance staff.

Sometimes people may use more than one type of mobility aid. They may be happy to use a stick inside the care home but prefer a frame when they are walking outside in the garden, for example. Likewise, somebody who becomes tired as the day goes on may find that they can use a stick during the day but then need the extra support of a frame when they are tired in the evening.

Wheelchairs

For those older people who cannot walk or are able to walk only short distances, wheelchairs become invaluable as a means of mobility.

If it is identified that a resident would benefit from using a wheelchair one of two things can happen. Care homes usually have a supply of their own wheelchairs but these are often shared and therefore not set up specifically for one person. If short distances only are involved and the resident will only be using it for transport, then this is acceptable. If, however, a resident is going to be spending a significant amount of time in a chair, it should be set up specifically for them. An appropriate person – for example, an occupational therapist, a physiotherapist or a representative from the local wheelchair service – can carry out an assessment and make adjustments.

Before using the chair a number of things should be checked:
• are the brakes both working?
• are there two leg rests?
• is there an appropriate cushion in the chair?
• is the back rest in the correct position?
• are both arm rests in position?
• are the tyres fully inflated (if appropriate) and in good condition?
• are the wheels all turning freely?
• is there a safety belt on the chair?
• is the chair clean?
• is the upholstery in good condition, no torn fabric?

This may seem like a long list but in reality it takes only a few seconds to look over the chair and check that every thing is as it should be.

When pushing someone in a wheelchair try to be aware all the time of how it may feel to be pushed around, not always knowing where you are going. It is vital that you talk to the person in the chair, warning them of uneven surfaces, when you are going to turn or even need to go backwards for a short distance. You should also warn them before tipping the chair back when negotiating a kerb or threshold. Never push someone along in a wheelchair in the tipped-back position (you may have seen this done when there are no footrests on the chair). Not only is it frightening and dangerous for the occupant, it is also dangerous for the staff member as the chair could very easily tip backwards. The golden rule is always talk to the occupant, even if they may be confused. Let them know what you are doing, and don't go too fast.

Even though someone may need to use a wheelchair it doesn't mean that they are totally incapacitated. They should be encouraged to put the brakes on and off themselves if possible, or move the leg rests or arm rests out of the way. Some people may even be able to move the chair themselves over short distances.

Wheelchair assessment

If it is decided that the resident needs a wheelchair, the following questions need to be considered when choosing the most appropriate chair for them to use:

- is the chair for indoor or outdoor use or both?
- what sort of tyres are needed, solid or pneumatic (air)?
- is the resident to be pushed in it or to propel it themselves?
- if they are to be pushing it themselves will they be able to use one or two arms?
- what is the height of the resident?
- what is the weight of the resident?
- does the resident have any particular problems with their posture?

- do they need a special type of cushion either for pressure relief or to aid their posture?
- what sort of leg rests are needed – standard or elevating? Are toe or heel straps required?
- is a calf strap needed on the leg rest to prevent the legs coming off behind the leg rests?
- is a lap belt necessary for safety?

Different types of wheelchair

The main choice is between self-propelled and attendant-propelled. Self-propelled chairs have big wheels at the back which enable the user to move the chair themselves. If the user has only one functional arm the chair can be given a single-handed drive. Attendant-propelled chairs usually have four small wheels. Electric chairs are very useful for those people who do not have the physical ability to self-propel a chair but have the mental faculties for operating an electric chair. These chairs are very expensive and not everyone can use them as they take a high degree of concentration, good spatial awareness and good judgement – for this reason they should always be tried out before purchase.

Although the basic features of a chair are the same, various modifications are possible:

- **Wheels** – solid or pneumatic? Pneumatic wheels give more cushioning and are therefore better if the chair is to be used outside
- **Backrest** – solid or folding, and sometimes removable to help in transfers. A tension bar can also be attached to the backrest to stop it bowing out, which helps maintain a better back posture for the occupant. Back rest extensions are also available for very

tall residents or those with very poor trunk and head control

- **Armrests** – permanent or removable to make transfers easier. Tray tables can be fitted to the arm-rests. These can be useful in helping to position an arm which may have been affected by a stroke, or may be needed just as a table to enable the user to carry objects or do crafts
- **Foot-rests** – permanent with swing back or removable. Elevating leg rests are also available, good for ankle swelling or if the person is unable to bend their knee
- **Footplate** (of leg rest) - can have straps for the heels and toes to keep feet in place. Larger footplates can be fitted for those with larger feet and a solid footplate can be placed on top of the two footplates providing a larger area for positioning. This is very useful for those residents whose feet tend to slip off the footplate. A calf strap can also be attached to leg rests to prevent legs getting trapped behind the leg rests. The height of the footplate can be easily adjusted with a spanner
- **Brakes** – usually positioned on the rear wheels. Brake levers can be extended, which is very useful if someone only has the use of one arm. This enables them to stretch over to the affected side and apply the brake
- **Anti-tip rollers** can be attached to wheelchairs. These allow the chair to rock backwards without tipping over. They can be very useful for confused residents or those with various neurological problems.

Wheelchairs come with instruction manuals. They should be kept in a convenient place and referred to whenever necessary.

Care of mobility appliances

It is essential to the safety of the person using the mobility aid that it is kept in good working order. The following is a checklist to help you care for the appliances.

- **Ferrules** – need to be checked regularly for wear and tear. Sometimes they wear unevenly – they can be turned to ensure more even wear. Any that have worn smooth should be replaced immediately.
- Mechanisms to adjust the **height** of aids should also be inspected regularly. The buttons should be sticking completely out of both holes.
- Any **nuts, bolts or screws** on the aid should be checked regularly as they do sometimes become loose. If you are unable to tighten them then you should take the aid out of use and report it to an appropriate person.
- Any **wheels** on frames should turn easily and those that pivot should be able to do so without getting stuck. Any problems should be reported to the appropriate person immediately after taking the device out of use.
- The **handles** on mobility aids sometimes get out of position and often end up with the ridged section for the fingers on top so that they dig into the palm. These plastic handles can usually be turned back to their correct position with relative ease.
- The **braking mechanism** on any mobility aid should be checked regularly to ensure that it is working properly. Take the aid out of use immediately if not working and report it to the appropriate person.

Given the number and types of mobility aids used in a care home, there is considerable potential for them to become mixed up. It is a good idea for all devices to be labelled with the user's name.

Last but not least, keeping mobility aids clean is vital: they very quickly become dirty and the handles sticky – unpleasant to use!

If in doubt about the safety of any mobility aid, take it out of use immediately and report it to a senior member of staff.

Useful books

Ruddlesden M (1995) *You Can Do It! Exercises for Older People.* Hawker Publications, London.

Skelton D (1998) *Exercise for Healthy Ageing.* Research into Ageing.

Phair L, Good V (1998) *Dementia, A Positive Approach.* Whurr Publications.

Chapter 10 - Exercise and aids to mobility

ESSENCE OF CARE						
None						

NMS						
Adaptations and equipment						
22.1	22.2	22.3	22.4	22.5	22.6	

NSF						
8.1	8.2	8.3	8.4	8.5	8.6	8.8
6.4						

TOPSS		
Induction		
4.1.5		

NVQ 2 CARE		
Z6.1		
All Performance Criteria	All range	All knowledge
Z6.2		
All Performance Criteria	All range	All knowledge
Z7.1 1A,1B		
Performance Criteria 3		
Z7.3		
Performance criteria 6		

Compiled by Adrian Muir

CHAPTER 11

Comfort, rest and sleep

Jane Slack & Wendy Goodman

*• What is pain? • How to assess it • Helping people who are in pain
or discomfort • Complementary therapies • Daytime rest
• A good night's sleep • Managing difficulties at night*

Rest, sleep and the relief of pain are all interrelated. Without rest and sleep, the body cannot renew or rebuild and thus relieve pain, and without the relief of pain the body cannot relax enough to sleep. This chapter will look at these three areas, showing how they work together and how the care assistant should use knowledge of them to enhance the quality of life of an older person.

Pain

Pain is an unpleasant sensory and emotional experience associated with actual or potential tissue damage. Pain can affect older people's physical, social and emotional well-being. A recent survey indicated that over 50 per cent of people over the age 70 reported high degrees of pain or discomfort. Older adults are more likely to experience pain as a result of developing chronic conditions such as arthritis, angina, stroke and Parkinson's disease, and it can have a serious affect on an person's mobility, sleep pattern, dietary intake and emotional state.

There are two types of pain: *acute* and *chronic*. *Acute* pain is pain that has come on recently and lasts for a limited time. It serves a useful purpose – signalling that something is wrong. Pain becomes *chronic* when it goes on beyond three months, but it may not be associated with any specific disease, injury or identifiable cause. Muscle and joint pain are very common in older people.

A few people who have had a stroke experience generalised pain. This is often a deep burning or crushing sensation, which may affect half or only a small part of the body. The person may feel more pain and react more sharply to something that would normally only cause a small amount of discomfort, such as a limb being incorrectly positioned, or touching a sharp object. People who have diabetic neuropathy and shingles sometimes experience this altered pain sensation.

There are some commonly held misconceptions about pain. One is that pain is an unavoidable consequence of growing older. This belief leads many older people to feel that there is no point in telling anyone that they are in pain, as nothing can be done about it.

Some older people feel it is a sign of weakness to admit that they are in pain – feeling they ought to be able to 'grin and bear it'. Different life experiences, gender or cultural background can affect both how they feel about pain and how they express it to others. A retired soldier with many battle injuries may not feel it is appropriate to complain about the level of pain he is experiencing now in relation to past experiences. The older person may be worried about the side-effects of pain-killing medication (analgesia), particularly constipation.

Another commonly held but incorrect belief is that older people experience less pain. This myth has probably arisen because so many older people don't complain about their pain.

Pain assessment

The aim of any pain assessment is to identify where the pain is being felt, what it feels like, when it started and what is affecting it – for example, does a particular movement cause it? Pain assessment is important as many older people will experience more than one type of pain.

When an older person is asked directly, 'Are you in pain?', they may well answer 'No', if they are not feeling any pain at that precise moment. However, they may experience a lot of pain whenever they move – to turn over in bed or get up and walk, for example. Using different words can help, eg 'Are you uncomfortable?', 'Are you feeling achey?', 'Does it catch when you breathe?', 'Does your chest feel tight?'.

Asking about how the pain changes at different times, or when the older per-

son is doing anything specific can also help.

Research has shown that older people who have dementia receive significantly less pain-relieving medication than other older people. This may due to the misconception that they do not feel pain – they do feel it just as much as anyone else, but may not be able to communicate what they are feeling. Some people with dementia may be able to answer questions about pain if given a lot more time to do so, but many will not be able to express it in words. Detective work and observation may be needed.

Observing the person's body language and facial expressions is extremely helpful; these can show that the person is experiencing pain even if they are unable or unwilling to tell the carer. Signs to watch for are:

- grimacing or frowning
- looking sad/anxious
- rigid body position
- flinching when touched
- aggressive behaviour
- restlessness
- crying out on movement.

Pain assessment tools can be more effective than simply asking an older person. There are a variety of pain assessment tools available. These may be diaries, pain logs, graphs or scales. Pain scales are questionnaires that ask the person to score their level of pain, usually on a 1-10 scale (1 being the lowest level; 10 the highest).

Helping older people in pain or discomfort

The attitude of the care assistant can make an enormous difference. Taking time to listen to the person's concerns and showing sympathy can itself have a powerful effect. The golden rule when helping people who are in pain is that **if they say they are in pain, then they are in**

pain. It is important to respond quickly to a request to move the position of the individual, such as repositioning in the wheelchair or returning the individual to bed. By reporting and documenting the pain experienced, an accurate assessment can be made that will assist effective intervention.

Emotional distress is just as painful to the individual as physical pain, and it needs to be treated with the same level of understanding, care and attention by the care assistant.

Anxiety, fear, depression, lack of sleep can all make the sensation of pain much more distressing.

Prescribed medication

Many older people are used to taking regular medication. Before they entered a residential care setting, they may have been accustomed to managing this independently. However, there is a lot of evidence that many older people do not take their medication in the correct way, as prescribed by the doctor. There are many reasons for this, such as:

- not being able to understand or remember the doctor's instructions
- no written information being supplied
- not being able to read the small print on the label
- the medication being labelled 'take as directed'.

In order for any of us to remember to take medication, information about what it is for and when and how to take it is absolutely crucial. For some residents an individual drug chart is helpful. This chart will have the name of the drug, what it is for, and when to take it. If a resident has had medication prescribed for pain relief but is unable to take it, this must be recorded and reported. Alternatives to tablets are often available – such as liquids, suppositories or patches on the skin.

Complementary therapies

Many people with chronic pain use complementary therapies in addition to or instead of painkillers. Concerns about the long-term effects of taking pain killers, and a reluctance to rely on regular pills, are reasons often given for using complementary therapies. Such remedies include meditation, aromatherapy, reflexology, acupuncture, massage, transcutaneous electrical nerve stimulation (TENS), and heat therapy. Some training or experience is required for all of these therapies, and the care assistant should not undertake any of them without it.

- **Meditation/relaxation**

Meditation can be very useful in managing the anxiety and stress caused by chronic pain. Relaxation techniques are often taught to people who have experienced heart attacks or suffered with chronic pain for some time.

- **Acupuncture**

Acupuncture is based on a series of energy lines (meridians) in the body, which are said to flow from the head towards the feet or hands and return to the head. Penetration of the skin by small needles, it is believed, helps the body to correct itself by realigning or redirecting the energy. As yet no Western scientific theory has managed to explain how acupuncture works.

- **Reflexology**

The basis of this therapy is that the application of pressure to one part of the body produces an effect in another part. Pressure is usually applied to the feet but the hands can also be used.

- **Homeopathy**

This is a method of treating disease by prescribing tiny doses of natural drugs

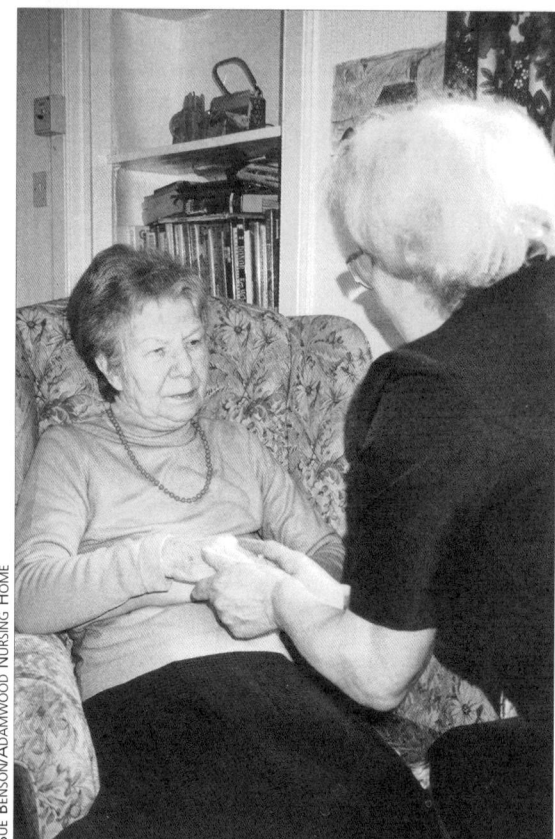

A hand massage, perhaps with aromatherapy oil, can be most relaxing

• Massage

Stimulation of the skin for the purpose of pain relief has been practised for centuries. It is thought to alleviate stress by relaxing muscles, and is particularly helpful for pain that involves muscle tension or spasm such as headache or backache. Recently a small study of older people in long-term care showed a reduction in anxiety following back massage. Massage is not suitable for people with pain caused by damage to the nervous system, such as that experienced by many people who have had a stroke.

• Heat therapy

This is perhaps the most common form of complementary therapy for relieving pain, and can be applied in many ways. It is very effective for musculoskeletal disorders such as rheumatic pain. There are health and safety issues to think about when a client is using heat devices such as hot water bottles/electric heat pads/wheat pads and gel packs.

that in maximum dosage would produce symptoms of the disease. The body then naturally learns to fight the cause of the pain and so relieve the symptoms.

• TENS

This is often recommended and applied by a physiotherapist or specialist staff working in pain clinics. However, the electrical devices can often be bought via mail order or from large chemists. Electrodes, applied and taped to the skin over the pain site, emit a mild electric current that is felt as a tingling, buzzing or vibrating sensation.

Ointments are very popular with older people, and are often used surreptitiously in addition to any prescribed methods. However, it is important to check the ingredients of the ointment, as there is a danger of over-dosage of medication. For example, ibuprofen is a very commonly used painkiller that can be bought over the counter (as well as being prescribed) as pills or in an ointment version where the drug is absorbed through the skin when massaged into the affected joint. The ointment should should not be used in addition to taking the tablets, as serious side effects (bleeding from the stomach) could result.

REST AND SLEEP

All human beings spend the day and night over a period of 24 hours moving between states of wakefulness and sleep. The number and length of times spent in each of these states depends on many factors, the most important being our age and occupation.

A baby spends most of its time sleeping, interspersed with short periods of wakefulness. As the child matures, more and more time is spent awake and as a working adult we may spend most of the day awake and have one main sleeping period during the night of around 8 hours. As age increases and work decreases, daytime naps may be taken to supplement the night-time sleep which reduces as we grow older. Within these generalised work/sleep patterns there are many individual differences.

Most people can give their own reasons for the importance of sleep: it refreshes the body, takes away tiredness and irritability, makes us feel better. There is evidence of sleep deprivation and disturbance being used as a form of torture, and some recent research studies have highlighted the hazards of working nights.

Everyone agrees that sleep is a good thing, but much research has taken place over the years to examine what happens during sleep and discover what its exact functions may be.

Sleep has been found to consist of two types: rapid eye movement (REM) sleep and non-REM sleep. Non-REM sleep has four distinct phases and accounts for approximately 75-80 per cent of sleep. The four phases move from drowsiness to light sleep to deeper sleep, ending with a period of deep sleep. This deep sleep period is also called slow-wave sleep (SWS). It coincides with the time when growth hormone is produced and the cells of the body repair themselves.

It conserves energy and allows brain cells to recover. Brain tissue only recovers during sleep.

REM sleep accounts for the remaining 20-25 per cent of sleep and it is during this period that dreaming takes place.

The phases of sleep occur in a pattern starting with phase one of non-REM sleep, progressing through to phase four, and then reversing back up to phase two which is followed by REM sleep. Each complete phase takes about 90 minutes to complete. It appears to be the slow-wave, deep sleep of phase four that is reduced as we become older, being replaced by longer periods of light sleep from which we are easily rousable. This can lead to fragmented sleep with more frequent awakenings and less of the restorative deep sleep.

Preparing for sleep

Everyone prepares for sleep in different ways, yet individual preparation often follows a similar pattern each night, perhaps with a bedtime drink; maybe warm milk or a tot of whisky; a wash, shower or bath; cleaning of teeth or dentures; or just going to the toilet and getting into bed. Once in bed the person may read, watch the television or have a cuddle.

What about the bed? Does the person prefer a soft or hard mattress, duvet or blankets, one, two or three pillows, hot water bottle or electric blanket? Do they like to have the window open or closed? Total darkness or a night light? Does the person like to go to bed early or late? Do they wake early or late? Do they like a drink before they rise or have to dash to the toilet straight away? There are numerous choices here, made without thinking in everyone's own home.

How do people feel when they have to change their rituals? Maybe they 'don't sleep a wink'. A common comment following an absence from home is 'I can't wait to sleep in my own bed'.

Recognising bed-time rituals is vital in working with older people in a care setting. When a person comes to live in a care home, staff should ensure that a full assessment is made of their night habits and wishes as well as their daytime rituals. The needs and wishes of the person should be recorded and documented on a night care plan, so that all staff know how best to help the resident settle.

A good night's sleep

Most people would feel they had had a good night's sleep if they went to sleep quickly, woke only a little during the night and woke up at the appropriate time in the morning feeling rested and refreshed. This does not happen every night and yet people still manage to function well and do not consider themselves to be insomniacs. Everyone experiences a variety of sleep patterns without thinking them abnormal. However, if a person sleeps badly every night, they might start to feel irritable and function less well than they should.

Several factors have been found to prevent a good night's sleep. Most of them can be changed in order to improve sleep.

Pain

A study of nursing home residents found that one third of the residents cited pain as a major cause of sleep disturbance. Pain can be more intrusive at night because there are fewer ways of taking your mind off it. There are also some illnesses and diseases where the pain is worse at night than during the day.

Noise

As people get older they are less able to sleep through noise and are more easily woken. Strategies should be in place to ensure that noise is kept to a minimum during the night. The residents should be asked what it is that wakes them. One of the biggest problems for patients trying to sleep in a hospital at night is the noise of the nurses' shoes!

Temperature

The body temperature drops naturally during the night and the resident may be at risk of feeling cold; this can cause them to wake during lighter periods of sleep. In some centrally heated homes it is also possible to be too hot. It is therefore important to be aware of the residents' needs and sleep patterns.

Feeling hungry and thirsty

Some people may feel hungry or thirsty at night. Older people should always have access to food and drink at any time. In some care settings there is a long gap between supper and breakfast. The gap should not be more than 12 hours and snacks should always be available for night staff to give to people if they feel hungry. These could include simple high energy foods like bananas, milk or chocolate biscuits.

Day time activity

One common problem experienced by people in care settings is that they either doze all day and can't sleep at night or they sit and do nothing all day and so have a sleepless night.

Good sleep at night will be enhanced by encouraging both physical and mental activity during the day. This may include exercises, quizzes, singing or good quality chat.

Residents who cannot take themselves outside should be given the opportunity to get some fresh air, which will help the body in requiring a good night's sleep.

Many older people enjoy a rest in the

middle of the day – for some this is a long-established habit. Some people become exhausted and need to lie down and sleep on the bed. Others may like to be made comfortable in a chair with a footstool to have a nap. Care staff should understand the difference between people napping in a chair because of boredom, lack of involvement or stimulation, and the need for the resident to have a short but good quality sleep in the daytime.

Sometimes a daytime nap seems to result in the person not sleeping well at night. If so this must be assessed and discussed first with the resident and then the whole care team (including both night and day staff). Rest and activity should be balanced with the agreement of the resident in order to promote the most positive lifestyle possible.

Depression

Depression can prevent someone from going to sleep and also wake them early in the morning. It can lead to lethargy, which prevents the daytime activity that can help the sleeping process. It is therefore important that care staff monitor sleep patterns as they may be the first to spot symptoms of depression in a resident. The medication prescribed for a resident with depression may also upset sleep patterns.

Medication

Older people are likely to be prescribed a variety of drugs. Many of these are likely to have an effect on sleep patterns, including drugs prescribed for heart problems, high blood pressure, respiratory problems and parkinsonism.

One of the most important culprits for causing sleeplessness is caffeine, contained in several mild analgesics and some cough remedies. It is also contained in many drinks such as coffee, chocolate and cola. Caffeine-free herbal teas or other drinks should replace these. If a resident has been used to taking large amounts of caffeine, the intake should be reduced slowly to prevent withdrawal symptoms.

Alcohol, except in small amounts, and nicotine are also drugs that cause sleep problems and should be reduced if possible. If a resident is experiencing sleep problems, it may be a good opportunity to request a review of the medication by the district nurse or doctor.

Nocturia

Many people need to empty their bladder at least once during the night (nocturia) and will soon get back to sleep. However, for a frail, older person with poor mobility, getting to the toilet at night may be more of a challenge. Strategies will need to be in place to ensure that the resident is able to visit the toilet safely to avoid falls.

Urgency may lead to incontinence if the toilet cannot be reached quickly. It must be remembered that the ageing bladder has less time from first awareness of the need to void until the need is urgent. Assistance should always be available at night to assist with the need to pass urine. Any resident with a bladder or bowel problem should be referred to the district nurse for a continence assessment.

Other causes

More complex and unusual issues of insomnia include sleepwalking (which occurs more commonly in children), sleep terrors and bruxism (teeth grinding) which may prevent sleep in others rather than the sufferer and need referral to a specialist.

Managing a crisis at night

- Always remember that the night time can be frightening for a resident who may not be able to see or hear so well, and may misunderstand shapes and shadows, sounds and actions of others

- The resident will probably be more distressed than you

- An older person may be confused (even momentarily) due to poor lighting, strange noises, a bad dream or ill health

- Try and understand what is happening from the resident's point of view

- Use the skills learned in communication and managing aggression to defuse the situation

- Stay calm

- Ask yourself whether it is a 'rule' being imposed on the resident that is causing the difficulty. If so, decide whether the rule is sensible for safety or just to suit the home and the staff, and if it can then be dropped

- Always call for assistance

- Always report any incidents in the care plan, and to senior staff

- Help the resident as much as you can, asking them how you can help. 'Bossy' staff only make the situation worse

- If there has been an accident, always use correct first aid procedures

- After the incident, think about the problems and try to identify what may have contributed to the situation, from the staff, the home, the environment, other residents and the resident themselves.

Problems loom large

There is little doubt that when something untoward happens at night, whether at home or at work, the problem always feels bigger, more insurmountable and sometimes more frightening than if it occurs during the day.

Furthermore, noise carries, making the situation worse. With fewer staff to assist, good management and communication skills are essential in night staff.

Every situation will be different – from a person falling over, or not sleeping, to someone becoming frightened and aggressive. A few practice tips may assist when managing a crisis at night (see box, left).

Person-centred care

The role of the night worker is to support and care for people at night, whether they are asleep or awake. All residents should be able to go to bed and get up at times that suit them. This is person-centred care at night time. Practices which were common in the past, such as residents being encouraged to go bed before the night staff come on duty, or getting a certain number of residents up and dressed in the mornings 'to help the day staff' are examples of the bad old culture of care.

Unless a resident wants to get up early they should not be woken before 7am. Forcing a person to wake up before this time (against their wishes) can constitute abuse. The most common reason for staff to call residents at 6.30am is to give them an early morning drink before the night staff go home. This is an example of how an institution is run to suit the staff or the organisation; it is not person-centred practice.

Residents may want to get up in the middle of the night for a stroll or a cup of tea. They may want to talk. They may be disorientated or distressed and so may need comforting. Whatever the person needs, the night staff are there to provide the care and support required, continuing the care given in the waking hours.

The role of the night care worker is to promote good sleep by creating the right environment, but it is also to support residents who may want to be up and about as their own needs dictate.

The care assistant and sleep

Residents will not be cared for properly at night if the care staff looking after them do not manage to sleep and rest properly themselves. All the strategies discussed for older people can apply to everyone, and care staff have a responsibility to themselves, the residents and their employer (under Health and Safety law) to take care of themselves.

It is known that lack of sleep reduces vigilance, leads to slowing of mental processes and can lead to irritability and reduced motivation. If care assistants are going to work a full shift, day or night, which includes the need for vigilance, an alert mind, motivation and a calm manner, then it follows that they must be aware of their own sleep patterns and the need to have a good night's or day's sleep.

Shift workers have extra difficulties in managing their sleep patterns. Some useful tips for managing to sleep in the daytime might be:

- sleep as soon as possible after a night shift
- work shifts in blocks rather than changing all the time
- move shifts forwards so that early shifts are followed by late shifts followed by nights
- ensure you are offered the annual occupational health assessment for night workers. This health check should be offered under the European Union Working Time Directive
- ensure you eat correctly
- ensure you take regular exercise
- do not expect to be able to work all night and stay awake all the next day, however tempting it is.

Sleep has an important role for everyone if they are going to function at optimal levels. The knowledge now available from research can help to ensure that those with the responsibility for caring for others can take steps to enable each person to have the best sleep possible.

Bibliography and further reading

Morgan K, Closs SJ (1999) *Sleep management in nursing practice: an evidence-based guide.* Churchill Livingstone.

Ersser S *et al* (1999) The sleep of older people in hospital and nursing homes. *Journal of Clinical Nursing* 8 360-8.

Davis C (2002) Secrets of successful night nursing. *Nursing Times* 98 (27) 24-6.

Chapter 11 - Comfort, rest and sleep

ESSENCE OF CARE

Self care
1   2   3   7   8   9

Food & nutrition
6

Pressure ulcers
6

Safety
1

Privacy & dignity
1   3   5   6

NMS

12.1   12.2
14.1
15.3
3.1

NSF

2.1   2.27
6.11
8.8

TOPSS

Induction
1.1.1
3.2.1

NVQ 2 CARE

Z19.1
All performance criteria, range and knowledge
Z19.2
All performance Criteria   All range   All knowledge   *Compiled by Adrian Muir*

CHAPTER 12
Care for the dying person and their family

Ruth Sander & Phil Russell

Thinking about death and dying • Important aspects of care • Don't worry about finding the right words – just be there • Cultural and religious considerations • Supporting the family • Care after death • Supporting self and others

Death is a very important part of our lives but it is a subject that many of us prefer not to think about. Being with somebody at the very end of a long life is a great privilege but it is not always easy. Each occasion is different so there are no easy answers. This chapter aims to give you some hints, a little knowledge and some support in a challenging role.

Working with people who are dying can raise unexpected emotions. You may find that you can give confident, objective care to one person but on another occasions you will find yourself an emotional heap. This may take you by surprise and can be for all sorts of different reasons. Perhaps this person reminds you of your own grandmother, perhaps you had a special relationship with them or maybe there is something about this

• Think about how you might want your death to be. If you were old and reaching the end of your life, how and where would you like to be cared for?

particular death that reminds you that one day you too will die. It often helps to have a friend or colleague to chat to about your feelings. The important thing is to remember that this range of emotions is completely normal.

Ask a group of care workers which aspect of working with dying people they find most daunting and they will all give you different answers. For some it will be seeing and touching a body. For others it will be talking to a person who is dying or their relatives after death. Whatever it is that you find most difficult, try not to hide from the challenge but, at the same time, be kind to yourself. Do your best, but do not expect too much from yourself and ask for help when you need it.

Older people often talk about dying or refer to the fact that they might not be here much longer. This can seem hard to deal with and it is tempting to jolly them out of thoughts of death with comments such as 'don't talk like that' or 'there are years left in you yet'. Although they are well meaning, there is a danger that comments like these will stop people discussing something that is very much on their mind. Death of friends and family becomes a greater part of life as we grow older. One woman in her eighties said that every year she takes out her Christmas card list and crosses out the names of friends who have died since last year. We cannot shelter older people from death and we need to be able to listen if they want to talk about it. You do not have to say anything profound. Just listen and let them talk.

Some people like to feel that they are still in control by making sure that they have their affairs in order before they die. They may want practical help such as arranging for them to go home to collect useful documents or contacting a solicitor to draw up a will. While you should give every possible assistance, care workers are advised not to act as witnesses to legal documents. This avoids the possibility of becoming embroiled in family disputes.

Drawing up a living will is the way some people choose to maintain a sense of control. The will states choices they would like made on their behalf if they become too ill too speak for themselves. They might say that they do not wish to be resuscitated or kept alive by any artifi-

> • Imagine you are asked to look after a 82-year-old woman who is in the terminal stages of an illness. What would be your main concerns over how to care for her?

cial means. Living wills are not legally binding in the UK but health professionals have a duty to take account of the views they express. It is important that all relevant staff are aware that a living will has been drawn up and know where it can be found.

Caring for the dying person

When it is decided that the resident's condition can no longer be adequately treated it does not mean that there is nothing more that can be done. There is much that we can do to care for the person and make their life as comfortable and meaningful as possible. This care is usually termed 'palliative care'. It is very important to begin this care early and not wait until the terminal stages of the illness. Starting pain and symptom control too late often means the person suffers unnecessarily and that the symptoms are poorly controlled.

The physical care of a terminally ill person is about keeping them as comfortable as possible. To do this you need

Palliative care

The World Health Organisation's (1990) definition of palliative care is:
'The active total care of patients whose disease is not responsive to curative treatment. Control of pain and other symptoms, and of psychological, social and spiritual problems is paramount. The goal of palliative care is achievement of the best quality of life for patients and their families'.

Palliative care:
• affirms life and regards dying as a normal process
• neither hastens nor postpones death
• provides relief from pain and other distressing symptoms
• integrates the psychological and spiritual aspects of care
• offers a support system to help patients live as actively as possible until death
• offers a support system to help the family cope during the patient's illness and in his or her own bereavement

to prevent unnecessary problems and minimize symptoms from any underlying disease. One thing you should do is keep skin clean and free from sores. Avoid the drying effects of too much soap and water but remove any soiling and keep skin folds clean and dry. A little of their favourite scent on the bedclothes may be appreciated.

Dying people have a greatly increased risk of pressure sores. All dying older people should be nursed on a pressure relieving device such as an alternating pressure mattress. Regular turning is also important but try to minimize disturbance and discomfort during turns. Use pillows behind the length of the back to shift the person so the weight lies through the right or left buttock rather than turning them right over from hip to hip. This is a technique known as the 30 degree tilt.

Teeth and gums should be gently cleaned with a small-headed, soft toothbrush. If this is not possible, moistened gauze wrapped around a gloved finger is an effective and simple alternative. Oral thrush, making the mouth and tongue red and sore, is common in dying people and can cause considerable discomfort. Thrush is easily treated with anti-fungal medication, so a doctor should be alerted as soon as possible. Sips of whatever fluid the person seems to enjoy should be given for as long as they are wanted but should never be forced on a dying person. Recent research has suggested that dehydration in the last hours of life does not cause additional discomfort.

Disease-related symptoms are many and various. Pain, constipation , nausea, breathlessness, itching and agitation are common. All these problems can be managed with appropriate medication, so it is important that you report anything that seems to be causing discomfort. Do not wait until the symptoms become severe. Early intervention is the secret of good symptom management.

While waiting for professional advice there may be something you can do to make the person more comfortable. A breathless person may feel easier if they can sit up and be near an open window. Pain may be more bearable if there is something else to think about. Anything that provides a distraction, such as playing favourite music, is worth considering. Gentle massage or warming or cooling the affected part may be helpful – but these techniques could have the opposite of the intended effect so you must be guided by the person's wishes or response.

Physical care is only half the story. Good emotional care can be an even greater challenge. You may be worried that you do not know the right things to say. It is not the words you use that matter: it is showing that you care. A smile or touch can sometimes be more important than talking. Visit the dying person whenever you can. Touch their hand and say a few words to let them know you are there even if they cannot respond. **Do not worry about finding the right words. Just be there.**

It has been suggested by Elizabeth Kubler-Ross (1969) that dying people go through five stages:
• denial
• anger
• bargaining
• depression
• acceptance.

This can help you to understand what may seem like irrational behaviour but does not mean that the dying person will progress neatly from stage to stage. None of these stages are right or wrong

> • *'The nurse has just brushed my hair, how do I look?'* (Patient in care home, who died a few hours later.)

and certainly not everyone goes through all of them. It is better to think of them as different reactions people might have at different times in the dying process. They are part of the person trying to cope with life's final and, for some, difficult journey.

Cultural and religious views of death and dying

The moment of death holds immense spiritual significance for most people. Our spiritual beliefs revolve around the way we give meaning to our lives. This may be determined by religion but issues of spirituality are equally important to people who do not belong to any religious group. Providing person-centred care means accepting the beliefs of the dying person even if they conflict with your own. One way you can help older people is to listen to them, show an interest and encourage them to talk about their life. Everyone has a meaningful life but older people may no longer have anybody to tell about it. Be careful not to probe. Let the person choose the direction of the discussion.

It is important that different religious and cultural needs are met with care and sensitivity. A Catholic may need to see a priest before they die; an orthodox Jew may not wish their body to be touched after death; and a Muslim, as they approach death, may wish to face Mecca. Many religions have different sub-sects with different requirements. Even people who do not subscribe to a particular faith may have strong feelings about what should happen to them around the time of their death. The panel on the next page gives a very brief outline and some of the considerations required by four religions but be careful not to use a 'fact file' approach to religious customs. With so many different needs the surest way to know what to do is to ask. If necessary ask relatives when death occurs or is imminent but, ideally, you should try to ask the older person himself or herself. This is not an easy topic to raise. Do not pursue it if the person seems uncomfortable. However, many older people will welcome the chance to tell you how they would like things to be. With their permission, make sure that relevant details are recorded so that they can be easily found when the time comes.

Supporting the family

Facing the death of a family member can be very distressing. Relatives' emotions can be confused and very 'up and down'. Try to give time to them to talk about their feelings and give them as much space and as much information as you can. This is about building trust and a partnership of care between the patient, the nursing and medical staff, and the relatives. Don't assume that relatives only need to be told about major issues. Small things matter too: things the patient has said or done; what sort of night they had; how their symptoms are being managed. Good communication is vital if relatives are to feel supported.

Some relatives feel less distressed if they can make an active contribution to the care of the dying person. Involvement can vary from the relative wishing to control and organise total caregiving to them simply wanting to wash the older person's face and brush their hair. If this accords with the wishes of the dying person, the relatives should be given every support.

Losing somebody close to you can be devastating; this is no less true if they

> • Find out if the setting in which you work has details of local religious leaders who can be contacted to give help and advice and the correct procedures to follow in death and bereavement.

Religious and cultural considerations

Hinduism

- The family will want to be present. A Hindu priest and family will say prayers from the holy books. They may want the person to be laid on the floor to be close to Mother Earth. A basil (tulsi) leaf is dipped in holy water from the Ganges and placed on their lips. The priest may tie a sacred thread around the person's neck or wrist. Every effort should be made to allow them to die at home.
- When death occurs loud shrieks may be expressed. The family will usually perform ritual washing and preparing of the body. If healthcare workers have to wash the body they should wear disposable gloves. Jewellery and any religious objects should not be removed from the body.
- Cremation as soon as possible.

Islam

- The family may wish to say prayers and recite from the Qu'ran. If possible allow the dying person to face Mecca (south east from the UK).
- Ask permission before touching the body. If permission is granted disposable gloves should be worn. The body should normally be washed and prepared by a same sex Muslim and dressed in a white shroud called a Kaffon. Post mortems should be avoided where possible.
- Burial – where possible within 24 hours but most Muslims accept that this may be impractical in this country.

Christianity

- Prayers, anointing and Communion may be performed by an appropriate minister.
- There are no special requirements but prayers may be said for the deceased and the bereaved.
- Burial and cremation are acceptable.

Sikhism

- A dying Sikh will be comforted by reciting hymns from the holy book. If they are too ill then a relative or reader from the local temple may do so. A Sikh will want to die with the name of God being recited. They may also want to have Amrit (holy water) in their mouth.
- Non-Sikhs may perform last offices but permission must be gained from the family and the family must be given the opportunity to do this. The body should be covered in a plain white sheet. The five Ks should not be disturbed. They are: kesa ('hair') no hair or beard should be cut; kangha ('comb'); kacch ('drawers'), worn by soldiers; kirpan ('sabre'); and kara ('bracelet') of steel, commonly worn on the right arm.
- Sikhs are always cremated.

are very elderly. The process of supporting a dying person can take a large physical and emotional toll on the relatives and friends who have cared for them. They are at greater risk of developing ill health. Guilt is an emotion commonly expressed by relatives, perhaps because they felt they could have done more, perhaps because they persuaded the person to go into a care home, or perhaps for things said and not said in the past. Such feelings can lead to depression and self neglect and may make bereavement all the more difficult.

There are many theories of grief. Colin Murray Parkes, for example, suggests that people pass through stages such as shock and alarm, searching, anger and guilt and, it is hoped, eventually resolution. Another theory suggests we have to work through a series of tasks:

• To accept the reality of the loss
• To experience the pain of grief
• To adjust to an environment no longer containing the loved one

• To relocate the deceased and move on.

While these are helpful in that we can recognise these emotions and behaviours as normal, it is important not to expect people to fall in with theoretical models. Just as people who are dying show a whole variety of emotions and behaviour, so do people who are bereaved. There is not a 'right way' and people's emotions are often confused. Try to accept that some people will show little outward emotion while others might be distraught and others again may seem angry and confused. It is important that you do not make judgements but accept the emotions expressed. Families are complex and death can reawaken hidden tensions. You need to put your own emotions and beliefs to one side so that you can offer support to all those who have been bereaved. There are no words that can take away grief, so just show them that you care. A hug or a squeeze of the hand can sometimes say more than words ever could.

CARING FOR THE PERSON IMMEDIATELY AFTER DEATH

When somebody dies you need to think about who needs to be informed. When death is expected, the first people you think of are the close relatives. Ideally they will have nominated one person who should be contacted and can then tell the rest of the family. The relative may have specified that they would prefer to wait until morning if the death occurs at night.

For an unexpected death the doctor must be called immediately but, where death has been expected, most doctors would prefer not to be called during the night.

There are no hard and fast rules about how 'last offices' should be carried out. A lot of myths tend to surround them

and you should be guided by local protocol. However, the following procedure and the dos and don'ts listed in the box opposite should act as a useful guide.

The main points to remember are that you need to:

• Show concern for friends and relatives
• Show respect for the person who has died
• Follow local policies, particularly regarding paperwork.

Occasionally a relative might want to be involved in performing the last offices. These wishes should be accommodated if at all possible.

As a care worker you may have your own beliefs about death. Some people, for instance, like to open a window for

A few guiding dos and don'ts for last offices

- Do cover any wounds with a clean dressing
- Don't feel you must wash the body unless it is soiled
- Do close the eyes, but do not put pennies on them to keep them closed or tape them down. If they open slightly do not worry
- Don't tie the person's feet together
- Don't pack body openings (orifices). If there is any leakage of body fluids, just use a pad
- Do be careful not to do anything that would have been out of the ordinary for someone had they been alive. For instance don't put lipstick on a woman who normally never wears it
- Do put the person's dentures in
- Don't bandage up the jaw
- Don't wrap the person in a sheet. Just leave them clean and in a clean nightdress or pyjamas
- Do remember to observe any religious or cultural needs
- Don't remove jewellery unless you are sure that it is what the person or their family would have wished
- Do take account of any special requests from the person or their family.

the spirit to leave. Actions like these are fine provided that they do not conflict with the beliefs and wishes of the older person or their family.

Friends and relatives may wish to see the deceased person before they are taken to the mortuary. It is always best to make this assumption and make the person look their best. It may be necessary to cover the deceased person's face with a sheet, especially in the summer when there may be flies around. Turn the covers back before relatives come into the room and put the person's arms on the outside of the sheets so the relatives can easily hold their hands. It is also worth thinking about the other staff including domestic and catering staff who may also wish for a chance to say goodbye.

Caring for the body after death is an opportunity to show your care and respect for the person who has died. Relatives have said how comforting they found it to overhear nurses talking to their deceased father as they washed his body. Another relative said how pleased

he was that nurses did not switch off the light as they left the room where his wife's body lay.

Collecting belongings can be a stressful task so presenting them clean and well-ordered is another important part of the care you can give to bereaved relatives.

Paperwork is vital so that there is no opportunity for mistaken identity and to ensure that accurate checks and records are kept. Different areas will have their own policies about what forms should be completed. Some hospitals may specify that the body should be wrapped in a specific way and forms attached to these coverings. Care homes are more likely to leave the deceased person in their own night clothes but it remains equally important that documents are carefully completed and given to the relevant people.

You should take all normal precautions regarding infection control. This means wearing gloves when dealing with body fluids. The risk of contracting

Some of the reasons for referral to a coroner

- Has not seen a doctor during his or her last illness
- The doctor has not seen the person during the 14 days prior to death or seen the body after death
- The death may have been caused by an industrial disease
- Any unexpected or unexplained death
- Any death in suspicious circumstances
- Any death which an accident may have caused or contributed to
- Any death due to neglect, poisoning, or misuse of drugs
- Any death which may be related to surgery or anaesthetic.

infection is no less and no greater than when the person was alive. If you were following special precautions before death these need to be continued but you do not need to take any additional precautions.

Tubes and catheters can be removed to improve appearances but should be left in place if this was a sudden death that will need to be referred to a coroner. A coroner enquires into those deaths reported to them. It is their duty to find out the medical cause of the death if it is not known, and to enquire about the cause of it if it was due to violence or was otherwise unnatural. Details of how to contact your local coroner should be kept available, but it is normally the doctor who decides whether the case needs to be referred or not – see the box above.

Working with other agencies

It is up to the family to specify which funeral director is to be used. For expected death this is usually known in

- If you work in a care home it might be useful to talk to residents and other members of staff about how best to manage death so that it is not hidden and forbidden but a shared experience in which all staff and residents can say goodbye

advance so that they can be contacted at the appropriate time. Some funeral directors make an extra charge if they are called out of office hours but they will normally have an on-call service so that they can be contacted at any time. They will need to know if the body is for funeral or cremation so that they can arrange the required doctors' certificates.

The funeral director will work with the family to organise the burial or cremation in the way that they would wish. They will be able to respond to any special cultural needs such as witnessing the actual process of cremation. They will also give advice on such diverse topics as whether or not the body should be embalmed and how to plan the funeral ceremony.

The funeral cannot be conducted until the death is registered. The family, or somebody acting on their behalf, does this at the local registry office. They will need to take the death certificate that will have been completed by the doctor shortly after the death occurs. It is useful if you know the whereabouts of the local office and can direct the relatives.

Organ donation and transplants

The older person may have expressed a wish for their body to be used for organ donation or medical science. For kidney donation there is an upper age limit of 70 and for heart and lung transplants the age limit is as low as 50. Donation of the cornea (part of the eye) may still be possible from older people and can be made up to 24 hours after death.

Leaving the body to medical science usually means for anatomical dissection. A wish for this to happen must have been expressed during life. The next of kin technically own the body and must also agree to it.

The approach would normally be made to the local medical school. Their objective is to explore normal structures, so they may reject a body if there are severe arthritic changes or if there has been major surgery.

Supporting self and others

It is not just family and friends who grieve when somebody dies. Staff and other residents may also feel the loss. One of the issues with staff is remembering to inform those not on duty. Some care homes have developed systems such as putting a discreet marker on the bedroom door. Another home took the photograph from the drug chart and pinned it to the staff notice board. This way staff who have been on holiday or away for a few days would have the information as soon as they return.

Residents in care homes are often sheltered from the fact that a fellow resident has died. This may be appropriate if the death was of a resident not well known to the others. Death of a long-term resident is a different matter. At one home the residents' committee complained that they felt left out. They wanted to be treated as any other close friend who would be kept informed when somebody was ill. They wanted the opportunity to visit the dying person, to attend their funeral and to mark their loss once they had gone. This was partly because they wanted their grief acknowledged but also because they wanted to know that their own death would be marked in some way. Some care homes insist that the patient came in through the front door and they should leave through the front door and do so in a dignified way. It is worth talking to residents, staff and local funeral directors to see how this can be best managed. It is also worth thinking about whether some form of memorial such as a memorial book where pictures and details of those who have died can be kept. If residents know that the staff really care when someone dies then they may be reassured that they will receive the same treatment when their time draws near.

Caring for a dying person and their family is never easy. Every person's hopes and fears at the time of death are different so there can be no blueprint of what to do and what to say. The event belongs to that older person and their family. Your role is to support them in the best way you can. The emotional demands on you will be high but there is great satisfaction in knowing that you have made even the slightest difference.

Further reading

Cooke H (2000) *When someone dies: A practical guide to holistic care at the end of life.* Butterworth Heinmann, Oxford.

Twycross R (2003) *Introducing Palliative Care* (4th edition), Radcliffe Medical Press, Oxford.

Kubler-Ross E (1969) *On Death and Dying.* Macmillan.

Russell P (2002) Dying, death & spirituality, in Hogston R & PM (eds), *Foundations of Nursing Practice.* Macmillan Press Ltd, Basingstoke.

Sander R & Russell P (2001) Care for dying people in nursing homes. *Nursing Older People* 13(2) 21-6.

Tschudin V (1997). *Counselling for loss and bereavement.* Ballière Tindall, London.

World Health Organisation (WHO) (1990) Cancer Pain Relief and Palliative Care Technical Report Series 804. WHO, Geneva.

Chapter 12 - Care for the dying person and their family

ESSENCE OF CARE

None

NMS

| 11.1 | 11.2 | 11.3 | 11.4 | 11.5 | 11.6 | 11.7 | 11.8 | 11.9 | 11.10 | 11.11 | 11.12 |

NSF

None

TOPSS

None

NVQ 2 CARE

Z15.1
All performance Criteria range and Knowledge met
Z15.2
All performance Criteria range and Knowledge met

NVQ 3 CARE

NC3.1
All performance Criteria range and Knowledge met
NC3.2
All performance Criteria range and Knowledge met
NC3.3
All performance Criteria range and Knowledge met   *Compiled by Adrian Muir*

CHAPTER 13

Supporting residents and relatives

Brendan McCormack

Moving into a care home – a major life change • Easing the transition: the environment, support and respect, making sense of what is happening, encouraging participation in care • Giving and gathering information • Welcoming the resident • Supporting the family

Being old is not some kind of illness but a position of pride and respect that you have earned. People should want to be old. They should look forward to it. (Taylor 1992)

This chapter will explore the role of relatives and families in helping the older person adjust to life in a care home. It will particularly focus on the idea of 'transition', that is, the adjustments made in order to come to terms with a significant change in one's life. The chapter will describe approaches to working with older people that can help them adjust to this transition to life in a care home.

The role of families in care decisions

Families play an important role in all of our lives. For older people, the ageing process means that for many, their role in the family network changes. Family participation in care decisions often centres on the balance between promoting independence and controlling the degree of risk that an older person can take. Sometimes people think that someone closely involved with an older person, other than a care professional, is in the best position to act on their behalf and make decisions for them. Indeed, sometimes it is argued that people who are not employed as health professionals should work with older people to protect them from the power and control of care staff.

While we do know that care workers can exert a lot of power over older people, it is also true that family members themselves could do this. Because family members can be so powerful, care staff often give in to family members even though it might not be in the best interest of the older person. Family members can become another form of power that older people have to fight against, and this can be very difficult for them to do.

It is important that family members are involved in decision-making, and the government insists on this through legislation and policies such as the Care Standards Act. This approach is based on the idea that family members are important sources of information about their relatives' values and previous life choices and can confirm the views expressed by residents in conversations with care staff. However, we need to be cautious about this, as not all family members know their relatives well enough to make the same the choices for them that the person would make for themselves.

For example, I have a good relationship with my mother but I have not lived with her for a long time – so I would be unfamiliar with the kind of choices she might make every day for herself. It would be inappropriate for me to try to represent her in decision-making. Another issue to consider is that a son or daughter may lack the interest or skill to be an active player in their parent's health care. Children in this situation may be motivated by different things which could influence their decision: they may be overwhelmed with the demands of being a carer, with guilt, or financial burdens.

So we can see that involving family members in decision-making is difficult. As care workers, we can place too much emphasis on the decisions made by family members and so take away the older person's right to make decisions for themselves.

What is a 'transition'?

The word 'transition' means moving from one place, state or stage to another. So, in our context, a transition can be thought of as a process of adapting to a change in circumstances and the way the older person experiences that change. For example, the person deciding to move to a care home is experiencing a major change in circumstance (in giving up their own home).

Some transitions may be planned, such as retirement. Other transitions occur suddenly and without opportunity to make preparations, such as developing an illness. However, in both cases a transition is started because the person's current reality (circumstance) is disrupted. Individuals differ in their ability to adapt to such disruption. In many cases the transition to nursing home care will occur with ease as the older person recognises the need for care and support and identifies the potential for new opportunities, while for others it may signify failure, despair and loss of identity. However the individual copes with their change of reality, the transition requires the person to adapt and this will occur over a period of time. The 'stages of death' model offered by Kubler-Ross (1969) describes a process of adaptation that may be experienced by people who are dying (see Chapter 12).

Sex and relationships

Some of us hope that sex won't rear its ugly head in patients and residents, and even if it does we would rather translate the sexual needs of older people as social needs (such as being lonely) because it's more comfortable for us.

A recent story of a family trying to find a suitable nursing home placement for their parents demonstrated this attitude. The couple had never slept apart from each other except during periods of hospitalisation and therefore wanted a room together with a double bed.

The difficulties experienced by the family in finding such a place were enormous, as the logic went: if the couple were well enough to sleep together, then did they really need care in a nursing home? These kind of attitudes and beliefs work against older people and their friends and family making a successful transition to a care home setting.

Facing the prospect of long-term care

Joan and Brigid are two patients on a rehabilitation ward being faced with the reality that they will require long-term care in the future. They are both trying to come to terms with their disabilities following a stroke. For both of them it is a psychologically and socially painful prospect.

Joan has ample resources to help her cope with the inevitable losses this will bring. She is a determined woman who has always been in control of her own affairs. She has a supportive family who are committed to finding her the home that exactly suits her values and needs. She also has the financial security to make such decisions. She further believes that life will be easier for her in a care home as she won't have to worry about the 'daily drudges' of life but instead can concentrate on her own particular interests. She has for some time found main-taining her large Victorian property to be too much for her.

Brigid, however, has low resources at this time in her life. She finds the daily help she needs intolerable as she has always been a private person. Her husband had previously been the only person to see her naked and she now feels 'dirty' and 'undignified' because of her circumstances. However, her husband is dead and her speech problems prevent her from being able to explain to the nurses her beliefs and values. She is financially insecure and will have to rely on the state to pay for her care. She has heard 'bad reports' about the home she is being moved to, but because of a lack of available places elsewhere, she knows she has to accept it. Therefore the losses far outweigh the resources in Brigid's case.

As the older person adapts to living in a care home, not only does he or she experience considerable change, but the lives of family members, 'significant others' (people who are important to them) and carers are affected. The extent of the change experienced depends on the roles and relationships in place before the transition. However, some people cope better with the transition to a care home than others.

Consider the examples of Joan and Brigid in the box above. They demonstrate the importance of addressing the issue of resources and losses when considering how well a person will adapt to change, and begin to clarify why two people may adapt to the same transition in very different ways. Such considerations are essential when assisting the older person to make the transition from independent living to continuing care.

Easing the transition

Considering a care home placement can be very emotionally charged and complex. Placing a loved one in a home can evoke family guilt, anger and resentment and the family member being placed may also feel helpless, abandoned and rejected. The situation is not helped by the negative image of care homes that still exists in our society, negative reports about the conditions in some care homes and the financial reality of the decision. Good care home placement requires everybody to acknowledge the problems and difficulties such a decision brings. How can this be done? I would suggest that five issues need to be considered:
• The environment
• Support
• Respect
• Helping the older person make sense of what is happening
• Encouraging participation.

The environment

It is important that the home provides an environment that the older person finds to be 'healing'. By that I mean an environment which helps the person come to terms with what is happening to them in their life. While the provision of comfortable, pleasant and homely living conditions goes some way towards the creation of a healing environment, the relationship between resident and carer can guarantee it. However, this is not a one-way relationship, ie carer to resident and family. It is the kind of relationship where all parties grow as a result of their relationship with each other. This kind of care is itself a kind of healing art, a clinical art that is creative. It involves 'being with the person' and doing things 'with' the resident rather than 'to' them.

In addition, the older person's surroundings and approaches to their care should recognise the unique journey they are making, which began with their detachment from their family. To an older person, their own home and the presence of a clutter of familiar possessions helps to preserve a sense of security in a world that moves too fast. It may be that older people are disturbed by changes in their physical environment as much as they are about loss of contact with friends or family. Their new home should offer a stable environment on which the person can stamp their own individuality. Acceptance of the individual way in which the person lives their life is perhaps one of the best qualities to show in caregiving, and goes some way towards preserving the person's sense of their own identity.

Support

To be supportive, the care worker must believe in the worth of the resident as a person and build on their strengths and capabilities by assisting them to make decisions that are consistent with their beliefs and values. Once a decision has been made, it is the role of the care worker to provide the support necessary for the person to reach their desired goal(s). This calls for flexibility and creativity in the way care services in the home are organised. Activities such as providing comfort during periods of pain and distress; providing appropriate, accurate and timely information to the resident and their family; giving emotional support; and staying with the person when they feel alone and helpless are all forms of supportive activities. If care workers show sensitivity and interest in each person as an individual, that will in turn encourage and enable the family to feel a part of the care process.

Respect

One of the most effective ways that care workers can show they do care, is through behaviour that makes the older person feel they are respected and cared about as a human being. This kind of respect acknowledges the many years of experience the older person has. Older people who have experienced this genuine respect report that it feels like a form of healing in itself, and that it helps them to come to terms with the changes in their lives.

The focus should then be on helping the older person to see themself in the context of being a citizen of the home, rather than through the limited context of a 'resident' (which can suggest being present in someone else's home, ie being a lodger!). Examples of how to help the older person to feel more like a citizen of the home include:

• Care planning between staff, resident and family/friends
• Residents' committees
• Involvement in menu planning
• Special interest groups

- Involvement in staff selection interviews
- Involvement in quality meetings (about how the home is run)
- Social events that include family and friends
- Involving families in caregiving.

All of these examples come from care homes in the UK. Good person-centred care will ensure that organisation of the home includes the older person being part of the planning and decision-making of the place where they live.

Making sense of what is happening

The emphasis here is on helping the person to cope with losses in their social identity, and make the transition to their new world. It is important to avoid making assumptions about the individual or imposing rules and regulations before they have established their own identity in the home. When an older person moves to a care home, the care worker should work with the person and their family to find out what the experience means to them and what kind of support they need. When this understanding is achieved, it is easier to work out how to respond in practice to the person's individual behaviour and emotional responses.

It is important to approach assessment from the resident's viewpoint. If the focus of assessment of older people's needs is purely on activities of daily living, an understanding of the person's uniqueness can never be gained. Is that person really just a collection of body systems, one or more of which now fails to work properly? Or can we see that person as an individual who has marked out a unique journey in order to reach this stage of their life, and now requires help to move on to the next stage?

By taking what is called a 'biographical approach' to assessment, we can build up a unique, individual picture of the person. A person's biography can be seen as an account of events that have influenced and directed their life. It is the history that gives meaning to the way the older person deals with particular situations and experiences, and knowing this history helps the care worker make better decisions. Involving family and friends in constructing the biography is a good way of helping them cope with the transition of the older person to residential care.

Encouraging participation

Older people should be actively involved in their care programme, with every effort made to maximise their physical and mental independence. This means we should always aim to do things *with* the resident, not *to* them. This active involvement provides a form of rehabilitation that is aimed at improving independence with such things as walking, washing and dressing; preventing secondary complications (such as pressure sores); and promotion of psychological well-being, confidence and self-esteem. In our current finance-driven world, savings in care staff time, pressure area treatments, wound dressings, incontinence pads, mobility aids and drugs could also be made through an emphasis on rehabilitation.

Giving and gathering information

The understanding and knowledge of why people react in different ways when they have to move into a care home, must be used in practical ways to ensure the person and their family are supported through a difficult time.

Although care staff are not often directly involved in the arrangements for the admission of a new resident, they may be involved in the preparation of the room, some aspects of the assessment, or when the person comes to view the home. All of these encounters will make an impression on the person, and will influence their decisions. For some people, the choice of the home will be very limited because of their special needs, the area where they live or because of cost. This must not affect the efforts that staff make to ensure that the resident and their family feel that the home is the right choice for them.

Supporting a family and the potential resident begins before they have even chosen the home. When a person is thinking about moving to a care setting, the home should supply the person and their family with information. This should be written in a way that is easy to see and easy to understand. It should not be written in professional jargon. There should also be information given about the type of people the home cares for, the facilities and size of the home, the qualifications of the staff and a copy of the most recent inspection report.

This brochure can give other information, perhaps about activities, social events or how relatives are encouraged to stay involved.

The older person and their family should be encouraged to visit the home and view it as anyone would who was thinking of moving. Care staff who see visitors should remember all of their communication skills, especially that first impressions are the most important.

Visitors should be offered information about how independence is encouraged, how each person will be enabled to live their life as far as possible in their own way, meal arrangements and menus, in a warm and welcoming way.

Residents may be happy to talk to visitors looking around the home, giving their opinions of what it is like to live there.

A full pre-admission assessment will be carried out by a senior member of the team. This will ensure that all the care needs of the older person can be assessed, and a plan made for their admission. The assessment will include finding out about the person and their life, their activities and what they would like to carry on doing when they move in. Discussion about the decoration of their room, choice of new carpet or plans for their furniture to be moved will all assist in helping the older person feel involved in the plans.

Plans for admission should be worked out so that everyone knows what is happening. This may involve a number of different agencies, and can sometimes take weeks to arrange. Care staff who receive messages must record the information and tell the relevant people. All documents sent from other care providers should be put in the files. Rules of confidentiality apply, and there is a balance between ensuring the new resident feels welcome by telling existing residents about them, and giving away information which is confidential.

Welcoming the resident

When a person moves into a care setting it will inevitably be an anxious time. The room should be welcoming. Some homes write a welcome card, while others leave some flowers. The room must be warm and clean and smell pleasant. Helping the person to unpack will allow conversation, and an opportunity for questions.

Always be aware that the person may not remember things that have been said, either because of a memory problem or because there is too much new information.

Another resident may be happy to act as a 'buddy' for the first few days; alternatively staff must ensure that the care plan shows the person will need more support and guidance at first.

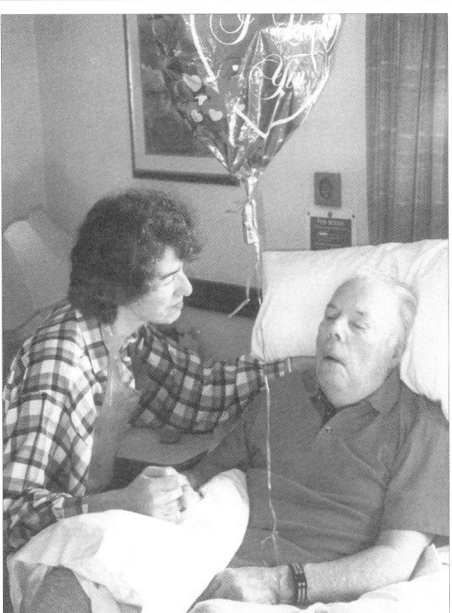

SUE BENSON/AGECARE

A spouse should be invited to visit at any time, have meals at the home or assist in care

Some questions are obviously important while others may seem silly to the care staff. All questions are important to the person asking them, and staff must respect that. Equally, they must ensure that the new resident does not feel that the staff don't want them because they are too much work, or that the staff have taken a dislike to them. If a staff member is finding that they are having difficulties with a new resident, it is the staff's problem to solve.

The new resident may need extra support over the first few weeks, so staff should be alert and sensitive. Emotional support is vital as people come to terms with the change in their lives.

Supporting the family

The decision to move to a care home will affect many people. Care staff must ensure that the family is supported in both practical and emotional ways. Most important is to show that the new resi-

dent is cared for and cared about. The relatives have entrusted their loved one to people they don't know well, and trust can only be developed if the care team prove worthy of it. It may come through making sure small but essential things are done – being helpful to the person in some way, ensuring they have washed if they cannot help themselves, that they have drinks or that glasses are being worn. Any of these small issues could become enormous if the family do not feel the staff care.

A spouse should be invited to visit at any time, have meals at the home or assist in the care. The home should ensure that any family member who wants to remain involved is able to do so, in whatever way that is possible.

Care staff should think about what the family won't know or might want to know. Families should be able to ask questions of anyone, but a key worker could be specifically appointed to help them. Some homes have a slightly different welcome pack for the resident as well as one for the family. This is an excellent way of communicating a number of small but important pieces of information.

As the person settles and is no longer considered 'new', it is important to continue to offer means of support and communication with the families. This can be through social events, regular family meetings, or a key worker telephoning if the family lives a long way away. Family members could also play a more active role through planning and quality assurance committees, a league of friends or even staff interview panels.

Conclusion

Working with an older person, their family and their friends in the way that is described here can be thought of as a shared process of learning; that is, I as a care worker am learning from the older person as well as them learning from me. In this way the resident is given a real part to play in helping the care worker discover new ways of working, and a real partnership can be established. Fresh insights emerge and the tendency to fall back on to the old ritualised ways of doing things is avoided. There are, of course, other times when firmness in approach has to be taken and sometimes without this firmness the person would feel insecure and at risk. However, as long as the reasons for this are made clear in the plan of care, the sense of partnership can still be maintained.

In working with older people and their families it is important that care workers strive to understand the *whole* person. We need to adopt approaches that focus on individuals and their different ways of living, learning from them in order to create the appropriate care environment – not expecting people to fit in to a set of rules and routines just because they now live in a care home. The approach to care described here tries to give the older person as many opportunities as possible to exercise freedom of choice, to express opinions, to make decisions and to talk while we really listen.

References

Kubler-Ross E (1969) *On Death and Dying.* Macmillan, London.
Taylor A (1993) *Older Than Time.* Harper Collins Publishers, London.

Useful reading

The Relatives Association (1997) *As others see us.* 5 Tavistock Place, London WC1H 9SN.

Chapter 13 - Supporting residents and relatives

ESSENCE OF CARE			
Privacy & dignity			
1	2	3	
Record Keeping			
2			
NMS			
5.1			
7.6			
12.1	12.2		
13.1	13.2	13.3	13.6
14.1			
NSF			
2.1	2.13		
8.2			
TOPSS			
Induction			
1.1.1	1.1.	1.2.1	1.2.2
2.3.2	2.3.5		
3.2.1	3.2.9		
Foundation			
1.1.1	1.1.2	1.2.1	1.4.1
2.5.3			
3.1.1			
5.2.1	5.2.3		
NVQ 2 CARE			
W3.1			
All Performance Criteria, Range and Knowledge			
W3.2			
1 All Performance Criteria, Range and Knowledge			

Glossary of terms

Abuse. Physical, verbal or emotional mistreatment or exploitation of another person.

Accreditation of Prior Learning (for NVQ). The assessment of an individual's past achievements against national standards.

Acute. Used to describe an illness or condition that is of relatively short duration, and usually severe.

Advocate. A person who supports, encourages, defends and negotiates on behalf of another by representing them where they are unsure or unable to represent themselves.

Agitation. An extreme state of distress where the person may experience physical signs of restlessness and feel uneasy and tense.

AIDS (Acquired Immunodeficiency Syndrome – see also HIV). A condition caused by a virus called Human Immunodeficiency Virus (HIV). It damages the defence system so that the body cannot fight infection. AIDS can cause people to develop certain forms of cancer, and to get serious infections of the lungs, digestive system, the brain and skin. It is passed on by exchanging body fluids such as blood, semen and vaginal fluids.

Allergy. A reaction to a substance to which a person is sensitive. Examples include fur, dust, alcohol, certain foods, insect stings and medicines. Usually causes skin rashes, but can be more severe causing difficulty with breathing due to swelling of the throat and airway. Death can occur. (See also Anaphylaxis).

Alzheimer's disease (see also Dementia). A form of dementia characterised by changes to the brain. Disorientation, loss of memory and intellectual function, apathy and difficulty with coordinating movement, speech and thoughts are common features.

Amnesia. Loss of memory.

Anaemia. Shortage of the oxygen-carrying part (haemoglobin) of the blood's red cells. This may be because the body is losing too much haemoglobin (eg due to bleeding) or because it is not making enough (eg due to a shortage of iron in the diet).

Anaesthetic. A substance that can cause temporary loss of the sensation of pain or consciousness. As a "local" anaesthetic it numbs a specific part of the body only. As a "general" anaesthetic it causes the patient to lose consciousness.

Analgesics. Medicines that provide relief from pain.

Anaphylactic shock. A severe reaction causing swelling of the airway and possible respiratory and cardiac arrest. It can occur when a medicine or injection is given. It can also occur if people are allergic to a particular food or are bitten or stung by an insect.

Angina. Chest pain due to oxygen shortage in the heart muscles. Caused by narrowing or blockage of the coronary arteries which supply the heart muscle with oxygen.

Anorexia. This is the loss of desire to eat. Emotional disturbances, such as depression, may induce a chronic state of anorexia.

Antibiotics. Medicines which either kill bacteria or stop them multiplying. They have no effect on a virus.

Anticonvulsant drugs. Medicines which are used to treat epilepsy.

Anti-depressant drugs. Medicines that are used in the treatment of depression. These drugs act upon and stimulate parts of the nervous system.

Anti-emetics. Medicines that are used to prevent nausea and sickness.

Anti-histamine. Medicines and creams used to counter the symptoms of an allergic reaction, eg irritation and itching of the skin.

Anus (see also Colon and Rectum). The muscular ring at the end of the intestinal canal.

Anxiety state. A condition in which the individual is so worried about a certain situation, that their life is severely restricted. The main characteristic is the inability to relax.

Arteriosclerosis. A gradual loss of elasticity in the walls of arteries due to thickening and the build up of calcium and cholesterol deposits. This may cause decreased blood flow and oxygen supply to essential parts of the brain and body.

Artery. A blood vessel carrying blood containing oxygen around the body.

Arthritis (see also Osteoarthritis and Rheumatoid Arthritis). Inflammation causing pain, stiffness or swelling in one or more joints. There may be several different types including osteoarthritis and rheumatoid arthritis. Main causes are inflammation, and the effects of wear and tear.

Aseptic. Free from germs and bacteria that cause infection.

Assessment. The systematic collection of information by observing, interviewing and examining an individual and their social environment in order to develop a plan of care.

Assessment (for NVQ). The process of collecting evidence and making judgements on whether national standards have been met.

Assessors (for NVQ). Individuals approved by assessment centres to judge evidence of competence.

Asthma. A condition in which the tubes of the lung have a fluctuating and reversible tendency to narrow causing breathlessness, coughing, wheezing or chest tightness. It may be triggered by an allergy.

Audiometer. A machine used to test a person's ability to hear normally.

Audit (see also Standards and Quality Assurance). A methodical process of examining (for example, practical care, record keeping and client satisfaction with services) against agreed standards.

Autopsy. See post mortem.

Barrier cream. A cream, usually water based, that is applied to the skin to prevent drying or damage, for example when a person is incontinent.

BCG. A vaccine given to prevent people contracting Tuberculosis (TB). See also Immunisation.

Benign. When describing a tumour means favourable, non-cancerous, usually contained within a capsule and not spreading to other parts of the body.

Bereavement. The human response to loss, usually as a result of a person dying. It also occurs when a person has lost something personal and important to them, such as their home, or a limb.

Blood pressure. The force of blood in the arteries measured in millimetres of mercury by a machine called a sphygmo-manometer. Blood pressures are written down as two figures. The top figure is called "systolic" and the bottom figure is called "diastolic". How high or low the blood pressure is depends on the strength of the heart beat and the condition of the arteries.

Bradycardia. A marked slowing of the rate of the heart.

Braille. A system of writing and printing by means of raised points representing letters which allows blind and partially sighted people to read by touch.

Bronchitis. Inflammation of the air tubes of the lungs. It may be "acute" due to infection, or "chronic" due to excessive production of mucus caused by many factors including pollution and smoking.

Bronchodilators. Medicines used to widen the lung airways.

Cancer. A large group of diseases which are linked together. In each case there is uncontrolled new abnormal tissue growth of the affected part/s of the body. The outlook for each cancer sufferer is dependent upon the site and type of the growth.

Capillaries. Tiny blood vessels that lie between arteries bringing blood to the tissues, and veins taking blood away.

Cardiac arrest. Used to describe a situation in which the heart suddenly stops beating.

Cardio-pulmonary resuscitation (CPR). The technique used to try and restart a heart after a person has had a cardiac arrest. It includes breathing into the person's lungs and externally massaging the heart in a regular and systematic way.

Carer. The term usually applied to a person who provides care at home without receiving a salary or wage. Most often it is a female relative of a dependent person.

Cataract. A clouding of the lens of the eye preventing light passing through it. Vision becomes very dim or is lost altogether.

Catheter. A tube which is passed into the body to drain away fluids. The most common is the urinary catheter for draining the bladder.

Cerebrovascular accident (CVA). See stroke.

Cervix. The neck of the womb.

Chemotherapy. The treatment of disease by medicines or chemicals. The term is often used for cancer treatment, which can make the person feel very unwell, nauseous and cause hair loss.

Chronic. A term used to describe a long standing and continued disease process. There may be progressive deterioration (sometimes despite treatment).

Chronic obstructive pulmonary disease (COPD). A lung disease in which a combination of chronic bronchitis and emphysema causes persistent obstruction of airflow in and out of the lungs. Patients are invariably short of breath.

Coeliac disease. Sensitivity to gluten, a protein found in cereals (wheat, rye and barley). In adults the disease tends to show as a deficiency of one or more nutrients because these are not absorbed properly. Other symptoms are weight loss, tiredness and irritability.

Cognition. Consciously knowing, understanding and having insight into personal and environmental events. The person may not necessarily be able to take action.

Colic. A sharp pain resulting from spasm of a muscle, commonly the stomach and gut.

Colon (see also Anus and Rectum). A part of the large intestine that absorbs nutrients and fluid from the diet. It ends at the anus.

Colostomy. See Stoma.

Compliance aid. A storage box for tablets. Contains sections for each day and the time that the medicine should be taken. Helps to remind people of when to take medicines.

Competence (for NVQ). The ability to perform an activity to the agreed standard. The assessment of competence forms the basis for NVQs and SVQs.

Compress. Soft pad of gauze or cloth used to apply heat, cold or medications to the surface of the body.

Concussion. A temporary loss of consciousness due to a knock on the head. The person becomes pale, has a feeble pulse and shallow breathing.

Confusion. Condition in which consciousness is clouded, so that the individual is unable to think clearly or act rationally. Confusional states may be temporary, due to acute illness (toxic confusional states), or long term and irreversible.

Connective tissue. The supporting tissues of the body, found under the skin, between muscles, and supporting blood vessels and nerves. Their functions are mainly mechanical, connecting other active tissues and organs.

Constipation. Incomplete or infrequent action of the bowels, due to lack of muscle activity, insufficient fluids or inadequate diet.

Continence (see also Incontinence). The ability to control the functions of passing urine or faeces when desired.

Contra-indication. A reason for not doing something, such as giving a medicine as this could have an adverse effect on the person.

COPD. Chronic obstructive pulmonary disease.

Coronary artery disease. Narrowing or blockage of the arteries supplying the heart with oxygen. Usually due to blockage of the coronary arteries. Also known as coronary heart disease or coronary vascular disease.

Counselling. A skilled method of listening to and talking with a person or a group of people, to enable them to overcome a problem, make a decision or accept their circumstances.

Cramp. Painful contraction of a muscle, associated with salt loss. Failure to replace salt or fluids, a lack of oxygen reaching the muscle, or poisons of various kinds may be the cause.

Crohn's disease. See Inflammatory bowel disease.

Culture. The values, attitudes, lifestyle and customs shared by a group of people and passed from one generation to the next.

Cyanosed. Bluish discolouration of the skin, particularly the lips, due to shortage of oxygen supply.

Cytology. The microscopic study of the cells of the body.

Defaecation. The act of opening the bowels.

Dehydration. Excessive loss of fluid from the body caused by vomiting, diarrhoea or sweating or because of inadequate fluid intake.

Dementia (see also Alzheimer's disease). An organic mental illness caused by changes to the brain. This may be a result of disease or damage. The principal changes include inability to learn and retain information, inability to recall recent events, and feelings of anxiety and depression. This may lead to disorientation and confused behaviour.

Depression. A profound sadness, distinct from normal bereavement or loss. Its features include reduced enjoyment, slowness and a lack of interest in life or the lives of others.

Dexterity. The ability to use fingers and hands to undertake everyday activities.

Diabetes. Failure of the pancreas in the body to produce insulin, or failure of the body to use the insulin correctly. Insulin breaks down sugary foods, allowing the body to use it for energy. Diabetes results in too much sugar circulating in the blood. Normal body functioning, for example wound healing, is affected by the condition. It is treated by diet alone, medicines or insulin.

Digoxin. One of the earliest discovered medicines which was found to have a beneficial effect on the failing heart.

Disorientation. A state of confusion in which an individual has lost a sense of where they are, what time it is and what they are doing.

Diuretic. A medicine which stimulates the kidney to produce more urine.

Diverticulitis. A condition in which there is inflammation of small pockets (diverticulae) of large bowel which stick through the muscle surrounding the bowel at weak points. Generally caused by long-standing constipation.

Down's syndrome. A congenital disorder caused by an extra chromosome. The person may have marked learning difficulties and heart problems.

Dysarthria. A speech disorder caused by poor muscle movement or poor muscle co-ordination, often following a stroke.

Dyslexia. Difficulty with reading and writing.

Dysphagia. Difficulty with swallowing.

Dysphasia. A language disorder which may affect understanding, speaking, reading and writing (often due to a stroke).

Eczema. A condition of the skin causing dryness, flaking and extreme itching.

Elimination. The removal of waste matter from the body.

Encephalitis. Inflammation of the brain, usually due to a virus.

Enema. Procedure involving the introduction of a fluid into the rectum for cleansing or therapeutic purposes.

Enteral feeding. Provision of nutrients through a tube directly into the stomach when the person cannot chew or swallow food but can digest and absorb the nutrients.

Epilepsy. A condition in which excessive or unregulated electrical activity in the brain causes fits. These may involve the whole body with loss of consciousness – "grand mal" – or parts of the body, involving perhaps a short loss of full consciousness, known as "petit mal" fits.

"Focal fits" are said to occur when only one part of the body, eg arms or legs, is affected.

Ethnicity (see also Culture). A group's sense of identity associated with race, heritage, upbringing and values.

Evidence (for NVQ). Proof in support of the judgement made by an assessor that a candidate is competent.

Exertion. The amount of effort a person puts into carrying out a task. This may be physical, in walking or getting out of bed. It can also be mental, for example struggling to remember recent events.

Faeces. Waste matter which is indigestible such as fibre, excreted by the bowel.

Fainting. A temporary loss of consciousness due to a fall in blood pressure. The person usually falls to the floor, as this is the way in which the body attempts to restore the blood circulation, so that oxygen can reach the brain.

Fatigue. State of extreme exhaustion or loss of strength.

Fibre (in diet). Used to describe food that is high in roughage, indigestible, and which stimulates the action of the intestine (bowel).

Flatulence. Excessive wind, usually causing discomfort and pain.

Fracture. A broken bone. The signs and symptoms include pain, swelling, loss of power and shortening of the affected limb.

Gangrene. Death of body tissue usually due to loss of blood supply.

Genital. Relates to the sexual organs of the man or woman.

Glaucoma. An illness in which abnormally high fluid pressure inside the eye can cause permanent damage.

Guardian. A person who assigns themselves or is appointed legally to look after and take responsibility for another.

Guarding. A defensive action that a person may take to safeguard themselves or to prevent any pain. It may include not wishing to talk about difficult subjects or holding oneself in a comfortable position that prevents physical pain.

Haemorrhoids. Piles.

Health education. Educational activities aimed at enhancing or maintaining the health and wellbeing of others.

Heart attack. Damage to an area of the heart muscle due to obstruction of the artery supplying this area with blood. Usually preceded by extreme chest pain.

Heart failure. The failure by the heart to pump blood around the body efficiently. The most common symptoms are breathlessness, tiredness and swollen ankles.

Hemiplegia. Paralysis of one side of the body. Usually caused by stroke or as a result of injury or disease to the brain.

Hernia. Protrusion of an organ from its normal position in the body into another. The most common is the inguinal hernia in which bowel pushes through defects in the muscle of the groin. Also known as a "rupture".

HIV (Human Immunodeficiency Virus). The virus that causes AIDS. It is not one virus, but a family of many similar viruses. It weakens the body's defence system by entering and destroying white cells that normally protect our body from infection.

Homeostasis. The tendency of the normal body to return to a steady state at all times. This is achieved by physiological control and feedback mechanisms.

Hydrocephalus. Accumulation of fluid in and around the brain.

Hypertension (see also Blood pressure). A condition in which the blood pressure is higher than it should be for an individual person. Blood pressures are written down as two figures. The top figure is called the "systolic" and the bottom figure is known as the "diastolic".

Hypotension. A condition in which the blood pressure is lower than it should be.

Hypothermia. Body temperature below the usual value of 37 degrees centigrade. At about 35 degrees centigrade confusion and listlessness may begin. Below 33 degrees centigrade the breathing and pulse rate and blood pressure may start to fall. If prolonged, death may occur.

Ileostomy (see Stoma).

Immunisation. The process by which a small safe dose of an infectious disease is given to build up body immune resistance.

Impairment. A reduction or weakening of any body function.

Incontinence (see also Continence). The inability to control the passage of urine or faeces until a suitable time and place is found. Urinary incontinence may occur when abdominal pressure, through coughing or lifting heavy weights, causes urine to leak from the bladder and urethra. Faecal incontinence is caused by a loss of control of the anus. Disorientation may also cause incontinence.

Infarct. An area of the body which is damaged or dies as a result of not receiving enough oxygen from its arteries. This supply failure is usually due to a blockage of or haemorrhage from the artery. Frequently used as "coronary" or "myocardial" infarct to describe the damage done to heart muscle after a heart attack.

Inflammatory bowel disease. Disorders where the bowel becomes red and inflamed. In *ulcerative colitis* the lining of the large bowel is involved. In *Crohn's disease* any part of the digestive tract can be affected and the full thickness of the bowel wall can become inflamed.

Infusion. Introduction of a substance, such as a medicine in fluid form, directly into a vein or under the skin. May be attached to a mechanical pump to ensure that the correct amount is given over a period of time.

Insomnia. Difficulty getting to sleep or staying asleep for a long time.

Intestine. The bowel.

Intractable. Commonly used in reference to pain, that is difficult to control or cure.

Larynx. The voice organ. Vocal cords of elastic tissue are spread across it. The vibrations and contractions of these produce the changes in the pitch of the voice.

Laxative. A medicine to encourage passing faeces.

Legislation. Acts of Parliament passed by the Government that must be upheld under the law.

Local authority. A body responsible for a range of public services, such as housing and recreation provided in a given area, usually a geographical Borough or Council.

Malabsorption. The failure of the gut to absorb nutrients and food. It can lead to malnutrition.

Malignant. A type of tumour that spreads and grows uncontrollably.

Malnutrition (see also nutrition). Under-nourishment due to poor diet or disease that prevents absorption of essential nutrients.

Medication (see also Sedation and Tranquilliser). Used to describe tablets, liquids or injections used with the aim of improving a person's physical or mental condition.

Melaena. The production of black, tarry stools containing blood from the upper part of the gut.

Meningitis. A serious infection of the tissues surrounding the brain.

Metabolism. The sum total of the chemical processes that occur in living organisms, resulting in growth, production of energy, elimination of waste material.

Micturition. The act of emptying the bladder of urine.

Monitored drug dosage system. A system of providing medicines that are dispensed and sealed by the pharmacist in weekly or monthly packs.

Motor neurone disease. A disease in which there is progressive destruction of some of the nerves responsible for stimulating muscles. This causes weakness and problems with movement, breathing and swallowing. The cause is unknown.

Motor strength. The strength of the muscle which stimulates the limbs and body to move.

Mucous membrane. A mucus-secreting membrane that lines body cavities (eg lungs) or passages that are open to the external environment (eg mouth, nose, vagina).

Mucus. The slimy protective secretion of the mucus membranes.

Multiple sclerosis. An often fluctuating, sometimes progressive disease of the brain and spinal cord in which plaques replace normal nerve tissue. This can cause a range of symptoms, including difficulty with coordinating movement, incontinence and problems with vision and speech.

Muscular dystrophy. A group of muscle disorders which are usually passed on through families and become apparent in childhood and adolescence.

Nausea. The sensation of feeling sick.

Nebuliser. Equipment that adds drops of water or medicine to compressed air or oxygen so that it can be absorbed more effectively or dislodge mucus in the air passages and lungs.

Neurological. Relating to the body's brain and nerves.

Neuro-transmitters. Chemical substances that help to pass a signal down a nerve.

Nutrition. The intake of nutrients (in food and drink) and their assimilation into body tissue.

NVQs – National Vocational Qualifications. Practical competency-based qualifications in England and Wales.

Occupational therapist. A health care practitioner who is qualified to diagnose and teach people with an illness or disability to use aids and adaptations for everyday living and working.

Oedema. Excess tissue fluid, often around ankles, at the base of the spine or in the heart and lungs.

Osteoarthritis (see also Arthritis & Rheumatoid arthritis). A form of arthritis occurring in the joints of older people. It is usually very painful. There is destruction of the spongy pads between bones, and small bony growths at the edges of the bone joint.

Palliative. Treatment that relieves or reduces uncomfortable symptoms, such as pain, but does not provide a cure.

Paralysis. Loss of movement (but not sensation) in a muscle or group of muscles normally under the person's control. May be due to damage to the muscle itself or to its nerve supply.

Parkinsonism. Symptoms such as shaking or trembling, rhythmical muscular tremors, rigidity and a mask-like face that shows no emotion. Thumb and fore fingers may move in a "rolling" fashion. It can be caused by tranquillisers.

Peak flow. The measurement of air as it is expelled from the lungs.

Performance criteria (for NVQ). A set of outcomes related to an element of performance by which an assessor can judge that a candidate can work to the required standard.

Personality. The mental make-up of a person. The way that they respond is influenced by life events and experiences, and their attitudes to situations.

Pharmacist. Practitioner trained to make up prescribed medicines and provide advice and information on side effects and contra-indications.

Photophobia. Intolerance to light.

Physiotherapist. A health care practitioner who is qualified to diagnose, teach and apply therapies, usually involving muscles and bones, to people who are ill, have an injury or disability, in order to restore them to health.

Pneumonia. Inflammation of the lungs due to bacterial, viral or fungal infections.

Presbycusis. The gradual loss of hearing which commonly occurs with age. The deafness is due to loss of hair cells and nerve fibres in the inner ear, resulting in sounds becoming less clear, especially higher tones.

Presbyopia. Loss of the eye's ability to accommodate for near vision. More common in middle and old age when the focusing power of the eye weakens.

Prescription. A legal document that must be used and signed by a doctor for issuing medicines. It must contain the name, dose and frequency of the medicines.

Pressure sore. An area of skin and underlying tissues which dies as a result of pressure persistently preventing the flow of blood through its blood vessels. It can cause an ulcer or sore to develop, particularly if the skin is broken.

Prognosis. The outlook for a person with a disease, in terms of disability and death.

Prostate. A gland at the base of the bladder in men. It may become enlarged due to disease or old age, causing difficulty in passing urine.

Prosthesis. Manufactured substitute for a part of the body (for example an artificial leg, false teeth, breast).

Pruritus. Itching.

Pulse. The regular expansion and contraction of an artery produced by waves of pressure as blood is pumped from the heart.

Pyrexia. Raised body temperature.

Quality Assurance (see also Audit and Standard). A system of evaluating and auditing the standards of a service

to ensure that the best possible service is provided in terms of value for money and client satisfaction.

Racism. Discrimination against a person on the grounds of skin colour and/or ethnic origin.

Range statements (for NVQ). The breadth of contexts in which a candidate is expected to demonstrate competence (linked to an element of competence).

Reality orientation. The way in which older people with mental illness are helped to keep in touch with the world around them. This may be through the use of large clocks, signs on doors, and newspapers.

Recovery position. The safest position in which to place a person who is unconscious. See chapter 13.

Rectum (see also Colon). The lower end of the bowel leading out to the anus.

Rehabilitation. The process by which a team of workers restores a person who has had a serious illness or injury to as near as possible their previous state of health.

Reminiscence therapy. Active participation by individuals or groups, using past life events to understand the reasons for their mental health problems. The past can also be used as a basis to share concerns and anxieties, since people with dementia are more likely to have a better memory for long term events than for more recent events.

Respiratory arrest. A situation in which a person stops breathing, but before the heart stops beating. There can be more than one cause.

Respite. Temporary relief services for the main carer of a dependent person in the home or other setting.

Rheumatism. The term is loosely applied to any pain of unknown cause in the joints or muscles. Small swellings may appear under the skin, particularly around bony ridges. There may be fever, sweating and pain and stiffness in the joints.

Rheumatoid arthritis (see also Arthritis and Osteoarthritis). Arthritis occurring in the small and large joints of people of all ages. The cause is unknown.

Role reversal. A situation in which a person exchanges a pattern of behaviour with another. For example a daughter may have to take on a mothering role to her own mother if she requires care.

Sacrum. Part of the lower end of the spine.

Sedative (see also Medication and Tranquilliser). Having a calming or soothing effect.

Sexuality. A part of the human personality that relates in physical, emotional and social dimensions to the way a person identifies and values themself. It includes their gender, appearance and sexual preferences.

Sharps. Any piece of equipment used that could cause injury by stabbing or cutting a person if not disposed of safely.

Shock. This may arise out of fear or pain, it may also be the result of loss of blood, as a reaction to medicines, or contact with electrical currents. It is the condition in which there is a sudden fall in blood pressure, which if untreated will lead to a lack of oxygen in the tissues.

Social services. A department of the local authority that employs social care workers to enable people to live independently at home by providing practical help and advice. Examples include social workers, welfare rights officers, disablement officers and care assistants.

Social worker. A professional trained to counsel clients and families, helping them seek community and financial resources to enable them to live independently in the community or other setting.

Sphincter. A muscular ring which surrounds the opening of a hollow organ, such as the bladder. It controls the escape of the content of the organ until a suitable time.

Spina bifida. A congenital disease in which there is a defect in the bones of the spine. This can be mild and cause no symptoms. In more serious forms the spinal cord can be damaged causing paralysis of the legs and incontinence of urine and faeces, often accompanied by hydrocephalus and mental retardation.

Sprain. An injury to a ligament when the joint it is supporting is forced through a range of movements greater than normal, without dislocation or fracture.

Sputum. Excess secretion from the lungs that contains mucus and saliva. It may also contain bacteria.

Standard. A guide that serves as a basis for measuring how good or bad a particular service or practice is. (See also Audit and Quality Assurance.)

Stereotype. A commonly held belief about a behaviour, individual or group that is not always true.

Stethoscope. A device for listening to sounds within the body, such as heart beat, bowel sounds and breathing, that cannot otherwise be heard by the human ear.

Stoma. A surgical procedure in which an opening is made on the abdominal wall to allow the passage of intestinal contents (colostomy and ileostomy) or urine (urostomy) from the bladder.

Stool. Formed faeces passed from the bowel..

Stress. Stress reactions, both physical and mental, occur when the individual is unable to cope with all the demands made upon them. If extreme, it may be called "burn-out".

Stroke (see also Cerebrovascular accident). A rapid brain disorder usually caused by a blockage in or haemorrhage from one of the main arteries of the brain. Speech and movement are commonly affected. Other functions may be damaged depending upon which artery is affected. Recovery depends on the extent of the damage.

Subcutaneous. Relates to an injection or infusion given into the skin tissue at a 45 degree angle, rather than into the muscle (intramuscular).

SVQs. Scottish Vocational Qualifications (the Scottish equivalent of National Vocational Qualifications).

Syringe driver. A battery-driven device for giving drugs (usually pain killers) over a period of time via a subcutaneous needle under the skin.

Systole. The maximum level of blood pressure measured between heart contractions.

Tachycardia. A marked increase in the rate of the heart.

Thrombosis. The formation of a blood clot on the lining of an artery or vein which may partially or completely block the blood flow through it.

Thrush. A fungal infection usually affecting mucous membranes such as the mouth or vagina.

Tinnitus. An abnormal buzzing, ringing, whistling or clicking noise in the ears.

Toxin. Any poisonous compound. It may be caused by bacteria multiplying in the body.

Tracheostomy. A temporary or permanent surgical opening above the Adam's apple. It allows a person to breathe when the throat or upper airway is diseased or damaged.

Tranquilliser (see also Medication and Sedation). Medicines that allay anxiety and have a calming effect on the person. They may also prevent them from feeling pain.

Trauma. A wound or injury, physical or emotional. Emotional trauma can be a cause of mental illness.

Tumour. A lump or swelling in the body that is not inflamed. A benign tumour does not grow in other parts of the body. A malignant tumour may spread to other organs.

Ulcer. An erosion and inflammation of the skin or mucous membranes. Examples include venous leg ulcers, caused by poor skin condition and poor return of blood to the heart. Arterial leg ulcers are caused by poor blood supply.

Ulcerative colitis. See Inflammatory bowel disease.

Universal precautions. The wearing of gloves and protective clothing, and correct cleaning and disposal of waste, to prevent the spread of infection from blood and body fluids.

Ureters. The tubes which drain urine from the kidneys into the bladder.

Urethra. The tube that carries urine from the bladder to outside the body.

Urine. Waste products in liquid form that are produced in the kidney and emptied from the body via the bladder.

Urinary tract infection. An infection that affects the bladder or the urethra. It may result in the person wanting to pass urine frequently, cause pain and a stinging sensation.

Urostomy See Stoma.

Value base unit (for NVQ). This is the "O" Unit which embeds in NVQ awards in care the principles of good practice: anti-discrimination, confidentiality, rights and choice, respect for beliefs and identity and effective communication.

Varicose veins. A condition, usually of the lower leg, in which the veins are swollen and may be twisted due to structural changes in the walls or valves of the vessels. These veins have difficulty returning blood back to the heart . Knocks to varicose veins commonly cause leg ulcers in older people which can be painful.

Vascular. Relating to blood vessels, usually arteries or veins.

Vein. A vessel carrying blood from the capillaries back to the heart after oxygen has been removed by the tissues and organs that need it.

Vertigo. A feeling of dizziness accompanied by a feeling that either oneself or one's surroundings are spinning.

Visual acuity. A measurement of how much a person can see at a particular distance, usually six metres, to identify whether they are short- or long-sighted.

Useful resources

All these organisations welcome a stamped, self-addressed envelope sent with your enquiry.

Action on Elder Abuse, Age Concern England,, Astral House, 1268 London Road, London SW16 4ER, Tel: 020 8679-8000.

AgeCare, Royal Surgical Aid Society, 47 Great Russell Street, London WC1B 3PB. Tel: 020 7637 4577.

Age Concern Cymru, 4th Floor, 1 Cathedral Road, Cardiff CF1 9SD. Tel: 029 2037 1566.

Age Concern England, Astral House, 1268 London Road, London SW16 4ER. Tel: 020 8679 8000.

Age Concern Northern Ireland, 3 Lower Crescent, Belfast BT7 1NR. Tel: 028 9024 5729.

Age Concern Scotland, 113 Rose Street, Edinburgh EH2 3DT. Tel: 0131 220 3345.

Age Exchange Reminiscence Centre, 11 Blackheath Village, London SE3 9LA, Tel: 020 8318 9105.

AIDS Helpline National, Healthwise Helpline Ltd, 1st floor, Covern Court, 8 Matthew Street, Liverpool L2 6RE, Ethnic minority language lines also available, Tel: 0151 227 4150, Tel: 0800 567123 (free line).

Alcoholics Anonymous, Hanley Health Centre, Huntbach St Hanley, Stoke-on-Trent, Staffs, ST1 2BN. Tel: 01782 266366.

Alzheimer Scotland – Action on Dementia, 22 Drumsheugh Gardens, Edinburgh EH3 7RN.. Tel: 0131 243 1453.

Alzheimer's Society, Gordon House, 10 Greencoat Place, London SW1P 1PH. Tel: 020 7306 0606. Helpline: 0845 300 0336.

Alzheimer's Society (Northern Ireland), 403 Lisburn Road, Belfast BT9 7EW. Tel: 028 9066 4100.

Alzheimer's Society Wales Development Office, Tonna Hospital, Tonna, Neath, Neath and Port Talbot SA11 3LX. Tel: 01639 633400.

Arthritis and Rheumatism Council (ARC), Copeman House, St Mary's Court, St Mary's Gate, Chesterfield, Derbyshire, S41 7TD. Tel: 01246 558033.

Arthritis Care, 18 Stephenson Way, London, NW1 2HD. Tel: 020 7380 6500.

Association for Continence Advice, 102a Astra House, Arklow Road, London, SE14 6EB, Tel: 020 8692 4680.

Association Of Continence Advisers, The Disabled Living Foundation, 380-384 Harrow Road, London, W9 2HU, Tel: 020 7289 6111.

BackCare, 16 Elmtree Road, Teddington, Middx, TW11 8ST, Tel: 020 8977 5474.

British Association Of Cancer United Patients (BACUP), 3 Bath Place, Rivington Street, London, EC2 3JR, Tel: 020 7696 9003.

British Colostomy Association, 15 Station Road, Reading, RG1 1LG, Tel: 0800 3284257 (free line), Tel: 0118 939 1537.

British Complementary Medicine Association, PO Box 5122, Bournemouth, BH8 0WG, Tel: 0845 345 5977.

British Deaf Association, 1-3 Worship Street, London, EC2A 2AB, Tel: 020 7588 3520.

British Dietetic Association, 5th Floor, Charles House, 148/9 Great Charles Street, Queensway, Birmingham, B3 3HT, Tel: 0121 200 8080.

British Epilepsy Association, New Anstue House, Gateway Drive, Yeden, Leeds, L519 7XY, Tel: 011321 08800.

British Federation of Care Home Proprietors, 44 Harpur Street, Bedford, Bedfordshire, MK40 2QT, Tel: 01234 271275.

British Heart Foundation, 14 Fitzhardinge Street, London, W1H 6DH, Tel: 020 7935 0185.

British Institute of Learning Disabilities, Campion House, Green Street, Kidderminster, Worcs, DY10 1JA, Tel: 01562 723010.

British Red Cross Society, 9 Grosvenor Crescent, London, SW1X 7EJ, Tel: 020 7235 5454.

BTEC Management Education and Training College, Lower Ground Floor, Regent House, 109-111 Brittannia Walk, London N1 7LU. Tel: 020 7253 4332.

Carers UK, Ruth Pitter House, 20-25 Glasshouse Yard, London EC 4JT, Tel: 020 7490 8818.

Centre for Policy on Ageing, 25-31 Ironmonger Row, London EC1V 3QP, Tel: 020 7253 1787.

Chartered Society of Physiotherapy, 14 Bedford Row, London WC1R 4ED. Tel: 020 7242 1941.

Chinese Mental Health Association, Oxford House, Derbyshire Street, London, E2 6HG. Tel: 020 7613 1008.

Citizens Advice Bureaux, Myddleton House, 115-123 Pentonville Road, London, N1 9LZ. Tel: 020 7833 2181.

City and Guilds, 1 Giltspur Street, London, EC1 9DD. Tel: 020 7294 2468.

CNEOPSA (Care Needs of Minority Ethnic Older Persons Suffering from Alzheimer's Disease), c/o PRIAE London, Boardman House, 64 Broadway, Stratford, London E15 1NG. Tel: 020 8432 0260.

Counsel and Care, Twyman House, 16 Bonney Street, London NW1 9PG. Tel: 0207485 7585, Advice Line 0845 300 7585.

Cruse Bereavement Care, Cruse House, 126 Sheen Road, Richmond, Surrey, TW9 1UR, Tel: 020 8940 4818.

Deafblind UK, National Centre for Deafblindness, John and Lucille van Geest Place, Cygnet Road, Hampton, Peterborough, PE7 8FD. Tel: 01733 358100.

Department Of Health, Richmond House, 79 Whitehall, London, SW1A 2NS, Tel: 020 7210 4850.

Diabetes UK, 10 Parkway, London, NW1 7AA, Tel: 020 7424 1000.

Disability Alliance, Universal House, 88-94 Wentworth Street, London, E1 7SA. Tel: 020 7247 8763 (Mon-Sat 2-4pm).

Disabled Living Foundation, 380-384 Harrow Road, London W9 2HU. Tel: 0870 603 9177.

Edexcel, Stewart House, 32 Russell Square, London WC1B 5DN. Tel: 0870 9800.

Equal Opportunities Commission, Arndale House, Arndale Centre, Manchester, M4 3EQ. Tel: 0161 833 9244.

General Social Care Council, Goldings House, 2 Hay's Lane, London SE1 2HB. Tel: 020 7397 5100.

Health and Safety Executive (HSE), Infoline, Caerphilly Business Park, Caerphilly CF83 3GG. Tel: 08701 545500.

Health Education Authority, Trevelyan House, 30 Great Peter Street, London SWC1P 2HW. Tel: 020 7222 5300.

Help the Aged, 207-221 Pentonville Road, London, N1 9UZ. Tel: 020 7278 1114.

Hospice Information Service, St Christopher's Hospice, 51-59 Lawrie Park Road, Sydenham, London, SE26 6DZ. Tel: 020 8778 9252.

Ileostomy Association, 19 Godman Road, Chadwell-St-Mary, Essex RM16 4SP. Tel:01375 858915.

Independent Healthcare Association, Westminster Tower, 3 Albert Embankment, Lonson SE1 7SP.Tel: 020 7793 4620.

Jewish Care, Stewart Young House, 221 Golders Green Road, London NW11 9DQ. Tel: 020 8922 1998.

Laryngectomy Clubs (national association), Ground Floor, 6 Rickett Street, Fulham, London, SW6 1RU. Tel: 020 7381 9993.

Limbless Association, Roehampton Rehabilitation Centre, Roehampton Lane, London, SW15 5PR. Tel: 020 8788 1777.

Listening Books, 12 Lant Street, London SE1 1QH.

Marie Curie Cancer Care, 89 Albert Embankment, London, SE1 7TP, 020 7599 7777.

Medic Alert Foundation, Ignors Cottage, By Pass Compton, Guildford, Surrey, GU3 1DT. Tel: 01483 810461.

MENCAP (Royal Society For Mentally Handicapped Children And Adults), 123 Golden Lane, London, EC1Y 0RT. Tel: 020 7454 0454.

MIND (National Association for Mental Health), Granta House, 15-19 Broadway, Stratford E15 4BQ. Tel: 020 8519 2122, Info line: 020 8522 1728.

Mobility Information Service, Unit B1 Greenwood Court, Cartmel Drive, Harlescott, Shrewsbury, Shropshire, SY1 3TB. Tel: 01743 463072.

Motor Neurone Disease Association, PO Box 246, Northampton, NN1 2PR. Helpline: 08457 626626.

Multiple Sclerosis Society, MS National Centre, 372 Edgware Road, London, NW2 6ND. Tel: 01582 760601.

Muscular Dystrophy Group, 2 Fennis, Dorridge, Solihull, W. Midlands, B93 8DH. Tel: 01564 777514.

National Association for Colitis and Crohn's Disease, 4 Beaumont House, Sutton Road, St Albans, Herts, AL1 5HH. 01727 844296.

National Asthma Campaign, Providence House, Providence Place, London, N1 0NT, Helpline: 0845701 0203. Tel: 020 7226 2544.

National Autistic Society, 393 City Road, London, EC1 V1G. Tel: 020 7833 2299.

National Care Homes Association, 45-49 Leather Lane, London, EC1N 7TJ. Tel: 020 7831 7090.

National Osteoporosis Society, Camerton, Bath BA2 0PJ. 01761 471771.

National Society for Epilepsy, Information Department, Chalfont St Peter, Buckinghamshire, SL9 0RJ. Tel: 01494 601300.

Dementia Services Development Centres

Each of these centres is a resource for local information on best practice, training and resources for dementia care. Centres in other areas of the country are planned. Latest information from The Journal of Dementia Care (020 7720 2108 ext. 206).

SCOTLAND
Dementia Services
Development Centre
University of Stirling
Stirling FK9 4LA.
Tel: 01786 467740
Email: mtm1@stir.ac.uk
www.stir.ac.uk/dsdc

NORTH EAST
Dementia North
Allendale House
Northumbria University
Newcastle upon Tyne
NE7 7XA
Tel: 0191 215 6110
Email: hs.dementianorth@
unn.ac.uk
http://online.northumbria.
ac.uk/faculties/hswe/
research/Dementia.htm

NORTH WEST
North West Dementia Centre
Dover Street Building
University of Manchester
Manchester M13 9PL
Tel: 0161 275 5682
Email: nwdc.man.ac.uk

CENTRAL
Trent DSDC (being developed)
Trent Dementia Services
Development Centre
Professor James Lindesay,
Psychiatry for the Elderly,
Leicester General Hospital,
Gwendolen Road,
Leicester LE5 4PW
Tel: 0116 258 8161
Email: jebl1@le.ac.uk

Dementia Plus West Midlands
Warstones Resource Centre
Warstones Drive, Penn,
Wolverhampton WV4 4PG
Tel: 01902 575056
Email: dementiaplus.wm@
whc-tr.nhs.uk
www.wmpmh.org.uk/
dementiaplus

Oxford Dementia Centre
Institute of Public Care
Roosevelt Drive
Headington
Oxford OX3 7XR
Tel: 01865 761815
Email:
dementia@brookes.ac.uk
www.brookes.ac.uk

SOUTH EAST
London Centre for
Dementia Care
UCL, Wolfson Building
48 Riding House Street
London W1N 8AA
Tel/fax: 020 7679 9588
Email:
margot.lindsay@ucl.ac.uk
www.ucl.ac.uk/lcdc

BRADFORD DEMENTIA GROUP

National resource for information, research, training (including Dementia Care Mapping) and publications.
Bradford Dementia Group
School for Health Studies
Bradford University
Unity Building
25 Trinity Road, Little Horton
Bradford BD5 0BB
Tel: 01274 233996
Fax: 01274 236395
Email: rj.woolley@bradford.
ac.uk
www.bradford.ac.uk\acad\
health\bdg

Dementia Services
Development Centre
South East
Canterbury Christ Church
University College,
North Holmes Road
Canterbury
Kent CT1 1QU
Tel: 01227 782702
Email:dsdcse@canterbury.ac.uk
http://dementiacentre.cant.
ac.uk

SOUTH WEST
Dementia Voice
Blackberry Hill Hospital
Manor Road
Fishponds, Bristol
BS16 2EW
Tel: 0117 975 4863
Fax: 0117 975 4819
Email: office@dementia-
voice.org.uk
www.dementia-voice.org.uk

WALES
DSDC Wales is based in both
Bangor and Cardiff
Details from:
Lesley Prendergast
Information Officer
Dementia Services
Development Centre
Neuadd Ardudwy
University of Wales Bangor
Holyhead Road
Bangor, LL57 2PX
Tel: 01248 383719
Email: dsdc@bangor.ac.uk
www.bangor.ac.uk/dsdc

REPUBLIC OF IRELAND
Ireland DSDC
St James's Hospital,
St James's Street
Dublin 8
Tel: 00353 1 416 2035
Email: dsidc@stjames.ie
www.dementia.ie

Nursing and Midwifery Council, 23 Portland Place, London, W1B 1PZ. Tel: 020 7637 7181.

Pain Society, 21 Portland Place, London, W1B 1PY. Tel: 020 7631 8870.

Parkinson's Disease Society, United Scientific House, 215 Vauxhall Bridge Road, London SW1V 1EJ. Tel: 020 7931 8080.

PAT Dogs (Pet Aided Therapy Scheme), c/o 10a Welldon Crescent, Harrow, Middlesex, HA1 1QT.

PRIAE (Policy Research Institute on Ageing and Ethnicity), 31-32 Park Row, Leeds LS1 5JD. Tel: 0113 285 5990.

Qualifications and Curriculum Authority, 83 Piccadilly, London, W15 8QA. Tel: 020 7509 5555.

Registered Nursing Homes Association, Calthorp House, Hagley Road, Birmingham B16 8QY. Tel: 0121 454 2511.

Relatives Association, 5 Tavistock Place, London WC1H 9SN. Tel: 020 7916 6055.

Royal College of Nursing, 20 Cavendish Square, London W1G 0RN. Tel: 020 7409 3333.

The Royal College of Speech and Language Therapists, 2 White Hart Yard, London, SE1 1NX, Tel: 020 737 81200.

Royal National Institute for the Blind, 224 Great Portland Street, London, W1N 6AA. Tel: 020 7388 1266.

Royal National Institute for the Deaf, 19-23 Featherstone Street, London EC1Y 8SL. Tel: 020 7296 8000.

Samaritans, 40 Queens Road, Bounds Green, London, N11 2QU. Tel: 020 8889 6888.

Schizophrenia Association of Great Britain, Bryn Hyfryd, The Crescent, Bangor, Gwynedd, LL57 2AG. Tel: 01248 354048.

Social Care Association, Thornton House, Hook Road, Surbiton, Surrey, KT6 5AN. Tel: 020 8397 1411.

Speakability, Canterbury House, 1 Royal Street, London SE1 7LN, Tel: 020 7261 9572.

Spinal Injuries Association, 76 St James Lane, London, N10 3DF, Tel: 020 8444 2121. Helpline: 020 888 34296.

SPOD (Sexual and Personal Relationships of Disabled People), 286 Camden Road, London, N7 OBJ. Tel: 020 7607 8851.

St John Ambulance, Edwina Mountbatten House, 63 York Street, London, W1H 1PS,.Tel: 020 7258 3456.

The Stroke Association, Stroke House, 240 City Road, London EC1V 2PRJ. Tel: 020 7566 0300.

TFH, 5-7 Severnside Business Park, Severn Road, Stourport -on-Severn, Worcs, DY13 9HT. Tel: 01299 827820. Games, puzzles, pastimes etc for disabled/older people.

Thrive (previously **Horticultural Therapy**), The Geoffrey Udall Centre, Beech Hill, Reading, RG7 2AT. Tel: 0118 988 5688.

University of the Third Age, 26 Harrison Street, London, NWC1, Self help educational activities for older people, Tel: 91207837 8838.

VOICES (Voluntary Organisations Involved in Caring in the Elderly Sector), c/o The Association of Charity Officers, Unicorn House, Station Close, Potters Bar, Herts, EN6 3JW. Tel: 01707 651777.

Index

APPENDIX A

NVQ Level 2
Quick reference guide

Where to find the underpinning knowledge to support your studies

NVQ Level 2 Care Unit	Chapters
Mandatory Units	
O1: foster people's equality, diversity and rights	1,2
CL1: Promote effective communication and relations	3
CU1: monitor and maintain Health, safety and security in the workplace	4
Z1: Contribute to the protection of individuals from abuse	5
Option group A	
NC12: Enable clients to eat and drink	8
Z9 Enable clients to maintain personal hygiene and appearance	9
Z11 Enable clients to access and use toilet facilities	9
Z6: Enable clients to maintain and improve their mobility through exercise and the use of mobility appliances	10
Z19: Enable clients to achieve physical comfort	11
CU 5: Receive, transmit, store and retrieve information	1,2,3
W3: Support individuals experiencing a change in their care requirements and provision	13
Z7: contribute to the movement and handling of individuals to maximise their physical comfort	1,2,3,4,6,9
Option Group B	
Z15: Contribute to the care of the deceased person	12
Z5: Enable clients to maintain their mobility and make journeys and visit	1,2,3,4,7,9,10,
CU6: Assist in supplying and maintaining materials and equipment	4,10
Z13: enable clients to participate in recreation and leisure activities	1,2,3,4,10

To achieve an NVQ 2 in Care, a candidate must achieve all 4 mandatory units, plus 5 option units at least three of which must be chosen from option group A. (up to 5 units can be chosen from Group a, if appropriate)

Reference
Edexcel (1998) Candidate Assessment log Issue 1. Edexcel Publications, London.